SARTRE AGAINST STALINISM

BERGHAHN MONOGRAPHS IN FRENCH STUDIES

The Populist Challenge: Political Protest and Ethno-nationalist
Mobilization in France
Jens Rydgren

French Intellectuals Against the Left: The Antitotalitarian Moment
of the 1970s
Michael Scott Christofferson

Sartre Against Stalinism
Ian H. Birchall

SARTRE AGAINST STALINISM

Ian H. Birchall

Berghahn Books
New York • Oxford

First published in 2004 by

Berghahn Books

www.berghahnbooks.com

© 2004 Ian H. Birchall

Library of Congress Cataloging-in-Publication Data

Birchall, Ian H.
 Sartre Against Stalinism / Ian H. Birchall.
  p. cm. (Berghahn monographs in French studies)
 Includes bibliographical references and index.
 ISBN 1-57181-621-6 (alk. paper)
 1. Sartre, Jean Paul, 1905--Political and social views. 2. Communism--
France. 3. Communism and philosophy--France. 4. Communism--Soviet
Union. 5. Intellectuals--France--Political activity. I. Title.

HX264.7.S27B57 2004
335.43--dc22

                                                    2003063587

British Library Cataloguing in Publication Data

A catalogue record for this book is available from
the British Library.

Printed in the United States on acid-free paper

To the memory of Tony Cliff, a lifelong source of enlightenment
and encouragement.

CONTENTS

ACKNOWLEDGMENTS

Earlier versions of parts of this book were presented as papers to the U.K. Society for Sartrean Studies, the Society for French Studies and the London Socialist Historians Group; my thanks to all who participated in the discussions. The basic thesis was first set out in an article called 'Sartre and Gauchisme', published by the Journal of European Studies (XIX, 1989). I thank the editor for publishing me and especially Professor Max Adereth of the University of Lancaster for provoking me so sorely by his own article (Journal of European Studies, XVII, 1987).

Thanks also to staff at the British Library, the Bibliothèque Nationale and the London Library. Jean-René Chauvin, who worked with Sartre in the RDR (Rassemblement Démocratique Révolutionnaire), allowed me to interview him and gave me access to his personal archives; this was invaluable in giving me insight into this episode in Sartre's career.

For some twenty years I taught a course on Sartre at Middlesex Polytechnic (later University). It is a tribute to the power and relevance of Sartre's ideas that these were the liveliest and most interesting classes I ever taught. I hope the students learnt as much from me as I did from them; they certainly helped me develop the account of Sartre presented here. Thanks also to my former colleague Deirdre Welsh for a gift of books which made my task lighter.

I am grateful to Ronald Aronson, David Drake, Richard Greeman, Dave Harker, Chris Harman, George Paizis, Dave Renton and Jim Wolfreys for making searching and valuable criticisms of earlier drafts. I fear, however, that I shall have disappointed some of them, who wanted me to write a rather different book. While recognising that they were making an important point, I have obstinately persisted with my original intention.

Thanks also to Chris Harman for first encouraging me to write on Sartre back in 1970, and to David Caute, whom I asked a question about Sartre and Trotskyism at a meeting in Oxford in 1963. When he failed to give me a satisfactory answer, I realised I should have to find out for myself.

This book is dedicated to the memory of the late Tony Cliff. Cliff did not greatly approve of Sartre, but they may have had more in common than either would have liked to believe.

Ian H. Birchall
September 2003

BIBLIOGRAPHICAL NOTE

Since Sartre's plays exist in a large number of different editions, I have given references to act and scene rather than to the pages of any specific edition. All translations in the text are my own unless reference is given to a published English translation.

Sartre's works have been translated into English under a bewildering variety of titles; often different titles were used for British and American editions. Moreover, some English titles are highly misleading. Hence I have used the original French titles throughout in the text. I list below some of the English versions.

L'Age de raison	The Age of Reason
Les Chemins de la liberté	The Roads to Freedom, The Roads of Freedom
Les Communistes et la paix	The Communists and Peace
Critique de la raison dialectique	Critique of Dialectical Reason (first part published separately as: The Problem of Method)
Le Diable et le Bon Dieu	Lucifer and the Lord, The Devil and the Good Lord
L'Être et le néant	Being and Nothingness
L'Existentialisme est un humanisme	Existentialism and Humanism
Le Fantôme de Staline	The Spectre of Stalin
Huis Clos	In Camera, No Exit, Vicious Circle
L'Idiot de la famille	The Family Idiot
Les Mains sales	Crime Passionnel, Red Gloves, Dirty Hands

La Mort dans l'âme	Iron in the Soul, Troubled Sleep
Morts sans sépulture	Men Without Shadows, The Victors, No Tomb for the Dead
Les Mots	Words, The Words
Les Mouches	The Flies
Le Mur	Intimacy (a different item is chosen as title story), The Wall
La Nausée	Nausea, The Diary of Antoine Roquentin
Nekrassov	Nekrassov
Orphée noir	Black Orpheus
La Putain respectueuse	The Respectable Prostitute, The Respectful Prostitute
Qu'est-ce que la littérature?	What is Literature? Literature and Existentialism
Question(s) de méthode	The Problem of Method, Search for a Method
Réflexions sur la question juive	Portrait of the Anti-Semite, Anti-Semite and Jew
Les Séquestrés d'Altona	Altona, Loser Wins, The Condemned of Altona
Le Sursis	The Reprieve

ABBREVIATIONS

In the case of certain works and collections referred to frequently in the notes I have used the following abbreviations:

Adieux   S. de Beauvoir, *La Cérémonie des adieux*, Paris, 1981

C&R   M. Contat and M. Rybalka, *Les Écrits de Sartre*, Paris, 1970

Choses   S. de Beauvoir, *La Force des choses*, Paris, 1963

Compte   S. de Beauvoir, *Tout compte fait*, Paris, 1972

Force   S. de Beauvoir, *La Force de l'âge*, Paris, 1960

Raison   J.-P. Sartre, Ph. Gavi, P. Victor, *On a raison de se révolter*, Paris, 1974

Sit   J.-P. Sartre, *Situations* volumes I–X, Paris, 1947–76

TDS   J.-P. Sartre, *Un Théâtre de situations*, Paris, 1973

TM   *Les Temps modernes*, Paris, 1945ff

Other abbreviations used in the text:

CGT   Confédération générale du travail – largest French trade-union confederation, from 1945 under Communist leadership

CP   Communist Party

FIARI   Fédération internationale de l'art révolutionnaire indépendant – organisation of anti-Stalinist artists founded by Trotsky and Breton in 1938

FLN   Front de libération nationale – main Algerian nationalist organisation during Algerian War

FO   Force ouvrière – anti-Communist union confederation resulting from split in CGT 1947

MNA	Mouvement national algérien – Algerian nationalist movement led by Messali Hadj, rival of FLN
OAS	Organisation armée secrète – clandestine organisation opposed to Algerian independence
PCF	Parti Communiste Français – French Communist Party
PCI	Parti Communiste Internationaliste – main Trotskyist organisation during and after the Second World War
POUM	Partido Obrero de Unificación Marxista – left anti-Stalinist party in Spanish Civil War
PSU	(i) Parti Socialiste Unitaire – formed 1948; held positions very close to those of the PCF
	(ii) Parti Socialiste Unifié – left socialist party formed 1960
RDR	Rassemblement Démocratique Révolutionnaire – independent left organisation, 1948–49
SFIO	Section Française de l'Internationale Ouvrière – French Socialist Party until 1971

Chronology

1905	21 June	Sartre born in Paris
1933	30 January	Hitler comes to power in Germany
1933–34	September–July	Sartre in Berlin
1936	4 June	Formation of French Popular Front government
	17 July	Start of Spanish Civil War
1939	23 August	Hitler–Stalin Pact
	2 September	Sartre called up into army
1940–41	June–March	Sartre prisoner of war
1941	April–October	*Socialisme et liberté*
1943	2 June	First performance of *Les Mouches*
1944	25 August	Liberation of Paris
1945	January–May	Sartre in United States
	15 October	First issue of *Les Temps modernes*
	29 October	Lecture: *L'Existentialisme est un humanisme*
1946	June–July	'Matérialisme et révolution'
	December	Start of Indo-China War
1947	5 May	PCF ousted from government
	October–November	*Les Temps modernes* radio broadcasts

1948	March	Launching of RDR
	2 April	First performance of *Les Mains sales*
	24 July	Berlin blockade begins
1949	4 April	Foundation of NATO
	15 October	Sartre resigns from RDR
1950	25 June	Outbreak of Korean War
1951	7 June	First performance of *Le Diable et le Bon Dieu*
1952	January	Sartre campaigns on behalf of Henri Martin
	May	Demonstrations against Ridgway
	June–November	'Les Communistes et la Paix'
	August	Climax of Sartre–Camus dispute
	December	Sartre attends peace conference in Vienna
1953	5 March	Death of Stalin
1954	May–June	Sartre's first visit to USSR
	21 July	Geneva agreements end Indo-China War
	1 November	Beginning of Algerian War
1955	8 June	First performance of *Nekrassov*
1956	27 January	Sartre addresses meeting against Algerian War
	25 February	Khrushchev 'secret speech'
	October–November	Russian troops crush Hungarian Revolution
	October–November	Franco-British invasion of Egypt
1957	January	'Le Fantôme de Staline'
	April	'Questions de méthode' published in Polish
1958	6 March	*L'Express* with Sartre's article on torture seized
	May	De Gaulle returns to power

1960	February–March	Sartre visits Cuba
	6 April	*Critique de la raison dialectique*
	August	Manifesto of the 121
1962	3 July	Algerian independence
1964	30 August	Obituary of Togliatti
	22 October	Sartre refuses Nobel Prize
1965	7 February	U.S. begin bombing North Vietnam
1966	November	First meeting of Russell Tribunal on Vietnam
1968	May–June	French general strike
	20 August	Russian invasion of Czechoslovakia
1970	April–May	Sartre defends *La Cause du peuple*
1973	22 May	First issue of *Libération*
1974	7 May	*On a raison de se révolter*
	5 December	Sartre visits Baader in jail
1975	30 April	End of Vietnam War
1980	15 April	Sartre dies

Chapter 1

Introduction: Claiming the Corpse

Anyone proposing to write yet another book about Jean-Paul Sartre must do so with a certain sense of guilt. Given the huge number of books and articles that already exist, what justification can there be for adding to them? Moreover, any writer on Sartre lives with the melancholy awareness that Sartre himself insisted that he had never learnt anything from any of the books written about him.[1] Yet such is the richness and complexity of Sartre's work that there are still things that have not been said – as well, unfortunately, as some that have been said all too often, despite the fact that they are untrue.

One of Sartre's earliest political memories was of the Russian Revolution of 1917; he died just before the rise of *Solidarność* in Poland in 1980. His life thus encompassed the rise and fall of Eastern bloc Communism. After witnessing the early days of Hitler in power, he lived through the Popular Front, the German Occupation and the crisis years of France's disastrous colonial wars in Indo-China and Algeria, before participating in the rebirth of the left in 1968.

From a relatively unpolitical stance in the 1930s Sartre became increasingly involved in the politics of the left. He opposed fascism and colonialism, and aligned himself with the struggles of the oppressed at home and abroad. But after 1945 the political line-up became much more complicated. The hopes that the Liberation would usher in an age of libertarian socialism soon perished under the pressures of the emerging Cold War. For a generation the French Communist Party (PCF), with its dogmatic caricature of Marxism, its undemocratic practices and its slavish subordination to the political needs of its Moscow bosses, dominated the French left. And well beyond the ranks of the Communist Party the idea that the USSR represented 'socialism' on a world scale was prevalent.

If Sartre always distrusted Stalinism he was sometimes driven to ally himself with it, though only for one brief period did the alliance have any

---

Notes for this chapter begin on page 9.

real substance. Though he took a keen interest in the independent left (often influenced, to a greater or lesser extent, by ideas derived from Leon Trotsky), he remained unwilling to throw in his lot with it. Yet for a new political generation coming to maturity in the 1960s Sartre was a vital influence; his stress on individual responsibility, and his outspoken denunciation of imperialism and oppression, unmodified by the tactical considerations that trammelled the PCF, made him an inspiration for those who wanted to reinvent a revolutionary socialist politics.

From the 1940s onwards Sartre always had his critics from the right – and the left – who accused him of nourishing dangerous illusions about the nature of the USSR and other Stalinist regimes. This was a major theme in his notorious 1952 quarrel with Camus and above all in the way that that quarrel was publicly perceived. But after Sartre's death in 1980, and even more since the alleged 'death of communism' in 1989, the critical chorus grew ever stronger. Many, it seemed, would be only too glad to let Sartre's corpse fester under the ruins of the Berlin Wall. For those who made a simple equation between Marxism and Stalinism, the end of the USSR meant an end to the whole socialist project.[2] Sartre's basic message – that the world can be changed; that we are free to change it; and that if we fail to do so we bear the responsibility – could now only be an embarrassing anachronism liable to give the wrong ideas to the younger generation. Thus Norman Podhoretz has insisted that one cannot reject Stalinist Communism without also repudiating what he calls 'the utopian dreams of a transformed and redeemed world'.[3] Hunger, poverty and economic crisis, it appears, are to be always with us. As for former Maoist Bernard-Henri Lévy, his recent study of Sartre, while not unsympathetic, is based on total rejection of communism, not merely in its Stalinist manifestation, but in its very essence – 'the revolutionary ideal is a criminal and barbarous ideal'.[4]

Sartre undoubtedly made some colossal misjudgements about the nature of Stalinism, some of which will be analysed below. But a generalised reputation for being 'soft on Stalinism' has meant that a number of myths have grown up around Sartre, which are repeated from one historian or journalist to the next without reference to factual evidence, until they have been reiterated so often that it seems eccentric to question them.

Thus in his obituary of Sartre, George Steiner declared that Sartre was 'damnably wrong – on the Soviet camps for example'.[5] Now it is possible to query Sartre's analysis of the role of labour camps in Russian society, or his decisions on political alliances in opposing them. But contrary to the pervasive myth, there can be no doubt whatsoever that he publicly condemned the camps. Tony Judt, in a study of Sartre and other French intellectuals, referred to Sartre's 'famous warning "Il ne faut pas désespérer Billancourt"'[6] [we must not make (the workers of the Renault car factory at) Billancourt despair]. The warning was apparently so famous that Judt felt no need to give any source for it. In fact Sartre said no such thing, but no matter. It has been repeated so often that everybody knows he said it, just as everybody knows that Voltaire defended free speech for fascists when he – apocryphally – said: 'I disagree with what you say but I shall defend to the death your right to say it'.[7]

Many of Sartre's sternest critics in recent years have come from the ranks of those who once shared his alleged illusions. Michel-Antoine Burnier, who in 1966 published a pioneering account[8] of the politics of Sartre and *Les Temps modernes*, followed it in 1982 with a savage satire written in the first person in which Sartre confessed his pro-Communism, *Le Testament de Sartre*.[9] Former Maoists Claudie and Jacques Broyelle vilified Sartre at the expense of his old friend and antagonist Camus.[10] They did not have a difficult job. Sartre wrote an astounding quantity of material, published and unpublished; he made many rash and imprudent claims; and he frequently contradicted himself. It is not difficult to construct an indictment against him. To give a full and fair account of his merits as well as his defects is a rather more demanding task.

History has not been kind to the apologists of Stalinism, but an examination of the evidence is not particularly to the credit of the professional cold warriors of anti-Communism either. Their mission was always to use legitimate criticism of Stalinism to weaken socialism and working-class organisation. Their model of Stalinism as a monolithic society which could not achieve change from within was actually disproved by the whole process of popular revolt that helped to produce the collapse of Stalinism (and by the precursors of that revolt in East Germany 1953, Hungary 1956, Czechoslovakia 1968 and Poland 1980). Their defence of Western society was often naive in the extreme; for one example among many it is worth citing Karl Popper's claims from the 1950s that 'the problem of mass-unemployment has largely been solved' and that 'racial discrimination has diminished to an extent surpassing the hopes of the most hopeful'.[11]

Moreover, Sartre's critics fail to explain why, if he was in fact such an abject and sycophantic admirer of Stalinism, the PCF felt the need to launch such violent denunciations of him, notably those by such leading party intellectuals as Garaudy, Lefebvre and Kanapa in the period after the Liberation.

Indeed, as Sartre himself pointed out in 1948 in a preface to the American translation of *La Putain respectueuse*, the fact that he was being maligned by both sides in the emergent Cold War could only confirm his sense that he was in the right:

> It would be strange for me to be accused of anti-Americanism in New York at the very moment that *Pravda* in Moscow is energetically accusing me of being an agent of American propaganda. But if that were to happen, it would prove only one thing: either that I am very clumsy, or that I am on the right road.[12]

What follows is conceived of as a political defence of Sartre. Of course the very term 'political' raises problems. In 1979 Sartre's long-term associate Jean Pouillon reported Sartre as saying: 'Politics? That doesn't interest me.'[13] If politics is taken in its normal sense of ballot boxes and party manoeuvres in legislative assemblies, then Sartre was no doubt telling the truth. But he also told his young Maoist comrades in 1972 that 'everything is political, that is, calls into question society as a whole and leads to a challenge to it'.[14]

I have tried to bear in mind both the broad and narrow definitions of the 'political'. This book will confine itself to Sartre's political evolution and in particular to his relations to Stalinism and to the anti-Stalinist left. His literary and philosophical work – his major claims to distinction – will be touched on only inasmuch as they are relevant to that theme.

This study is not intended as an uncritical apologia for Sartre. Especially during his period of *rapprochement* with the PCF in the 1952–1956 period, Sartre did indeed make some quite unjustifiable statements. I have attempted to analyse the historical context, and to draw out the complexity of Sartre's position during this period, but an aim to understand does not imply justifying the unjustifiable. Sartre's own excuses for the period are particularly abject. In an interview in 1975 he admitted that after visiting the USSR he had 'lied' – but went on to add, firstly, that his secretary Jean Cau had finished off the incriminating article because he was ill (the previous year he had told de Beauvoir that Cau wrote the whole thing), and secondly that he was bound by obligations of courtesy: 'I thought that when you've been invited by people, you can't throw shit over them as soon as you get home.'[15] Whatever the exact circumstances, Sartre had authorised the publication of the appallingly pro-Stalinist articles (including the absurd claim that there was total freedom of criticism in the USSR) under his name, and they were his responsibility; the excuses fall neatly into the category of what Sartre himself described as 'bad faith'.[16]

There were great weaknesses in Sartre's political stance. All too often he made choices in terms of the short-term alternatives available, and ended up siding with the big battalions of the established left rather than looking to the longer-term potential in the situation, though to his credit he did so primarily out of a belief that without the mass of the working class nothing could be achieved. But the balance sheet of his political commitments, from 1941 to 1968 and after, is very much positive. In insisting that a radical alternative to the status quo was possible, and in stressing the necessity for practical deeds, Sartre stood for a model of political action far superior to the scepticism and passivity of the postmodernists who succeeded him in popular fashion. For that alone Sartre deserves to be read and reread.

This still leaves open the question of his many tactical judgements and misjudgements. In general the argument hinges on the question of whether there was in fact an alternative. For Sartre's liberal and pro-Western critics, Marxism and indeed any kind of revolutionary socialism was identical with Stalinism; hence in order to renounce the evils of Stalinism Sartre would have had to reject the whole revolutionary tradition.

Thus Tony Judt chose a particularly tasteless metaphor with which to rubbish the anti-Stalinist left in France:

> Like a battered wife, the non-Communist intelligentsia of the Left kept return-ing to its tormentor, assuring the police force of its conscience that 'he meant well', that he 'has reasons'. And that, in any case, 'I love him'. And like a violent husband, Communism continued to benefit from the faith its victims placed in their initial infatuation.[17]

That Judt had not studied the French anti-Stalinist left very carefully is shown by the fact that the names Colette Audry, Daniel Guérin, Maurice Nadeau, Pierre Naville and Alfred Rosmer are all absent from the index to his book.

In fact, as will be shown in what follows, there was a lively and vigor-ous anti-Stalinist left in France throughout the period of Sartre's adult life. The main components of this left can be listed as follows:

1. The organisations of 'orthodox' Trotskyism. While these were always very small, they occasionally had some impact on the course of events, notably in the Renault strike of 1947. The virulence of the Communist Party's attacks on 'Trotskyism' shows that they were not wholly insignificant.
2. Dissident Trotskyists, especially the grouping known as *Socialisme ou barbarie*. Although very small in numbers this tendency exercised an important influence on some of the leaders of the student movement in 1968, especially Daniel Cohn-Bendit, as well as on the Situationist Guy Debord. Some of its members – notably J.-F. Lyotard – were later to be influential in postmodernist circles.
3. Anarchists and syndicalists, in particular the survivors of revolu-tionary syndicalism, grouped round the journal *La Révolution prolé-tarienne*, including such veterans of the early Communist movement as Alfred Rosmer and Pierre Monatte. Albert Camus retained links with this current, while not sharing all their views.
4. The left of the Socialist Party. In the 1930s this was constituted by the *gauche révolutionnaire*, led by Marceau Pivert, and including such activists as Daniel Guérin and Colette Audry; later its members formed the *Parti socialiste ouvrier et paysan*. A far left of sorts survived in the postwar SFIO (Section française de l'internationale ouvrière) especially among the youth, though many were expelled or resigned with the rightward move of the party in the late 1940s.
5. Those surrealists who did not follow Aragon into Stalinism, notably André Breton, Benjamin Péret and Michel Leiris.
6. The independent left press. In the few years after the Liberation the papers *Combat* (edited by Camus and Bourdet, with its slogan 'From the Resistance to the Revolution') and Altman's *Franc-Tireur* had a combined print run higher than that of the Communist *L'Humanité*.[18]

In the 1950s the weekly *France-Observateur* appealed to a similar audience, as to some extent did also *L'Express*, at least on the Algerian question.

7. The *nouvelle gauche* of the 1950s and its successor, the *Parti socialiste unifié* (PSU), founded in 1960.

8. A number of individuals who had emerged from the Trotskyist movement – Pierre Naville, Maurice Nadeau, Gérard Rosenthal, David Rousset – many of whom remained faithful to their revolutionary principles.

These groupings did not constitute a mass movement, but they were not wholly insignificant in French political and intellectual life. Of course, they did not form a homogeneous current, and they were often sharply divided among themselves. Individuals developed radically – David Rousset from Trotskyism to Gaullism, Daniel Guérin from *pivertisme* to anarchism. Yet it is possible to establish that there was a distinct grouping of the French left which at one and the same time was strongly and openly critical of the various Stalinist regimes but supported working-class struggles at home and opposed French imperialism, notably in Indo-China and Algeria; this left advocated a model of socialism based on direct democracy utterly different from the authoritarian state power of Stalinism.

Yet there is not, to the best of my knowledge, any systematic study of Sartre's relations with this current. To a very considerable extent the blame for that must lie with Sartre himself, who in his last years repeatedly justified his previous positions by the claim that before 1968 there had been nothing to the left of the Communist Party:

Have you ever wondered why people who were *gauchistes* [supporters of the far left] in the PCF and who were expelled for *gauchiste* positions were later to be found to the right of the PCF, in the Socialist Party or worse? Because there was *nothing* to the left of the PCF.[19]

The Communists have always maintained – and it was true until now [1968] – that revolutionary movements which claimed to be located to the left of the PCF contributed to dividing the working class and always ended up by being 'objectively' further to the right than it was.[20]

Yesterday there was no *gauchisme*. To the left of the Communist Party there was nothing. In 1936, in 1940–1941, there was only one solution, which was to take the side of the Communist Party.[21]

As the following account will show, these claims by Sartre are quite simply false. There was an independent anti-Stalinist left throughout the period from the early 1930s to 1968, and Sartre was well aware of it. He debated with it, cooperated politically with it on occasion, and encouraged its members to contribute to *Les Temps modernes*.

In a 1974 discussion with Simone de Beauvoir Sartre made a partial self-criticism: 'There were, to the left of the Communists, groups who challenged official Communism, and who were sometimes right on a mass of questions; I did nothing to find out more about them. Until 1966 I ignored everything to the left of the Communist Party.'[22]

Again, unless Sartre was asleep when he wrote some of his most important polemics, this is simply untrue. Sartre was well aware of the positions of the anti-Stalinist left, and, as I hope to show, much more influenced by them than he was willing to admit.

There was, however, an important factor which led Sartre to feel closer to the big battalions of the PCF, despite his distrust of their politics, than to small groups like *Socialisme ou barbarie*. The choice of a small revolutionary group is always the choice of the future against the present. Such groups were far too small to have any direct impact on the course of events. Of course individual far left militants could lead a strike in a particular workplace, but the group as such could have no impact on the balance of forces in French society as a whole. The wager (rather like Pascal's wager on a future life) was that at some point in the future the correct anti-Stalinist politics would attract enough workers to challenge and replace the PCF.

For Trotsky and his generation there was what can be called the Zimmerwald syndrome. In 1915, at the time of the first anti-war conference in Switzerland, the internationalist left could be seated in four stage-coaches, but within five years it had become a worldwide movement of mass parties. Trotsky clearly believed this would happen again with the Second World War – hence his preoccupation with infinitesimal sects, because he believed that within a few years they would attract millions of workers. We have the advantage of hindsight – it was not wholly implausible at the time. Within the Trotskyist tradition the syndrome survived – when one group of fifty denounced another group of thirty it was because of the hope that within the foreseeable future it would become half a million.

But Sartre was quite outside this tradition. For him to opt for a small revolutionary group would have meant opting for the more or less distant future at the cost of abandoning any possibility of affecting the present. But Sartre's philosophy insisted that alternatives were available in the present; he was impressed by the power of the working class, even when he distrusted those who claimed to be its political representatives. He thus found himself trapped in an uneasy triangle. He was repelled by the PCF, yet powerfully drawn to it; he was unable to throw in his lot with the anti-Stalinist left, yet equally unable to disregard the force of its arguments.

But with few exceptions[23] most of Sartre's commentators have taken his statements about the anti-Stalinist left at face value. Many commentaries on Sartre's Marxism simply ignore his exchanges with such anti-Stalinists as Pierre Naville or Daniel Guérin; if the latter do get a name check there seems to be no recognition that their Marxism was qualitatively different from that of the PCF. As a result many commentaries on Sartre's Marxism in the *Critique de la raison dialectique* largely miss the point, since they never identify what was the 'Marxism' that Sartre was in dialogue with. Was it the Marxism of Marx or of Stalin? All too often Sartre's intellectual development and his move towards Marxism are seen as taking place within the confines of his own skull, rather than in the context of the prolonged crisis of French Stalinism, as its hegemony was shaken by the international crisis of 1956, and then destroyed by the revolt of 1968.

The following book will examine Sartre's relations with the anti-Stalinist left over the different phases of his development, giving particular importance to such individuals as Colette Audry, Maurice Nadeau, Pierre Naville, David Rousset, Claude Lefort and Daniel Guérin. In so doing I hope to rescue Sartre from those who would like to bury him. It also provides the opportunity to give an account of a number of important independent Marxist writers and activists whose intellectual contribution has all too often been ignored in accounts of the French left since the 1930s.

In an important recent study of George Orwell, John Newsinger has sought to rescue Orwell from the cooption of the Cold War anti-Communist right and to show that he remained a committed socialist.[24] In a sense, I hope to have accomplished a parallel task, by rescuing Sartre from those who would try to transform him into a mere fellow traveller of Stalinism.

The method of this book is quite simply to place Sartre's various political writings in context. Sartre himself stated that books were like dates or bananas, which should be eaten on the spot as soon as they are picked.[25] Those of us who were born too late cannot know what it was like to read Sartre straight from the news-stand – or to hear him lecture – in 1945. But by studying the context, discovering whom he was addressing and against whom he was arguing, we can avoid misunderstanding his meaning.

Like István Mészáros, I think 'it is Sartre's lifework as a whole that predominates, and not particular elements of it'.[26] Hence I have drawn particularly on Sartre's journalism and polemical writings rather than his 'major' philosophical or literary works. Sartre himself believed that the collection of essays, polemics, prefaces and interviews that make up the ten volumes of *Situations* would be more likely to survive than any other part of his work.[27]

Yet there is a problem with *Situations*. Sartre's polemics are reproduced without any commentary or indication of the context in which they were written. 'Replies' to Camus, Naville or Lefort are printed without any indication of what is being replied to. Often the other half of the dialogue exists only in the original journal where it first appeared. Sartre's 1952 debate with Camus has been endlessly reported, summarised and analysed, yet to the best of my knowledge the original review of *L'Homme révolté* by Francis Jeanson which sparked the quarrel has never been reprinted since it first appeared in *Les Temps modernes*.[28]

Though not always wholly reliable, Simone de Beauvoir's various volumes of autobiography were an invaluable aid to reinserting Sartre's writings in their historical and polemical context. But de Beauvoir gave no precise references, and her account often reflected her own prejudices, not always identical with Sartre's. It was the publication of Contat and Rybalka's *Les Écrits de Sartre* which first made possible the recreation of the living context of Sartre's work.

In this book I have tried, by identifying Sartre's opponents and consulting debates in the contemporary press, to reestablish Sartre's debate with the anti-Stalinist left, a debate all too often suppressed or ignored. If it encourages some readers to question the glib accusations hawked by Judt, the Broyelles and their like, it will serve its purpose.

Notes

1. *Sit* X, p. 188.
2. This position is not confined to the political right. Even some of those who remain very much on the radical left argue that since 1989 Marxism has become obsolete, and offer their allegiance to something called 'post-Marxism'.
3. N. Podhoretz, *The Bloody Crossroads*, New York, 1986, p. 28.
4. B.-H. Lévy, *Le Siècle de Sartre*, Paris, 2000, p. 477. Lévy even criticises Sartre for arguing in 1980 that the USSR was not a fascist country (p. 444) – something which even the most rigorous anti-Stalinist with an elementary respect for the meaning of words would do.
5. *Sunday Times*, 20 April 1980.
6. T. Judt, *Past Imperfect*, Berkeley and Los Angeles, 1992, p. 211.
7. See I.H. Birchall, 'Voltaire and Collective Action', *British Journal for Eighteenth-Century Studies*, Vol. XIII, No. 1 (Spring 1990), p. 26.
8. M.-A. Burnier, *Les Existentialistes et la politique*, Paris, 1966.
9. M.-A. Burnier, *Le Testament de Sartre*, Paris, 1982. In 2000 Burnier published an autobiographical account of his own relations with Sartre, *L'Adieu à Sartre*, (Paris, 2000), showing how idolisation gave way to disillusion.. It is a more balanced assessment, and, like Bernard-Henri Lévy's book, may be symptomatic of the fact that the worst period of Sartre-baiting is now over.
10. C. and J. Broyelle, *Les Illusions retrouvées*, Paris, 1982.
11. Lecture at Bristol University, 12 October 1956, in K. Popper, *Conjectures and Refutations*, London, 1972, pp. 370–71.
12. *TDS*, p. 244.
13. J. Pouillon, 'Sartre et la politique', *Études sartriennes* II–III (1986), pp. 121–28.
14. *Raison*, p. 27.
15. *Sit* X, p. 220; *Adieux*, p. 462. The articles in question appeared in *Libération* 15–20 July 1954.
16. It is interesting to note that Albert Camus, whose supposed total honesty is frequently contrasted to Sartre, made a very similar excuse after his visit to the U.S.A. in 1946: 'I don't intend, like Sartre, to spit in the bowl after agreeing to eat the soup offered me.' (O. Todd, *Albert Camus*, Paris, 1996, p. 412). Whatever the issue, politeness is not a revolutionary virtue.
17. Judt, *Past Imperfect*, p. 158.
18. Comparative circulation figures:

	L'Humanité	*Franc-Tireur*	*Combat*
January 1945	326,000	182,000	185,000
April 1947	450,000	350,000	128,000

    C. Bellanger et al., *Histoire générale de la presse française* Vol. IV, Paris, 1975, pp. 300, 357.

19. *Raison*, p. 41.
20. *Sit* VIII, p. 222.
21. J.-P. Sartre, B. Pingaud and D Mascolo, *Du Rôle de l'intellectuel dans le mouvement révolutionnaire*, Paris, 1971, p. 21.
22. *Adieux*, p. 504.
23. For a more critical account of Sartre's relations with Trotskyism see the obituary of Sartre by A. Krivine and D. Bensaïd (*Le Matin*, April–May 1980, translated in *Telos* No. 44, Summer 1980, pp. 193–94).
24. J. Newsinger, *Orwell's Politics*, Basingstoke, 1999.
25. 'Ecrire pour son époque' (1946) in *C&R*, p. 674.
26. I. Mészáros, *The Work of Sartre*, Brighton, 1979, p. 14.
27. *Adieux*, p. 215.
28. This is not wholly true of the later volumes of *Situations*. Volume VIII contains a letter from D. I. Grossvogel and Sartre's correspondence with de Gaulle about the Russell Tribunal. (*Sit* VIII, pp. 20–24, 42–45). The inclusion of Kanapa's article 'Un "nouveau" révisionnisme à l'usage des intellectuels' (A 'new' revisionism for the use of intellectuals) in *Sit* VII, pp. 94–98 was doubtless decided on because Kanapa's own text exposed his backbiting sectarianism more effectively than any critique could do.

PART I

The Making of a Rebel

Chapter 2

'LA COMMUNISTE'

> *The war really divided my life in two… That was when… I made the*
> *transition from individualism and the pure individual before the war to the*
> *social, to socialism. That was the true turning-point in my life.*[1]

Sartre has repeatedly insisted in interviews that he was apolitical until
1939 and that it was the experience of the Second World War that transformed him into a committed thinker and writer. Most commentators have
accepted his claims at face value, and in a sense they are quite right to do
so. Yet the question depends on what definition of 'political' is used.
Before 1939 Sartre joined no organisation, participated in no campaign; but
he thought, read and talked about power and wealth, about oppression
and about how society might be better organised.

Indeed, if we want to understand how Sartre became Sartre, how he
developed as he did after the traumatic experiences of 1939, it is necessary
to examine his experiences and the influences he underwent in the period
before 1939. It was not the war that made Sartre the committed writer, but
rather the interaction between the experience of war and Sartre as he had
already developed. What he saw depended on what he was already looking for. Every French person was affected by the Occupation, but not every
French person was Sartre.

The philosophical and literary influences on the young Sartre are familiar. Less well known are the political influences that affected him during
the 1930s, especially those from the anti-Stalinist left.

Sartre himself claimed that he had always been an 'anarchist'.[2] Yet if the
term is given any sort of rigorous definition, it is patently untrue – Sartre
had no links with political anarchism and works such as *Les Communistes
et la paix* are hardly inspired by the anarchist spirit. Yet if it is no more than
some loose reference to a rebellious temperament, it tells us little.

Arguably Sartre's first political experience came at the age of around eight. His mother had hired a teacher to give him private lessons; the teacher complained of her low pay and her inability to find a husband. But when the young Sartre reported her grievances to his grandfather, the latter merely laughed and said she was too ugly to marry. 'I did not laugh; could you be born condemned? In that case I had been lied to; the order of the world concealed an intolerable disorder'.[3] Sartre had learnt that his own family did not believe their own professed values, and from this we can trace two of the most important themes in Sartre's subsequent intellectual development. Firstly, his profound distrust of his own class, the bourgeoisie. And secondly, the quest for values that could be taken seriously, the unity of theory and practice.

Sartre was twelve years old at the time of the Russian Revolution. His only knowledge of it was through the distorted reports of the conservative press, but because his stepfather, whom he loathed, was so hostile to Bolshevism, the young Sartre naturally tended to sympathise with it.[4] At the age of nineteen, he said, he had felt 'disgust' at colonialism.[5] This was around the time of the Rif War, when in September 1924 French Communists Doriot and Semard caused scandal by making public a message of support to Moroccan nationalist leader Abd-el-Krim urging struggle against all imperialists, including the French. Hence he would doubtless have seen the PCF as the most forthright and consistent opponent of colonialism.

Anti-colonialism in the 1920s was but a short step from anti-militarism, and when Sartre was a student at the *Ecole normale supérieure* in the 1920s his political energies, such as they were at the time, seem to have gone into anti-militarism, albeit often of a somewhat frivolous nature. Jean Bruhat, a fellow student of Sartre's, has collected a number of anti-militarist songs probably written at least in part by Sartre.[6]

Thus Sartre's original acquaintance with the PCF came in its earliest period, at a time when, under the influence of the twenty-one conditions for affiliation to the Comintern, it was vigorously anti-colonialist and anti-militarist, but before the time when Stalin's ascendancy in Russia was able to dictate leftward and rightward swings to the PCF at will.

De Beauvoir records that for her and Sartre, the original flame of the Russian Revolution was extinct by 1929, and that they perceived Russia under Stalin as an 'engineers' civilisation'.[7] Obviously a period in which technological advance and economic planning had crushed the last remnants of working-class democracy held little charm for Sartre. Yet de Beauvoir also notes that during this period Sartre was 'vaguely tempted to join the PCF'.[8]

Sartre read copiously during the 1930s, and there is no doubt that he was well aware that there was a left alternative to Stalinism. As de Beauvoir recalled: 'We had the greatest esteem for Trotsky, and the idea of "permanent revolution" appealed to our anarchist tendencies much more than the idea of building socialism in one country'. Yet, she added, they were never tempted to join a Trotskyist organisation. Firstly, because they found the oppositional groupings afflicted with the same 'ideological dogmatism' as the PCF, and secondly because these groupings were so small as to be quite ineffective.[9] In the early 1930s Sartre read Trotsky's *My Life* and, possibly, his *History of the Russian Revolution*.[10]

Sartre and de Beauvoir took what the latter called 'a moderate interest' in the case of the writer Victor Serge, about which the 'anti-Stalinists felt passionately'.[11] Serge, a former anarchist who had held responsibilities in the Comintern before becoming a supporter of the Left Opposition, had been imprisoned in Russia. The case drew a clear dividing line between the Stalinists and anti-Stalinists. The latter, including some surrealists, veteran ex-Communists like Marcel Martinet and 'proletarian writers' like Henry Poulaille, campaigned vigorously in support of Serge, notably at the 1935 International Writers Congress for the Defence of Culture. PCF members – including Nizan – and fellow-travellers bitterly opposed them.[12]

An important figure from the anti-Stalinist left who had some influence at this time was Daniel Guérin, later to become a regular contributor to *Les Temps modernes*. At the time of Hitler's accession to power most of the left was hopelessly confused. The PCF saw social democracy as 'social fascism' and hence equally as bad as Nazism, while the mainstream of the Socialist Party (SFIO) displayed a fatal complacency, hoping that Nazism would simply disappear if nobody said anything about it. Guérin was a member of the *gauche révolutionnaire*, the far left current within the SFIO, led by Marceau Pivert, which was sympathetic to many of Trotsky's ideas. Guérin toured Germany in the summer of 1933, observing Hitler's new regime and smuggling out clandestine leaflets in the frame of his bicycle. He published a series of descriptive articles in *Le Populaire*, the SFIO daily,[13] and followed this with a major study of German and Italian fascism in *Fascisme et grand capital* (Fascism and Big Business, 1936). De Beauvoir notes that this book 'helped us a little to understand our age'. While Guérin gave central attention to the social and economic roots of fascism, he also lamented the fact that too many contemporary Marxists confined themselves to the economic level, and failed to study the psychological appeal of fascism; he argued that it was necessary to counterpose socialist 'idealism' to the fascist 'mystique'.[14] Sartre, in his story 'L'Enfance d'un chef' (1939, in the collection *Le Mur*), was to stress the psychological appeal of fascism; it is not inconceivable that the reading of Guérin was one of the factors which inspired this project.

Also of importance for Sartre had been the discovery, in his last years at *lycée*, of the surrealists.[15] His later writings show that he was profoundly ambiguous about surrealism, and he made many sharp criticisms of its aesthetics and politics. But in his 1960 essay on Nizan he looked back with nostalgia to the times of 'hatred, unsated desire and destruction' when 'André Breton, scarcely any older than we were, wished to see the Cossacks watering their horses in the fountain on the Place de la Concorde'. Such sentiments could not fail to appeal to Sartre's rebellious spirit and his profound hatred of the bourgeoisie. Moreover, his long footnote on surrealism in *Qu'est-ce que la littérature?* shows that he had observed its political evolution – entry into and exit from the PCF followed by *rapprochement* with Trotsky – with some care, and clearly regarded it as an important lesson, if mainly a negative one, for the practice of committed literature.[16]

But although Sartre observed the surrealist contacts with Trotsky there is no evidence that he took any interest in the establishment in France of the *Fédération internationale de l'art révolutionnaire indépendant* (FIARI). This was set up to propagate the ideas developed in the manifesto 'Towards a Free Revolutionary Art', jointly authored by Trotsky and Breton in 1938; in reality its sole activity was to produce two issues of a journal, *Clé*, in 1939. Sartre did not identify with either of the main groups who supported the FIARI, the surrealists and the 'proletarian' writers. However, Maurice Nadeau and André Masson,[17] both later to be friends of Sartre and contributors to *Les Temps modernes*, were supporters of the FIARI.[18]

Sartre's exposure to the political debates of the 1930s did not come entirely through the written word. He had a number of friends and acquaintances who gave him direct insight into the current arguments. Of these, the one who has been most discussed, and who was certainly of great importance, is Paul Nizan. Nizan was an active Communist Party member from 1927 till his dramatic resignation from the PCF at the time of the Hitler–Stalin Pact. He had been a close friend of Sartre's for many years and certainly played a major role in enabling Sartre to understand the nature of orthodox Communist thinking in the 1930s.

Nizan was a trusted propagandist, who wrote widely for the PCF press. He would not have been given such a role had his loyalty been in any doubt; it was obviously because he had played such an important public part that after his defection it became necessary for the PCF to vilify him and accuse him of having been a police informer. Since his death it has been argued that in private Nizan was critical of aspects of Stalinism.[19] In the film on Sartre made by Contat and Astruc in 1972, de Beauvoir claimed that Nizan was 'very disconcerted by the Moscow Trials', but Sartre insisted: 'He didn't talk about it… He said nothing, for or against'. [20]

It may be that Nizan communicated some of his doubts, explicitly or implicitly, to a close personal friend like Sartre. The fact remains that in public he was a loyal Stalinist, who extolled Stalin's 'humanism', defended the Moscow Trials and argued that the POUM (Partido Obrero de Unificación Marxista – anti-Stalinist Marxists who opposed the Comintern's Popular Front line) in Spain were acting in collusion with Franco's espionage services.[21] Michael Scriven has quite rightly argued that Nizan was 'clearly convinced of the necessity to adopt a strictly orthodox party line', that his defence of Stalinism sprang from deep commitment, and that the Stalinism of his political practice contrasted sharply with the 'rebellious, iconoclastic picture projected by Sartre' in his 1960 article.[22] Indeed, while the PCF's later vilification of Nizan was an act of contemptible dishonesty, it is only fair to say that he was paid back in his own coin.

To those, like Sartre and de Beauvoir, whose attitude was not shaped by any organisational loyalty, Nizan must have seemed a contradictory figure. He was undoubtedly a writer of great talent and had a degree of personal commitment utterly foreign to the prewar Sartre; yet the Stalinist message he was transmitting was clearly unacceptable in its totality. Hence his influence was less than is sometimes supposed. While admiring *Aden-Arabie*, Sartre disagreed with the political logic which had led Nizan to join the PCF. But as de Beauvoir puts it: 'In view of his friendship for Nizan, it was easier for Sartre to tone down this divergence rather than to give it its full importance. Hence we appreciated Nizan's virtuosity without giving sufficient importance to what he was saying'. [23]

Sartre also came into contact with a number of activists from the anti-Stalinist left. Among these were Aimé Patri (a Trotskyist in the late 1920s and subsequently a member of the *gauche révolutionnaire* in the SFIO), Michel Collinet (like Patri an ex-Trotskyist now in the *gauche révolutionnaire*, who came to argue that socialists should not defend the USSR), who taught at the *lycée* in Rouen, and Simone Weil,[24] who, before she developed towards a religious position, was involved with Trotskyist and syndicalist circles. Weil had met Trotsky during his exile in France; she was influenced by Lucien Laurat, who was one of the first to argue that Russia was a new kind of society that was neither capitalist nor socialist, but ruled by an exploitative bureaucratic oligarchy, and who therefore argued against Trotsky's position that Russia was still a 'workers' state'. Weil herself saw Russia as an 'oppressive state' that was neither capitalist nor proletarian.[25] Hence Sartre had the opportunity to become aware of the different positions circulating on the anti-Stalinist left.

But the most important of all Sartre's political friends in the 1930s was Colette Audry (1906–1990). Audry first met Simone de Beauvoir in October 1932, when they were teaching in the same *lycée* in Rouen. Audry was already an activist on the far left.[26] She had been deeply affected by reading Trotsky's *My Life*, and had moved beyond an early sympathy for the PCF. As a teacher she became involved in the *Fédération unitaire de l'enseignement*; this left-wing teachers' union and its weekly paper *L'Ecole émancipée* were very much in the hands of the anti-Stalinists left. Here she encountered a range of political tendencies, including anarchists and Trotskyists. She joined the SFIO and became, like Daniel Guérin, a member of the *gauche révolutionnaire*. Audry was thus the very antithesis of the disengaged Sartre; she was a trade-union activist and undertook regular street sales of the SFIO newspaper *Le Populaire*.

In her memoirs de Beauvoir states that Audry was a member of a 'faction of Trotskyist oppositionists',[27] and many commentators have taken this at face value and repeated it as established fact. Yet there seems to be no evidence that Audry was ever a member of a Trotskyist organisation.[28] She remained a member of the SFIO when the Trotskyists were expelled in 1935 and during the Spanish Civil War she supported the POUM (producing the French edition of its journal), of which Trotsky was highly critical. Yet if de

Beauvoir failed to pick up the finer points of doctrine and organisation, in essence she was correct. On the major issues of the 1930s – anti-fascism, the Popular Front government, Spain and the Moscow Trials – Audry stood clearly in the camp of the anti-Stalinist opposition to the PCF.

The relationship between Audry, de Beauvoir and Sartre became a warm personal one (even though Sartre enraged her on occasion by telling her that women should keep out of politics!)[29] When Sartre was in Berlin in 1934, Audry helped de Beauvoir to absent herself from her teaching duties on a spurious medical pretext in order to visit him.[30] On more than one occasion Audry pawned her typewriter in order to lend money to Sartre and de Beauvoir.[31]

Audry remained a close personal friend of Sartre in the postwar period, and she was a regular contributor to *Les Temps modernes*. She published two books on Sartre[32] and always identified herself as one of his closest associates. Yet despite the substantial body of evidence, commentators on Sartre have systematically underestimated the influence of Audry on the development of Sartre's political views.[33] And either through malice or ignorance, they have failed to draw out the distinctive features of Audry's political stance.

Sartre himself seems to have been somewhat obtuse about those distinctive features. In an interview with John Gerassi in 1973, Audry made no efforts to conceal the fact that the 1930s Sartre had been far behind her in his political development:

> I met Sartre… and we got into lots of political arguments. He used to call me *'La' Communiste…*, even though he understood full well that the Communist party opposed us. His main argument then was simply this: workers can only escape their condition by joining the CP, but we intellectuals have other means, so why commit ourselves to political sides?… I would say that he was a left-winger who was neither a revolutionary nor a rebel… Sartre didn't understand politics very well, in 1936… He couldn't understand why, since I was a communist and a revolutionary, I was not a member of the Communist party. In fact, he was so blunderingly naive about it that friends of mine kept asking me why I even bothered talking to him. (I remember answering one of them that 'I was preparing the man of the future'.) But these political simplicities on his part dealt with tactics. On fundamentals, we agreed. When I returned from Cataluña and described to him the situation there, he was certainly in favor of intervention by the democracies, on the side of the Republic.[34]

Sartre was obviously a slow learner, and Audry was miles ahead of him in political culture and sophistication. But it is impossible to imagine that Sartre derived nothing from these discussions. In particular he must have become familiar with the arguments current on the far left about the class nature of the USSR – we find echoes of those debates in his writings of the 1940s and 1950s. De Beauvoir reports these discussions in such a way as deliberately to belittle them: 'When Colette Audry told us that her grouping – which had a total of five members – was examining the opportuneness of a new revolution in the USSR, we made plain our scepticism'. [35]

The accuracy of de Beauvoir's memory may be questioned. It is not clear what the 'grouping' in question was; Trotskyist groups with five members are a popular urban myth. Admittedly, the disproportion between programmatic aspirations and the forces that can actually be mobilised is one that has always haunted the Trotskyist movement, and in this sense de Beauvoir's implied criticisms have some force. But clearly Audry and her friends were not actually proposing to organise an insurrection on Russian soil, but rather trying to develop an analysis of what had gone wrong with the Revolution and how such distortions might be corrected.

In 1935 Nizan, who had just spent a year in the USSR, dined in Rouen with Sartre, de Beauvoir and Audry. Doubtless this provided yet another opportunity for Sartre to observe the differences between the Stalinist left and its critics.[36] Memories of such arguments must have built up inside Sartre's skull, so that when he himself began to discuss the questions after the Liberation, he was already familiar with the positions available. Whatever positions he was to adopt later in life, Sartre did not do so in ignorance or in innocence. He had heard the arguments and he knew the alternatives.

On at least three major questions Audry was politically and intellectually in advance of Sartre and de Beauvoir, and her ideas and writings may well have exercised a significant influence.

Firstly, Audry discovered the question of women's oppression long before de Beauvoir. During their years working together in Rouen Audry frequently argued with de Beauvoir that it would be of value to write a book that would encourage women to reject their oppression. De Beauvoir was very sceptical, since in her own relatively privileged career she had not found women's oppression a major problem. Audry, of course, was far too involved in the day-to-day struggle to engage in the kind of research needed. But well over a decade later the project finally germinated in de Beauvoir's mind, and she wrote *Le Deuxième Sexe*.[37]

Secondly, Audry preceded Sartre onto the difficult and dangerous terrain of the study of Heidegger. In 1934 Audry published a short two-part study of Heidegger in *L'Ecole émancipée*.[38] This was not an academic journal, but a weekly paper aimed at the rank and file of the *Fédération unitaire de l'enseignement*. It carried trade union news, discussion of teaching materials, and general articles on political and literary topics. Politically it was very much under the control of the anti-Stalinist left.

The article was addressed to the typical readership of *L'Ecole émancipée*, schoolteachers whose professional and trade union commitments gave them little time for study, but who were anxious to keep up with contemporary events. Audry's article was modest in scope: less than two thousand words in – relatively – simple language; but in content it was highly ambitious, covering all Heidegger's major works to date, including *Being and Time*. Most of this material was available only in German, but Audry, a talented linguist, had ploughed her way through it.

Her title, 'A philosophy of German fascism', made clear the nature of the project. For most of the left German Nazism was a new and bewildering phenomenon. By examining the relations between fascist ideology and a prominent intellectual who had publicly identified himself with Hitler, Audry was making her contribution to a demystification of the phenomenon.

Audry began by attempting to situate Heidegger in his historical context. His work, she argued,

> constitutes a translation into philosophical language of the state of mind of the German people since the war, of the problems it has encountered and the solution it devised. By this I do not mean that Martin Heidegger (although he has recently given his solemn support to the Third Reich) has made a conscious effort to manufacture, for the needs of rather more demanding intelligences, a doctrine which the theoretical poverty of *Mein Kampf* and the absurdities of Alfred Rosenberg made very necessary. All he did was to follow, as a philosopher, a path parallel to that of the petty bourgeois masses.

Audry thus staked out her methodological ground. A philosophical system was not born in a vacuum, but came into existence in specific historical circumstances. Heidegger's public adhesion to Nazism was not 'irrelevant', as devotees of pure philosophy would argue; but nor was it sufficient to enable us to categorise and condemn his thought. A philosophical system had a certain autonomy within the philosophical system in which it originated. Audry was thus already confronting questions of method with which Sartre was to grapple twenty years later in the *Critique de la raison dialectique*.

Audry went on to examine what she saw as Heidegger's 'religion of man' and compared it with the Nazi attitude to religion, showing how the concept of 'totality' had been appropriated by Heidegger and Nazi thought for their own purposes. She noted that the idea of 'the complete man' was central to education in German schools and universities under the Nazis, and argued that Nazi ideas of race were rooted in this idea. She then passed on to the notion of destiny and anticipated later commentators on Heidegger by linking the theme of destiny in *Being and Time* to the Nazi idea of national destiny. In conclusion she saw Heidegger's thought as essentially pessimistic, and likened his 'tragic doctrine' to the underlying contradictions of the newly established fascist social order.

Sartre had spent the academic year 1933–34 in Berlin, but although he had devoted some time to Heidegger, he had concentrated primarily on Husserl,[39] and he studied Heidegger in depth only some years later. Audry's article was probably written around the time of Sartre's return from Germany, though there is no evidence that she consulted him about it. However, given Sartre's interest in contemporary German philosophy – and the fact that Audry was one of nature's paper-sellers – we can be fairly certain that Sartre read the article.

In raising the question of Heidegger's Nazi connections Audry was anticipating a debate which was to recur on a much wider scale, beginning with articles in *Les Temps modernes* just after the Liberation,[40] and erupting again in the last decades of the century. But perhaps the most important part of Audry's study of Heidegger was the final paragraph. Here she returned to the question of how Marxism should approach such a topic. She lamented the fact that Stalinist Marxism had become concerned with the economic and political to the exclusion of a more complex materialist account of the totality of human culture:

> Marxism had the means of achieving this synthesis. The bases had been laid. It is deplorable that in the fields of philosophy, morality and psychology, Marxists have stuck too closely to those foundations, failing to pursue the analysis, to respond to the needs of the moment, to enrich human experience; as a result they leave to their opponents the monopoly of intellectual audacity in everything which goes beyond the scope of the purely economic and political.

It is impossible not to see in this conclusion some of the themes that were to occupy Sartre over the next forty or more years, in the *Critique de la raison dialectique* and in his existential biographies, where he strove to understand the relation between the writer and the text in a way that avoided both the idealist irresponsibility of seeing the text as wholly autonomous and the crude reductionism which explained everything through a political or sociological alignment.

Audry's account may be contrasted with an article written a little earlier by Nizan. He had argued that 'the philosophy of Martin Heidegger may provide theoretical justifications for a fascist doctrine'. But Nizan – a polemicist rather than a philosopher – did little to prove the point. Writing at a time when the Comintern equated fascism and social democracy, he saw emergent fascism on all sides, and even listed Kierkegaard as one of the sources of a 'future fascist philosophy'. Such indiscriminate reductionism had little hope of actually demonstrating anything.[41]

A few months earlier Audry had contributed another article to *L'Ecole émancipée*. This was on a literary subject: 'Contemporary American Literature: John Dos Passos – William Faulkner – Eugene O'Neill'.[42] In fact the article was devoted almost exclusively to Dos Passos, whom Audry used to pursue a similar problem to the one she confronted in the Heidegger article – namely, was it possible to develop a form of literature that would be genuinely revolutionary without being crudely propagandist? Audry noted that Dos Passos was a Marxist, and more revolutionary than Faulkner or O'Neill. Yet his work was not that of a propagandist: 'He has done something much better than make propaganda: he has introduced Marxism into the literary domain, in a *specifically* literary form'.

She stressed the importance of technique – understood in a broad sense – in Dos Passos's work, thus grappling with the problem of a revolutionary art which united theory and practice without falling into the trap of party and state control that characterised 'socialist realism'. She went on to describe the methods used by Dos Passos in *The Forty-Second Parallel* and *1919*:

> The characters are not necessarily in any relation with each other; some never meet each other, others are brought together for a moment by chance, but never see each other again. Others come together, are separated and sometimes are reunited. We move from one existence to another (each chapter concerns only *one* character), then to a third, before returning to the first. All around gravitate a host of episodic individuals, who emerge from the shade and disappear back into it, without having their own story told in the book.

What is striking here is that Audry's account would serve as an excellent description of aspects of Sartre's novel *Le Sursis*.

Audry then noted that in Dos Passos 'the narrative is presented as a sort of interior monologue in the third person'. Four years later, in an essay on Dos Passos, Sartre was to write that: 'Dos Passos's man is a hybrid being, internal-external. We are with him, in him, we live with his vacillating individual consciousness and all at once it wavers, weakens and is diluted into the collective consciousness. We follow it there and suddenly we find ourselves outside without having noticed it'.[43] Once again Audry seems to have explored terrain on which Sartre was later to work.[44]

None of this is intended to suggest that Sartre plagiarised Audry, nor even that he was particularly influenced by her. There are few close resemblances between her writings on Heidegger or Dos Passos and his. But it is certainly interesting to note the coincidence of some of their preoccupations, and the fact that, in both the philosophical and the literary sphere, Audry was aiming to develop a Marxism that was relevant to contemporary struggle without being crudely reductionist. In that sense her influence on Sartre was certainly significant.

Notes

1. *Sit X*, p. 180.
2. *Sit X*, p. 155.
3. J.-P. Sartre, *Les Mots*, Paris, 1964, p. 66.
4. *Raison*, pp. 171–72; J. Gerassi, *Jean-Paul Sartre – Hated Conscience of His Century*, vol. I, Chicago, 1989, p. 57.
5. J.-P. Sartre and B. Lévy, *L'Espoir maintenant*, Lagrasse, 1991, p. 64.
6. J. Bruhat, *Il n'est jamais trop tard*, Paris, 1983, pp. 44–46, 261–64.
7. *Force*, p. 37.
8. *Force*, p. 140.
9. *Force*, p. 141. In the 1930s the French Trotskyists had no more than 100 members, and by 1936 the figure had grown only to just over 600. See T. Cliff, *The Darker the Night the Brighter the Star* (London, 1993, pp. 206, 222). They did, however, exercise an influence disproportionate to their numbers during their brief period of entry in the SFIO in 1934–1935.

10. *Force*, pp. 53, 154.
11. *Force*, p. 141. Readers of the English translation of de Beauvoir's memoirs will find no reference to Serge; the case is transmuted into the 'Stavisky Affair'. (Alexandre Stavisky was at the centre of a financial scandal in 1934; he used the pseudonym Serge Alexandre.) See S. de Beauvoir, *The Prime of Life* (Harmondsworth, trans. Peter Green, 1965, p. 135). This is symptomatic of the ignorance of Victor Serge in British culture.
12. See R. Greeman, 'The Victor Serge Affair and the French Literary Left', *Revolutionary History* Vol. 5, No. 3 (1994), pp. 142–74.
13. Collected in *La Peste brune*, Paris, 1969.
14. D. Guérin, *Fascisme et grand capital*, Paris, 1969, pp. 73–76.
15. *Adieux*, p. 180.
16. *Sit* IV, p. 141; *Sit* II, pp. 317–26. In 1926, Pierre Naville, who was to cross swords with Sartre on several occasions, was, as a young surrealist evolving towards Communism and then Trotskyism, scathing about what he saw as Breton's 'sentimental vision' of revolution: 'There's as little interest in seeing Mongols pitch camp on our squares as there is in seeing "socialists" taking their seats as ministers' (P. Naville, *La Révolution et les intellectuels*, Paris, 1975, p. 95).
17. See J.-P. Sartre, 'Masson', *Sit* IV, pp. 387–407.
18. See *Clé* No. 1, January 1939, p. 6; also *Revolutionary History* Vol. 7, No. 4 (1999), pp. 214–15.
19. A. Ginsbourg, *Paul Nizan*, Paris, 1966, p. 82.
20. A. Astruc and M. Contat, *Sartre*, Paris, 1977, pp. 46–47.
21. Ginsbourg, *Paul Nizan*, pp. 30, 76.
22. M. Scriven, *Paul Nizan: Communist Novelist*, Basingstoke, 1988, pp. 30, 40–43.
23. *Force*, p. 84.
24. *Force*, p. 126.
25. H. Bouchardeau, *Simone Weil*, Paris, 1995, p. 90; D. McLellan, *Simone Weil*, Basingstoke, 1989, pp. 60, 81; P. Dujardin, *Simone Weil – idéologie et politique*, Grenoble, 1975, p. 81.
26. Audry makes frequent appearances in de Beauvoir's memoirs. The fullest account of her political life is in J. Maitron and C. Pennetier, *Dictionnaire biographique du mouvement ouvrier français* (Paris, 1964ff. 17: 312–14), based in part on an interview given by Audry in 1979. See also Audry's autobiographical novel, *La Statue* (Paris, 1983).
27. *Force*, p. 126.
28. Maitron and Pennetier's authoritative *Dictionnaire biographique du mouvement ouvrier français*, 16: 481–84, contains a list of some 550 people known to have belonged to a Trotskyist organisation in France before 1939; Audry's name does not appear.
29. D. Bair, *Simone de Beauvoir*, London, 1990, p. 325.
30. Audry, *La Statue*, p. 209.
31. *Adieux*, p. 431.
32. C. Audry, *Connaissance de Sartre*, Paris, 1955; C. Audry, *Sartre et la réalité humaine*, Paris, 1966.
33. In her 850-page biography of Sartre (*Sartre*, Paris, 1985), Annie Cohen-Solal finds space for just *four* references to Audry, only one of which refers to the period before the Second World War.
34. Gerassi, *Jean-Paul Sartre*, pp. 111, 139.
35. *Force*, p. 141. The misrepresentation was increased in the English translation, which referred to a debate about 'the possibility of a new revolution inside Russia' (De Beauvoir, *The Prime of Life*, p. 135). The French term used was *opportunité*, meaning 'opportuneness'; that is, the issue at stake was whether the Stalinist bureaucracy could be removed by a process of reform, or whether it had become so firmly entrenched that only revolutionary action by Russian workers could replace it. The debate was to have a long history within the anti-Stalinist left. Until 1933, Trotsky had believed that the Communist International was still susceptible to regeneration; once Hitler was established in power, he decided that it was necessary to build a new revolutionary international. Situated in context, the debate was not as absurd as it seems at first sight, and indeed was essential to an understanding of the nature of Stalinist society.

36. Cohen-Solal, *Sartre*, p. 215.

37. Bair, *Simone de Beauvoir*, pp. 325, 379–80, 680.

38. C. Audry, 'Une philosophie du fascisme allemand: l'oeuvre de Martin Heidegger', *L'Ecole émancipée* 14 October, 1934, pp. 34–35; 21 October, p. 53. For a full discussion and partial translation, see I. Birchall, 'Prequel to the Heidegger Debate', *Radical Philosophy* 88 (March–April 1998), pp. 19–27.

39. See 'Une idée fondamentale de la phénoménologie de Husserl: l'intentionnalité', *Sit* I, pp. 29–32.

40. Articles by M. de Gandillac and A. de Towarnicki, *TM*, January 1946, pp. 713–24; article by Karl Löwith, *TM*, November 1946, pp. 343–60. See also Sartre's article in *Action*, 29 December 1944, reproduced in *C&R*, pp. 653–58.

41. P. Nizan, 'Sur un certain front unique',. *Europe* 121, 15 January 1933, pp. 137–46.

42. *L'Ecole émancipée*, 18 February 1934, pp. 337–39.

43. *Sit* I, p. 23.

44. While *Le Sursis* was clearly influenced by Dos Passos, there may well also have been French sources, especially in unanimism. In many ways the structure of *Le Sursis* resembles that of Marcel Martinet's novel of the First World War, *La Maison à l'abri* (Paris, 1919), in which the impact of the outbreak of war is traced through the fortunes of a loosely linked group of individuals living in the same house. I have found no evidence that Sartre ever read Martinet, but it is quite possible that he did so; Martinet was short-listed for the *prix Goncourt* in 1919 (the year it was won by Proust) and his novel was for a time well known.

Chapter 3

THE THREAT OF FASCISM

The most crucial influence on Sartre in the 1930s was that of events themselves. The decade was marked by the rise and consolidation of fascism in Italy, Germany and then Spain. Sartre developed a deep loathing of fascism, beginning from the year he spent in Berlin when Hitler's regime was consolidating itself.[1]

In the short term Sartre was little affected by the experience of Nazi Berlin. But this may be less surprising than it seems. Most of the European left was confused and disoriented by Hitler's victory. The Comintern, having allowed Hitler to take power by refusing to build a united front against him, initially believed that his victory would be very temporary, and would improve the prospects for Communist revolution. Social democrats were often equally complacent. Daniel Guérin recalled being criticised by an SFIO member who told him that he would bring fascism about by talking about it too much; the woman who reprimanded him perished in a Nazi camp.[2] Sartre remembered being told by Raymond Aron, 'who was still a socialist then… that Hitler and his horde could not possibly last another year'.[3]

Small wonder then that a political innocent like Sartre did not immediately grasp the full implications of what was happening. Only a handful of far-sighted individuals – Leon Trotsky, Daniel Guérin – grasped the full danger of Nazism from the very beginning.

The threat that Hitler's triumph might be replicated in France led to the creation of the Popular Front, and the election of a Popular Front government under Léon Blum in 1936. However, Sartre's attitude to the triumph of the Popular Front was curiously contradictory. De Beauvoir tells us that Sartre and she had 'set their heart on' the victory of the Popular Front and that the election results 'filled us with satisfaction'. And yet Sartre himself did not vote.[4]

Notes for this chapter begin on page 30.

De Beauvoir adds :

Our abstentionism derived mainly from our powerlessness, and we did not refuse on principle to participate in events. The proof of this is that when the strikes broke out and there were street collections for the strikers, we gave as much as we could. Pagniez criticised us for this... In his view, the strikes were compromising the Blum experiment, whereas we saw them as the only way to radicalise it.[5]

The line of the PCF was similar to Pagniez's position, namely to control the strikes and then bring them to an end so as not to endanger the Blum government. PCF leader Maurice Thorez summed it up in the sentence: 'We must know how to put a stop to a strike' – at the very time when the strike was posing a challenge to the whole established order.

Nearly thirty years later, in 1964, Sartre analysed the contradictions of 1936 as follows:

There was a sudden, brutal awareness, from below, on the level of demands, which found expression in a tidal wave of popular struggles. But it was blocked at the level of the leadership. So as not to frighten the middle class, they didn't dare pose the problem on its true ground, that of the class struggle. The headquarters and the press stifled the whole thing. For many young people who could have found there the opportunity for their political apprenticeship, the Popular Front, for want of analysis, of information, of slogans, appeared as nothing more than an adventure: they regarded the demands of the masses as 'fair'. But they didn't grasp the deep roots in the structures of French society. [6]

And looking back in the 1970s, with the comparison with 1968 clearly in mind, Sartre still saw the factory occupations as the best thing about 1936: 'In the workplaces, there was a festival, a fine festival. The women came to eat bread and sausage with the workers; the little shops in the neighbourhood where the workers normally bought food gave supplies in great quantities; there was a movement of enthusiasm which could be felt at every moment'.[7]

Yet if there were inconsistencies in Sartre's attitude to the Popular Front it was because there was a contradiction within the historical events themselves. Daniel Guérin, in his account of the French Popular Front, argued that the term 'Popular Front' covered 'two commodities of very different natures': one the one hand, 'the misalliance, on the parliamentary and electoralist level, of bourgeois radicalism and Stalinism, under the banner of national defence'; on the other hand, 'the powerful popular movement , the anti-fascist "unity of action", for which the political and trade-union organisations of the working class... had taken the initiative – a genuinely *popular* movement in the sense that it drew behind the working class a not inconsiderable layer of petty bourgeois and poor peasants'. He concluded: 'We were resolute opponents of Popular Front No. 1, and enthusiastic supporters of Popular Front No. 2'. [8]

It is unlikely that Sartre could have produced such an articulate formulation in 1936 (although these ideas were presented by Guérin as shared by the *gauche révolutionnaire*, and Sartre may well have heard a version of them from Colette Audry). But while his response was less politically analytic, his position was not all that different.

As an electoral alliance the Popular Front was, in essence, an agreement between the PCF, the SFIO and the Radical Party. The Radicals, as the most 'moderate' of the three were, to a very large extent, able to call the tune; the programme of the Popular Front contained nothing that they were unwilling to accept, so little of the 'socialist' programmes of the PCF or the SFIO survived, for example colonial freedom or nationalisation of industry and the banks. Indeed, the PCF sometimes advocated dropping the *Internationale* and the red flag in favour of the *Marseillaise* and the tricolour in order to identify with a mood of republican unity and so as not to offend or provoke their new-found allies.[9]

To Sartre all this must have been vaguely disconcerting, especially since he had been in Berlin at the time of the great popular anti-fascist strikes and demonstrations of February 1934 in Paris which had led to the birth of the Popular Front. Sartre, after all, was motivated not so much by an attachment to the working class – of which he as yet knew very little – as by a profound hatred of his own class. The PCF of the period 1929 to 1934 – which he had been 'vaguely tempted' to join – had had the line of 'class against class'. Sectarian and indeed – in the German context – suicidal as this line was, at least its anti-bourgeois credentials were unambiguous. Popular Frontism was a very different matter.

Sartre had a deep loathing of the Radical Party, which represented all that he found worst in the hypocritical values of the French republican bourgeoisie. His grandfather had been a Radical, and Sartre despised the 'bourgeois optimism' embodied in the Radical programme.[10] In later writings Sartre flayed the Radicals unmercifully. In *L'Existentialisme est un humanisme* he was scathing about Radicals who flaunted their anti-clericalism, but complacently failed to face up to the alarming implications of the nonexistence of God.[11] Small wonder Sartre felt little enthusiasm for voting for an alliance in which the Radical Party exercised such power.[12]

Sartre had little more sympathy for the SFIO. In *La Nausée* (1938) the Autodidact, a satirical portrayal of the tradition of bourgeois humanism stemming from the Enlightenment, was presented as a member of the SFIO since 'September 1921' – that is, since just after the Congress of Tours, when the Socialist minority split from the newly formed PCF.[13]

Sartre was equally unimpressed with the cultural aspects of the Popular Front. Louis Aragon, who a few years earlier had been urging the assassination of social democrats, was now writing what de Beauvoir contemptuously described as 'tricolour articles'.[14] Nor is Sartre likely to have been much impressed by the PCF's response to the tercentenary of Descartes' *Discours de la méthode* in 1937. Two PCF deputies – Cogniot and

Berlioz – found time amid the pressing issues of the period to put down a parliamentary motion calling on the government to organise a national celebration. Sartre's relationship to Descartes was complex and critical, and he cannot have thought much of the simple adulation of Descartes as 'one of the greatest geniuses France has given to humanity' or the claim that 'the immortal elements of Cartesianism live on... in the work of Marx and Engels, of Lenin and Stalin'.[15]

The Popular Front was the period when the PCF attracted around it a whole batch of literary and artistic fellow-travellers. Of these the most famous were André Gide, who became a sharp critic of Stalinism after a visit to the USSR in 1936, and Romain Rolland, who never retracted his support for Stalin. Sartre despised Rolland; he wrote in 1939: 'I admit with shame that *Jean-Christophe*, that vile laxative, brought tears to my eyes more than once when I was twenty'.[16] For Gide, on the other hand, Sartre retained considerable respect; as he wrote in his obituary in 1951: 'He had the courage to take the side of the USSR when it was dangerous to do so and the greater courage to publicly reverse his position when he considered, rightly or wrongly, that he had been mistaken'.[17] If Sartre himself was later to become a fellow-traveller, at least he knew what the options were and he did not fall into all the same traps.

But it was in Spain, not France, that Popular Frontism was to be put to its severest test. De Beauvoir described the Civil War as 'the drama which dominated our whole lives for the next two and a half years'.[18] Sartre was not involved in any practical support for the anti-fascist forces, but he was inspired to write one of his most striking short stories, *Le Mur*, of which he said thirty years later: 'When I wrote *Le Mur*, I was not in agreement with Marxist theses, I was simply in total revolt against the fact of Spanish fascism'.[19]

It is noteworthy, therefore, that Sartre chose as his 'hero', not a supporter of the Popular Front, but an anarchist, one who had joined the anarchist movement out of admiration for Pí y Margall,[20] a nineteenth-century writer and politician who was an anti-clerical, anti-colonialist follower of Proudhon. And in the opening pages of *L'Age de raison*, Mathieu was accosted by a beggar who gave him a postcard marked 'CNT. Diario Confederal' (i.e., the anarcho-syndicalist Confederation's daily newspaper) and addressed to an anarcho-syndicalist committee in France.[21] This apparent sympathy for the Spanish anarchists was something more than temperamental anarchism. In 1936 Nizan had written a series of reports on Spain for the Comintern journal *La Correspondance internationale* (*Inprecorr*). In these he had repeatedly claimed that the Spanish anarchists were 'objectively' and indeed to some extent consciously the allies of the fascists:

> The anarchists are, whether or not they wish it, the accomplices of Robles's CEDA [the leading Catholic conservative party], of the local political bosses, of the monarchist colonels, in this plot against the union of democratic forces... If, as I have been assured in Madrid, there is an agreement between certain anar-

chist leaders and the fascist groups, we risk seeing the anarchists unleashing a premature insurrectionary movement which might draw in substantial numbers of workers.[22]

This idea of 'premature' insurrection was to become an important theme in Sartre's 1951 play *Le Diable et le Bon Dieu*.

Despite their extensive working-class support and the willingness of their leaders to compromise, the Spanish anarchists were to be progressively isolated and crushed by the Communists. Even if Sartre did not actually read the Comintern journal, he must have been well aware that Nizan was propagating such slanders.

Certainly Sartre had some knowledge of the various political currents within the Spanish Civil War. His friend Fernando 'Tito' Gerassi (the model for Gomez in *Les Chemins de la liberté*) fought with the International Brigades, though he was not an orthodox Communist.[23] Colette Audry visited the POUM leaders in Barcelona.[24] In a letter of September 1939 de Beauvoir, writing to Sartre, referred to 'your poor German teacher Katia Landau'. Landau, a POUM supporter herself imprisoned in Spain and released due to pressure from Marceau Pivert and others, had written one of the most severe indictments of Stalinist crimes in Spain, *Le Stalinisme en Espagne*, in which she described various atrocities including the kidnapping and murder of her own husband, Kurt Landau.[25] The Landaus had been in France from March 1933, and were accommodated by the parents of Simone Weil, who was in contact with Colette Audry. Since Sartre still had difficulty with German after his return from Berlin, it is quite possible that she did give him German lessons. If Sartre remembered her, he might well have noted how her account of the Spanish events differed from that provided by Nizan and his friends.

At the time of the trial of the POUM leaders in Barcelona in October 1938 de Beauvoir recorded the severe doubts that she and Sartre had about Spain: 'Was it true that the Stalinists had murdered the revolution, or were we to believe that the anarchists were playing Franco's game?'[26]

Looking back nearly forty years later, Sartre summed up his position on the French Popular Front: 'Yes, we were extremists, but we did nothing... Others, like Colette Audry, had devoted themselves to left-wing politics; they didn't achieve much, because nobody could achieve much, but they were active, and we weren't'.[27] A trifle grudging, perhaps, but Sartre was clearly admitting that 'La Communiste' had been in the right. A number of seeds had been planted in Sartre's brain during the 1930s; the war provided the conditions under which they could take root.

Notes

1. *Sit* X, p. 178.
2. D. Guérin, *La Peste brune*, Paris, 1969, p. 9.
3. J. Gerassi, *Jean-Paul Sartre*, vol. I, Chicago, 1989, p. 120.
4. *Force*, p. 272. Philip Thody has written that neither Sartre nor de Beauvoir 'bothered to vote'. P Thody, *Jean-Paul Sartre*, Basingstoke, 1992, p. 43. De Beauvoir, whose tactical judgements did not always coincide with Sartre's, did not have the choice. French women first got the right to vote under article 21 of the unpublished Vichy Constitution of 1943 and did not exercise that right until after the Liberation.
5. *Force*, p. 273.
6. *Sit* VIII, p. 129.
7. *Raison*, p. 338. Although the factory occupations of 1936 involved far fewer workers than in 1968 (around two million as against at least nine), the element of spontaneity was much greater, since the occupations were not so tightly controlled by the PCF bureaucracy.
8. D. Guérin, *Front populaire – révolution manquée*, Paris, 1963, pp. 93–94.
9. G. Lefranc, *Juin 36*, Paris, 1966, p. 265; M. Dommanget, *Le Drapeau rouge*, Paris, 1966, pp. 425–27.
10. *Les Mots*, pp. 146, 196.
11. J.-P. Sartre, *L'Existentialisme est un humanisme*, Paris, 1966, p. 35.
12. Le Havre, where Sartre was resident at the time of the 1936 election, was not a particularly left-wing town. Its three constituencies returned one Radical deputy, and two *'républicains de gauche'* who, despite their label, opposed the Popular Front. There were, however, Communist candidates in all three constituencies. And it was at the Bréguet factory at Le Havre that the very first factory occupation of May 1936 took place.
13. J.-P. Sartre, *Oeuvres romanesques*, Paris, 1981, p. 137.
14. *Force*, p. 273. In 'Qu'est-ce que la littérature?', Sartre, while belabouring the surrealists, expressed some enthusiasm for Aragon's poem *Front rouge*. 'Here was a man quivering with indignation, demanding in clear and violent terms the death of the oppressor' (*Sit* II, p. 326). But as well as demanding violence against police, Aragon wrote 'Fire on the trained bears of the social democracy!' ('Feu sur les ours savants de la social-démocratie!') (L. Aragon, *Persécuté persécuteur*, Paris [1931], p. 12; translation by e.e. cummings, *The Red Front*, Chapel Hill, North Carolina, 1933, p. 7). The poem was a typical piece of 'Third Period' lunacy, the sectarian rejection of a united front with the Social Democrats, a 'strategy' which enabled Hitler to take power in Germany. Had Sartre actually read the poem, and did he believe that in 1931 the SFIO, with 107 deputies (out of some 600) in a right-wing Assembly was 'the oppressor?'
15. G. Politzer, 'Le Tricentenaire du "Discours de la méthode" ', *Correspondance internationale* No. 23, 1937; reproduced in G. Politzer, *Écrits I: La Philosophie et les mythes*, Paris, 1969, pp. 67–74.
16. J.-P. Sartre, *Les Carnets de la drôle de guerre*, Paris, 1983, p. 96. By a bizarre inversion, the 'laxative' becomes an 'emetic' in the English translation: *War Diaries: Notebooks from a Phoney War*, trans. Quintin Hoare, London, 1984, p. 73.
17. *Sit* IV, pp. 86–87.
18. *Force*, p. 283.
19. *C&R*, p. 59. Geneviève Idt has suggested a possible source for the story in 'Corvelise', a story in the collection *Faux Passeports* (Paris, 1937, pp. 217–56), by the Belgian writer Charles Plisnier, in which Corvelise sacrifices his life to save his 'double', Saurat, a leading Comintern cadre trapped by Nazis. See I. Galster, ed., *La Naissance du phénomène Sartre*, Paris, 2001, p. 78. Plisnier was expelled from the Belgian Communist Party in 1928 for supporting the Left Opposition and thereafter was a nonaligned anti-Stalinist with close links with Victor Serge. If Sartre knew his work it is yet another indication of his awareness of the anti-Stalinist left.

20. Sartre, *Oeuvres romanesques*, p. 225.

21. *Ibid.*, p. 394.

22. *La Correspondance internationale*, Nos 28 and 30, 1936; reproduced in *Paul Nizan: intellectuel communiste*, 2 vols, Paris, 1970, 2: 45, 62.

23. His son claims he was a 'genuine Spanish anarchist, by temperament at least', and says that during the war he maintained friendship with both Stalinists like Luigi Longo and anarchists like Durruti (Gerassi, *Jean-Paul Sartre*, pp. 15–16.

24. *Force*, p. 298).

25. K. Landau, *Le Stalinisme en Espagne*, Paris, 1938, preface by Alfred Rosmer; English translation as 'Stalinism in Spain' in *Revolutionary History* Vol. 1, No. 2 (1988), pp. 40–55.

26. *Force*, p. 364.

27. *Adieux*, p. 483.

Chapter 4

WAR WITHIN WAR

'So now I'm cured of socialism, if I needed to be cured'. Thus Sartre wrote in his notebook on 14 September 1939.[1] For Sartre the Second World War had begun with the Hitler–Stalin Pact of 23 August 1939. It is important to remember just what a shock the Pact was for all those on the left, whether inside or outside the PCF. For nearly five years the PCF's strategy had been centred on the idea of the Popular Front; it had argued indefatigably that the struggle against fascism must take priority over everything else, including the struggle for socialism, which could be postponed until later. Many on the left who had no illusions that Russia was a workers' paradise still found themselves drawn to the PCF because it seemed to be the most consistent fighter against fascism. Whatever contorted and jesuitical excuses might be offered, that claim to consistency had vanished in a single day. De Beauvoir summed up the bitterness which many thousands of leftists must have felt: 'The Pact revealed, quite brutally, that the Trotsky-ists, Colette Audry and all the left oppositionists were right: that Russia had become an imperialist power like the others, obstinately set on its own selfish interests. Stalin didn't give a toss for the European proletariat'.[2]

The Pact made war inevitable; with Russia safely neutralised, Hitler had no fear of taking on Western Europe. The whole left was thrown into confusion and upheaval. Sartre, it turned out, was not cured of socialism; the infection was much more profound than he could have imagined. But there could be no going back to the illusions of the 1930s.

Yet if the Pact was a traumatic shock for the disengaged Sartre, it was even more catastrophic for the PCF loyalist Nizan. Twenty years later, Sartre recalled his last meeting with Nizan:

> In July 1939 [in fact 3 August], at Marseilles, where I saw him by chance and for the last time, he was cheery: he was about to leave for Corsica; I read in his eyes the cheerfulness of the Party; he spoke of war, which he thought we would

---

Notes for this chapter begin on page 44.

avoid: immediately I made the translation in my head: 'The Political Bureau is very optimistic, its spokesman states that negotiations with the USSR are about to reach a successful conclusion. Before the autumn,' he said, 'the Nazis will be on their knees'.[3]

Nizan appears to have believed his own propaganda – always a dangerous thing for a Stalinist – and he was at least as shocked as Sartre by the Pact. He left the Communist Party, not because he believed that the Pact was 'wrong', but because the PCF lacked 'the necessary political cynicism and the political power of lying which would have been required to draw the greatest profit from a dangerous diplomatic operation'.[4] This was not a leftist position, but in some ways can be seen as an anticipation of an argument which was to arise in the Communist movement from the 1950s to the 1970s, namely that national parties should show greater independence of Russia. Sartre received at least one letter from Nizan after his departure from the PCF in which he explained his break with Communism.[5]

Sartre had developed his own ideas on the Pact before he knew anything of Nizan's resignation. In a letter to Louise Védrine written only days after the Hitler–Stalin Pact was announced he informed her that he had now decided on the plot outline for the fourth volume of his novel cycle *Les Chemins de la liberté*: 'Brunet, disgusted by the German-Soviet Pact, would resign from the Communist Party and would come and ask for help from Mathieu'.[6]

In fact the Hitler–Stalin Pact was to dominate both the second half of *La Mort dans l'âme* and the various fragments of the never-completed fourth volume. While Sartre claimed that the figure of Brunet was not aggressive enough to have been modelled on Nizan,[7] undoubtedly his many discussions with Nizan played a part in the formation of the character. But the fragments of the fourth volume also show that Sartre had carefully observed and analysed the impact of the new line on the PCF.

In the summer of 1940, after France's military defeat, the PCF was urging workers to welcome the occupying German soldiers,[8] and was engaged in negotiations to get its paper published legally.[9] It was true that the PCF had been made illegal on 26 September 1939 by its erstwhile Popular Front ally, the Radical prime minister Daladier, and that neither Vichy nor the Gestapo was particularly keen to reciprocate the PCF's offers of friendship. In any case, workers and trade unionists, the PCF's main source of support, were the first victims of the new regime. Hence there were conflicts between PCF members and the occupiers before Russia entered the war. But the PCF's political line was unmistakable.

Sartre showed Brunet discussing with another PCF member, Chalais, who defended the strategy of seeking legal publication for *L'Humanité* against Brunet's scepticism. He argued that the Party, as the only one which defended the German-Soviet Pact and opposed the war, retained wide support in the popular masses, and that the Germans needed its support. In addition he invoked the possibility of 'secret agreements' between Germany and Russia about the European Communist Parties.[10]

On occasion Sartre was sharply satirical about the PCF's undemocratic practice. Thus when Mathieu urged Brunet to stay in the Party to prevent it taking a position he disapproved of, Brunet responded acidly: 'Do you imagine I can prevent anything? You seem to think the Party is a Radical Party congress'.[11] And when Brunet asked Chalais if he was putting forward current Party policy or his own opinion, Chalais responded like a loyal Stalinist: 'I never have opinions; I'm telling you Party policy'.[12] Yet Sartre also had a sense of the desolating tragedy that the Pact brought to many PCF members; Brunet was shown as thinking: 'if the party is right, I am more alone than a madman; but if it's wrong, *all men* are alone and the world is screwed'. [13]

No wonder that when *La Mort dans l'âme* appeared in 1949 critics from the PCF had a pretty low opinion of it. The PCF, after all, was still basking in its Resistance reputation, and to remind it of its role in the first twenty-two months of the war must have seemed grossly tactless. André Wurmser called Sartre a 'liar' and a 'falsifier of history', while for Maurice Mouillaud he was a 'speculator' in literature comparable to the speculators on the Chicago Stock Exchange.[14] Whatever tactical choices Sartre might make in relation to the PCF in later years, it is quite clear to anyone who reads what he wrote on the Hitler–Stalin Pact that he did not do so naively.

With the outbreak of war Sartre had gone into the army. As *Les Carnets de la drôle de guerre* reveal, his work on weather balloons left him plenty of leisure for reading and contemplating the nature of the war. By March 1940 his assessment was as follows:

> It was the bourgeoisie which prevented war in 38 and decided on the Munich capitulation, fearing victory even more than defeat. It was afraid that the Communists would reap the benefit of a war. But in September 1939 the war was welcomed by the bourgeoisie because the German–Russian treaty had brought Communism into disrepute and it was recognised that this war which was being waged, directly or indirectly, against the Soviets, would be necessarily accompanied by an internal police operation. The Communist Party would be dissolved. What ten years of politics could not do, the war would do in a month. Such is, it seems to me, the main reason for bourgeois support for the war. Under the guise of a national war, it is to a great extent a civil war.[15]

Here we find enunciated a theme that was to recur in Sartre's political writing over the coming decades. The PCF, whatever its political errors and indeed crimes, remained a working-class organisation and hence for it to be made illegal represented a defeat in the class war. While he was clearly right to stress the importance of the PCF's working-class base, Sartre here showed signs of a fetishisation of the Party which was to persist in his thinking until at least 1956.

What Sartre underestimated was the continuing defeatism of the bourgeoisie; having achieved their aims by declaring war, they still found defeat safer than victory – 'sooner Hitler than Thorez'. Hence by the summer of 1940 France had a puppet pro-Berlin government, and Sartre was in a German prisoner-of-war camp at Trier.

For Sartre the war still had an anti-fascist content, and to that extent he was in favour of resisting the German Occupation. But just as he refused to see France as a single entity undivided by class antagonisms, so he did not put all Germans into a single category. Sartre had spent a year in Berlin under Nazi rule, and he knew that many Germans were just as much victims of Nazism as were the citizens of occupied countries. Marius Perrin, a fellow prisoner of Sartre's, recalled a discussion as to why the German camp authorities had allowed the performance of Sartre's play *Bariona* (1940), which expressed some obviously subversive sympathies. Sartre's response was, 'suppose many Germans thought the same as us'.[16]

Perrin also recounted that Sartre's experiences had left him with a profound distrust of all party political organisation: 'You can't join a party: they're all rotten, including the Communist Party. Nizan had to leave it'.[17] Yet here was a paradox. Sartre would not join a party, yet if he were to fight fascism, he could not remain an isolated individual. Organisation of some sort was necessary.

This problem became concrete when Sartre was released from captivity in March 1941 and returned to Paris. He immediately became involved in establishing the *Socialisme et liberté* (Socialism and Freedom) grouping with some of his friends and associates, including Merleau-Ponty, de Beauvoir, Bost, Pouillon, Jean Kanapa and the Desantis – Jean-Toussaint and Dominique. The name of the group showed that Sartre, far from being 'cured' of socialism, now saw socialism as integral to his political project; but also that, after long intellectual consideration, he had reached the conclusion that socialism and freedom were not incompatible.[18] All the publications of the group seem to be definitively lost, and so our knowledge of the organisation rests on the accounts given by the fallible memories of Sartre and other participants; some of those involved later joined the PCF and the limits of their memories may well be politically determined.

It would be wrong to overestimate the significance of *Socialisme et liberté*. It had some fifty members by June 1941, mostly students and teachers, divided for security reasons into cells of five.[19] But it would also be wrong to be excessively disparaging. Thus Nathalie Sarraute recalled: 'It was supposed to be a resistance group. In fact, we were writing essays about the France of the future! There were three or four meetings, that's all'.[20] Certainly *Socialisme et liberté* spent its time on discussion rather than on armed struggle. But it must be remembered that at the time the French left was in a state of complete disarray, and no political current was offering effective resistance. The Popular Front parliament, elected with such enthusiasm in 1936, had handed over power to Pétain in 1940 – one more reason why Sartre might not altogether regret his failure to vote in 1936. The PCF was still following through the logic of the Hitler–Stalin Pact; three-quarters of the SFIO deputies had voted for Pétain in 1940 and the Socialist Party was in a state of chaos. The *Parti socialiste ouvrier et paysan* [Workers' and Peas-ants' Socialist Party], founded by Pivert's *gauche révolutionnaire* when expelled from the SFIO in 1938, had disintegrated at the outset of the war. Prominent advocates of anti-fascist unity in the 1930s, like Jacques Doriot and Gaston Bergery, were now supporting Vichy. Even on the far left there had been some strange transmogrifications. Maurice Wullens, an anarchist and pacifist who had supported the FIARI in 1939, under the Occupation advocated *rapprochement* with the Third Reich and wrote for collabora-tionist journals; the CGT leader René Belin also backed the pro-Nazi regime. Careful thought and theoretical clarity were a priority at this time.

Moreover, the outcome of the hostilities was still quite unclear; neither Russia nor America had yet entered the war against Germany. In the first issue of *Socialisme et liberté* Sartre, while hoping for a victory by the democ-racies, envisaged the possibility of a Nazi victory; he argued that if Ger-many won the war, then the aim would be to make it lose the peace.[21]

The group had eclectic politics. According to Dominique Desanti, Sartre himself proposed a rather bizarre form of united front: 'Sartre at the time called himself a non-Marxist. Several members of the group were Marx-ists. It was therefore democratically decided that the editorial would be drafted on one occasion by Sartre, and the following time by a Marxist, in the event Cuzin or [Jean-Toussaint] Desanti'.[22] At the same time efforts were made to contact other resistance groups, again on a fairly eclectic basis; for example, there were discussions with the right-wing 'Pentagone' group.[23] Contact was also made with the PCF, although the date is obscure; in two separate accounts Sartre placed it before the formation of *Socialisme et liberté* and after the Russian entry into the war.[24] The PCF reply, however, was plain enough. It was alleged that Sartre had been released by the Ger-mans in order to act as a spy. On the basis of that totally unfounded accu-sation, the PCF refused any contact with Sartre. While his links with the 'traitor' Nizan may have been one factor, it is not wholly clear what the Party's motives were. Certainly after June 1941 Popular Frontism was revived in an even more all-embracing form. The PCF had few scruples about alliances with forces to its right; what it could never tolerate was the existence of any political current positioning itself to its left. The PCF's ret-icence towards Sartre, in part at least, may be explained by the fact that he was already perceived as being potentially to the left of the Party.

The episode can have served only to confirm Sartre in his distrust of the PCF. At the same time he had not forgotten the interest in the anti-Stalin-ist left which he had developed during the 1930s. From the very begin-ning, members of the Trotskyist left were involved in *Socialisme et liberté*. Dominique Desanti recounted that the founding meeting of *Socialisme et liberté* was held in a room in the rue Gay-Lussac belonging to a mathe-matician who walked with the aid of sticks; this was Raymond Marrot, who described himself as a Trotskyist without being a member of the Fourth International.[25] Certainly one Trotskyist, Louis Rigaudias (also known as Rigal) was actively involved with *Socialisme et liberté*. Rigaudias played an important role in reconstructing French Trotskyism politically and organisationally; however, he left for Marseilles in 1941 and subsequently spent most of the war period in Cuba.[26] (Dominique Desanti tells us that during this period she wrote a novel, 'Les Termites', which she showed to Sartre; he made stylistic, but not political criticisms of it. Later, on joining the PCF, she destroyed her only copy because it betrayed Trotskyist sympathies which she had apparently acquired in the *Socialisme et liberté* milieu.)[27]

Further efforts were made in the direction of the Trotskyists.[28] In an interview with Annie Cohen-Solal, Raoul Lévy described how he had been entrusted with negotiations not only with the PCF but also with the Trotskyists. In neither case did any concrete cooperation emerge.[29]

Another leading figure in the Trotskyist movement who had links with *Socialisme et liberté* was David Rousset, who had worked closely with Rigaudias in the SFIO in the 1930s. In 1948, when Rousset was cooperating with Sartre in the RDR (Rassemblement Démocratique Révolutionnaire) he recalled a 'clandestine journal of which a few issues appeared in Paris in 1941', and seemed proud to claim this as a *rassemblement* which was in some sense a precursor of the RDR.[30] However, in Rousset's memoirs, published many years later, there is no mention of this episode at all. By then, of course, Rousset had made a sharp political break with Sartre and had himself become a Gaullist, albeit one of the left. Perhaps he found it more convenient not to recall his involvement in *Socialisme et liberté*.[31] Probably, however, his role was marginal. According to Cohen-Solal, Rousset and the former *pivertiste* Jean Rabaut had a 'peripheral' role, supplying information rather than being fully involved in the activities.[32]

A more significant encounter was that between Sartre and Maurice Nadeau. Nadeau, journalist, critic and publisher, was an active Trotskyist from 1932 till the Liberation. Sartre was originally put in contact with him by Merleau-Ponty, through another member of the Trotskyist organisation. At their initial meeting in a café in the rue Gay-Lussac, Sartre's main concern seemed to be with Nadeau's contacts with the surrealists and especially with his role in the FIARI. But although the FIARI had had support from over sixty writers and artists, it had never held a general meeting and its members were by now thoroughly dispersed. Nadeau attended only one meeting of *Socialisme et liberté* before it was wound up.[33]

The short-lived *Socialisme et liberté* did not aim to become politically homogeneous, and its organisational level seems to have been chaotic to say the least.[34] But some important issues were discussed. For example: 'One day Dominique Desanti raised the question: "Should we, yes or no, distribute our leaflets to German soldiers? For there's a big difference between a German and a Nazi." ' Only Sartre supported her, and the proposal got lost.[35]

Given the organisational skills of *Socialisme et liberté* it is probably just as well that the idea was not taken up, but the issue was an important one.

When the PCF entered the struggle, it did so in the most nationalist fashion, reviving the Popular Front idea of the broadest possible alliance. Among its slogans was '*Chacun son boche*' (Let everybody kill a German), leading to the strategy of individual attacks on members of the occupying forces. This was a central point of difference between the PCF and the various Trotskyist groups, who, like Sartre and Desanti, argued that German workers (including workers in uniform) were also victims of Nazism. The Trotskyists opposed individual attacks on soldiers and favoured an approach of fraternisation with rank-and-file soldiers. The *La Vérité* group succeeded in distributing a revolutionary paper, *Arbeiter und Soldat*, to German soldiers; at Brest an international group was formed including German sailors.[36] One of the leading organisers of this activity, Paul Widelin, was later arrested and tortured by the Gestapo, and ultimately hunted down to a hospital bed and murdered by them.

Too much should not be made of this. But the suggestion that Sartre was thinking on lines similar to those of the French Trotskyists is partially confirmed by an account from a hostile source, namely Jean Kanapa. Kanapa was one of Sartre's former pupils and he became a member of *Socialisme et liberté* in the spring of 1941. His membership of the group did not last long, as his family moved to the unoccupied zone, but he used the experience as the basis of his first novel, *Comme si la lutte entière* (1946).[37]

By 1946 Kanapa had become almost pathologically hostile to Sartre, whether for psychological reasons or because he was under pressure from the PCF, which he had now joined, to make a sharp break with his former mentor. The novel was crude and malicious. One of the central characters was an intellectual called Labzac, a fairly transparent caricature of Sartre. He was shown as a dilettante who was more interested in theorising about the future than in involving himself in activity in the present. There was a fairly clear implication that his unserious attitude was responsible for the death of a Communist militant. Labzac was shown as hostile to any idea of cooperation with the PCF:

'We can never get anywhere with the Communists! We'll have to talk about the Homeland from one end of the paper to the other – and about hostages with quavers in our pen – and cuddle up to the priests. We won't be able to do what we want. And we'll think ourselves lucky if they don't make us go and chuck "sardine tins" into the German soldiers' leave centre. Then we'll have to go to ground, move house, use different cafés – and what will become of my novel? No thank-you: I'm not a kid – I don't need to be told what to do and what not to do'.

... Finally they adopted what Suzanne, with a sheepish smile, called a middle course: they would make contact with the Trotskyists. It was Labzac who proposed the compromise. He knew a Trotskyist who worked in the Office for Propaganda in favour of the Family.

Contact was duly made with the Trotskyist, who proposed putting leaflets into maps sold by hawkers to German soldiers.[38]

Kanapa was scarcely a reliable witness – we may think ourselves lucky that he did not make Labzac into a serial killer. And in the language of the PCF the term 'Trotskyist' had become a smear word to be used almost indiscriminately against political opponents or rivals. But it may be taken as an indication that Sartre was distrusted because he was regarded as 'soft on Trotskyism'. And together with Desanti's testimony it begins to create a picture of a Sartre who was unhappy with a Resistance conducted primarily in nationalistic terms. In fact, because the primary motivation for Sartre's involvement in the Resistance was not patriotic, he laid himself open to attack from both the orthodox left and the right.

It is noteworthy that in Sartre's play about the Resistance, *Morts sans sépulture* (1946), the most positive character among the group of Resisters was a veteran Greek militant, Canoris. In giving this role to a 'foreigner', Sartre was breaking with the orthodoxy cultivated by both the PCF and the Gaullists that the Resistance was essentially a question of French patriotism rather than of anti-fascism.[39] It is only relatively recently that the role of foreign militants in the French Resistance has been given prominence.[40] This is yet another indication of Sartre's distrust of the PCF's nationalism.

What is certainly clear is that Sartre, in his first venture into political activity, felt the need of an organisation quite separate from the PCF. In the beginning this was made necessary by the fact the PCF was not yet in the Resistance, and that the Communists refused to work with him. But when Germany invaded Russia on 22 June 1941, and the PCF almost overnight went through a total transformation, Sartre was not immediately persuaded that this meant the end for *Socialisme et liberté*. In the summer holidays, that is in July and August, after the German invasion of Russia, Sartre and de Beauvoir (who both worked as teachers), embarked on their most ambitious attempt to build *Socialisme et liberté*. They undertook a cycle tour through the Southern, unoccupied zone, meeting Colette Audry, now living in Grenoble, as well as Gide and Malraux, neither of whom offered very much support.[41] By now the PCF – under orders from Moscow to put Germany under pressure – had stepped up the armed struggle to a level that could be described as adventurist, provoking vicious reprisals from the German forces.

There is no evidence that Sartre was immediately convinced of the superiority of the PCF's political line at this point. His political reservations had not disappeared, but circumstances were changing rapidly. One the one hand *Socialisme et liberté* was tiny and insignificant by the side of the far more disciplined and well-organised PCF machine. On the other hand the new PCF strategy had intensified the level of repression. Whereas earlier in the year the rather amateurish efforts of *Socialisme et liberté* had not suffered severely in their brushes with the authorities, the risks were now very much greater, and could scarcely be justified by any results that *Socialisme et liberté* could hope to achieve.

In the autumn Sartre decided that the group would have to be wound up. However, he did so reluctantly; he still felt that an organisation politically independent of the PCF was required, but he had neither the personnel nor the organisational skills to construct one: 'It cost Sartre a lot to abandon this plan, which he had cherished for a long time while in the Stalag, and to which he had happily devoted his energies for weeks; but he did very reluctantly give it up'.[42]

Socialisme et liberté had not achieved any political clarity or homogeneity. A number of its members, Kanapa and the Desantis for example, joined the PCF. Rigal, Nadeau and Rousset remained with the Trotskyist organisations; Rousset was to be imprisoned in Fresnes and later in Buchenwald. Two members of the group did not survive the war – Yvonne Picard, who died after being deported, and François Cuzin, who was shot by the Germans.[43] As for Sartre, he could not have cooperated with the PCF even had he wanted to; as de Beauvoir recalled, they 'built an impenetrable barrier between us and them'.[44]

Sartre's role during the rest of the war requires less attention. He was never a Resistance hero and never claimed to be one. In a modest but accurate summary, Sartre later said of himself: 'I was a resister, I met resisters, but it didn't cost me much'.[45] In recent years there have been many attacks on Sartre, suggesting that in fact his role during the Occupation was discreditable. Michel Contat has pointed out that *Les Mouches* was performed at a theatre called after the actress Sarah Bernhardt (whose mother had been Jewish), but which had been forced to change its name by the pro-Nazi regime. He claimed this reveals Sartre's 'indifference to the persecutions from which the Jews were suffering'.[46] But the choice must have been a tactical one; was it worth the compromise in order to get performed a play which might bring some encouragement to the forces of Resistance? In any case, it is dubious whether one can project back onto a totally different situation an action which might have been appropriate in the later stages of Sartre's career. 'Jean-Paul Sartre refuses Nobel Prize' made headlines in 1964, but 'Unknown playwright withdraws play' in 1943 would not have given Vichy any sleepless nights.

A much more comprehensive attack was launched by Gilbert Joseph.[47] This adopted as a point of principle that all writers should have refused publication throughout the Occupation, while ignoring the possibility that others might have had good moral and tactical reasons for pursuing a different course.[48] A writers' boycott – even if there had been any possibility of such a thing – would not have brought Vichy to its knees, though a general strike would have done so. In 1941, when it appeared that German domination might last for many years, it was not surprising that writers on the left looked to a more long-term rebuilding of opposition within the structures of Vichy.

Joseph's standards of evidence were highly questionable. He cited uncritically a number of eye-witness reports given some forty years after the events described; he persistently attributed to Sartre and de Beauvoir motives which he presumed them to have had but of which there was no documentary evidence; and on occasion he falsified the evidence – for example, in order to argue that Sartre made concessions to anti-Semitism he omitted any mention of *Réflexions sur la question juive* from the text and the bibliography.

A more balanced and serious account has come from Ingrid Galster, who has set out to restore the complexity of Sartre's position and to rescue him from both detractors and defenders. In particular she has raised the question of the fact that Sartre took a teaching post previously held by the Jew, Dreyfus-Le Foyer. This argument continues to be hotly contested.[49] But there is no need to show that Sartre was above all criticism to insist on the positive features of his wartime record.

It is striking that the criticisms of Sartre's conduct under the Occupation have intensified with the passing of time. In the decade immediately following the Liberation Sartre worked closely with a number of people – notably David Rousset and Claude Bourdet – who had seen the inside of Nazi camps. Such people would indeed have had a moral right to question Sartre's Resistance record; but I know of no instance of their doing so.[50]

Eventually the PCF accepted that Sartre could work within the Resistance. Claude Morgan, who had been the Communist editor of the clandestine *Lettres françaises* (he broke with the PCF in 1958, but continued to see himself as a Leninist communist) told John Gerassi:

> Sartre was a tremendous guy. He never looked for what could divide, only for what united us all. He was ready to do anything for the Resistance. He was the kind of guy that, once he had decided something, he would go all the way. He faithfully attended all the meetings… Most people really liked and everybody respected Sartre – except our chiefs, people like Aragon who kept telling me not to trust him: 'Use him but don't trust him,' he kept saying.[51]

Sartre seems to have accepted the general political line of the Resistance. Thus his film scenario *Résistance*, published anonymously in 1944, gave a completely orthodox view of the Resistance.[52] However, he remained in dialogue with the anti-Stalinist left and was aware of the criticisms that could be made of the PCF line. As de Beauvoir put it:

> One day Marie Girard criticised us for not being able to see beyond the ends of our noses. 'The defeat of Germany will mean the triumph of Anglo-American imperialism,' she said. She reflected the opinion of most of the Trotskyist intellectuals, who remained at an equal distance from collaboration and Resistance; in fact, they were much less afraid of American hegemony than of the growth of Stalinist power and prestige. In any case, we thought that they had failed to understand the hierarchy of problems and their urgency: first of all Europe must be cleansed of fascism.[53]

Whether Marie Girard (in fact Marie Ville, wife of Jean-André Ville) can be taken as a representative of Trotskyism is questionable,[54] and de Beauvoir overstates the abstentionism of the Trotskyists, who despite their limited numbers had a regular clandestine press and organised a number of factory groups.[55] But the fact that Sartre and de Beauvoir engaged with such arguments and regarded them as legitimate subjects for discussion shows that they maintained an intellectual distance from the politics of the PCF. After all, the PCF used the term 'Trotskyist' as a term of vilification, not as a description of a political position. Indeed, on occasion they were quite willing to physically exterminate their political opponents, as in the case of the Italian Trotskyist Pietro Tresso and his three comrades, killed by their fellow 'Resisters' after escaping from a fascist jail.[56]

Many years later, Sartre summed up his view of the role of the PCF in the Resistance; the Communists, he said, were

> tough, courageous, valiant fighters and martyrs, but also hacks for the Russian politburo. They did not want power. Oh yes, they had excuses: America would intervene, de Gaulle and Leclerc had all the tanks, and so on. But the fact is, no Communist Party in a country whose borders did not touch Russia (or a satellite), ever wanted to seize power, because Moscow said not to. Communists never thought they could rule without Russian tanks to back them up, in case. Our great Communist resistance fighters – or rather their leaders – were not revolutionaries, only very brave Russian messengers.[57]

It is against this background that Sartre's 1943 play *Les Mouches* should be seen. This was based on the Greek legend of Orestes, who returned to Argos to avenge his father Agamemnon by killing the tyrant Aegisthus. But he failed to awaken the people of Argos to their own liberation, so that they cursed him for taking away the security provided by tyranny.

The play raised a number of issues relevant both to the Occupation and to more general questions. Orestes was a 'terrorist' in the tradition of the Italian Red Brigades or Baader–Meinhof. He attempted to liberate Argos through an act of what Marxists have traditionally called 'individual terrorism'.[58] This had particular resonance in 1943. As Sartre pointed out in discussion with a German professor in 1948, the Communist-led Resistance had a policy of physical attacks against members of the occupying forces. The Germans responded by taking hostages – most of whom had no connection with the Resistance, and to begin with most of whom were Jews. 'For three Germans, six or ten hostages were killed'.[59]

It was the moral and political implications of this that were exercising Sartre's mind at the time he wrote *Les Mouches*. As he told *Carrefour* just after the Liberation: 'The real drama, the one I would have liked to write, is that of the terrorist who, by shooting down Germans in the street, brings about the execution of fifty hostages'. [60]

Interviewed by John Gerassi in the 1970s, when he was frequenting Maoists, Sartre argued that *Les Mouches* should have been written differently: 'But mind you, I was no revolutionary... Today I understand Orestes. After he killed the King and Queen he should have taken command. That he didn't was not just politically stupid. It was immoral'. [61]

But in his quest to sound more 'revolutionary' to Maoist ears, Sartre seemed to have misunderstood his own play, and to be advocating that revolutionaries should substitute themselves for mass action. In its original version *Les Mouches* argued that human beings cannot give freedom to others; each individual must find their own freedom for themselves. Though Sartre was still far from being a Marxist, this is quite compatible with the proposition that 'the emancipation of the working classes must be conquered by the working classes themselves'.[62]

The Sartre who understood this realised that 'socialism' and 'freedom' were inseparable, as the very name of *Socialisme et liberté* implied. It was because he did so that he did not wholly trust the Stalinists of the PCF – and they distrusted him equally.

Notes

1. *Choses*, p. 15.
2. *Force*, p. 386. De Beauvoir showed her relative ignorance of Trotskyism here; most Trotskyists at the time believed Russia to be a 'degenerate workers' state' and hence not imperialist. But in spirit, if not in doctrine, she was absolutely right.
3. *Sit* IV, pp. 181–82.
4. *Paul Nizan intellectuel communiste*, Paris, 1970, 2: 114.
5. *Adieux*, p. 493.
6. J.-P. Sartre, *Lettres au Castor*, 2 vols, Paris, 1983, 1: 269; *Force*, p. 387.
7. J. Gerassi, *Jean-Paul Sartre*, vol. I, Chicago, 1989, pp. 19, 155.
8. *L'Humanité*, 4 July 1940; cited J.-P. Sartre, *Oeuvres romanesques*, Paris, 1981, p. 2112.
9. P. Robrieux, *Histoire intérieure du parti communiste* 4 vols, Paris, 1980, 1: 510. After the war the PCF denied having made approaches to the German authorities; this was not publicly admitted until 1967; see the official history *Le Parti communiste dans la résistance*, Paris, 1967, p. 73. Hence there was considerable consternation at Sartre referring to the episode.
10. Sartre, *Oeuvres romanesques*, pp. 1496–97.
11. *Ibid.*, p. 1653.
12. *Ibid.*, p. 1493.
13. *Ibid.*, p. 1515.
14. *Lettres françaises*, 3 November 1949; *La Nouvelle Critique*, April 1950; both cited in Sartre, *Oeuvres romanesques*, pp. 2019–20, 2022.
15. J.-P. Sartre, *Les Carnets de la drôle de guerre*, Paris, 1983, pp. 375–76.
16. M. Perrin, *Avec Sartre au stalag 12D*, Paris, 1980, p. 103.
17. *Ibid.,*, p. 127.
18. *Adieux*, pp. 447–48, 452, 494.
19. A. Cohen-Solal, *Sartre*, Paris, 1985, p. 301.
20. A. Rykner, *Nathalie Sarraute*, Paris, 1991, p. 174.
21. F. Jeanson, *Sartre dans sa vie*, Paris, 1974, p. 130.
22. The fullest account is given in D. Desanti, 'Première rencontre avec Sartre', in I. Galster, ed., *La Naissance du phénomène Sartre*, Paris, 2001, pp. 338–48. See also D. Desanti, 'Le Sartre que je connais', *Jeune Afrique*, 8 November 1964, pp. 27–29, and D. Desanti, 'Sartre et l'engagement', *Adam* 343–45 (1970), pp. 32–35.
23. *Force*, p. 495.

24. *Adieux*, pp. 493–94; *Raison*, pp. 24–25.
25. Desanti, 'Première rencontre avec Sartre', p. 340.
26. See obituary by Paolo Casciola in *Revolutionary History* Vol. 7, No. 3 (2000), pp. 289–97.
27. D. Desanti, 'Sartre: une leçon de roman à une débutante en 1942', *L'Année sartrienne* No. 15, Paris, June 2001, pp. 137–40.
28. At this stage of the war the French Trotskyist movement was divided into four groupings; three of them fused in 1944 to form the *Parti Communiste Internationaliste* (PCI); despite their divergences all rejected the Moscow-dominated policies of the PCF both before and after Russian entry into the war, and argued for resistance to the Nazis on the basis of class rather than of nationalism.
29. Cohen-Solal, *Sartre*, p. 314.
30. J.-P. Sartre, D. Rousset and G. Rosenthal, *Entretiens sur la politique*, Paris, 1949, p. 70.
31. D. Rousset, *Une Vie dans le siècle*, Paris, 1991.
32. Cohen-Solal, *Sartre*, p. 303.
33. M. Nadeau, *Grâces leur soient rendues*, Paris, 1990, pp. 55–59.
34. See Desanti, 'Le Sartre que je connais'.
35. Cohen-Solal, *Sartre*, p. 303.
36. Rousset, *Une Vie dans le siècle*, p. 59.
37. G. Streiff, *Jean Kanapa*, Paris, 1998, pp. 28–31.
38. J. Kanapa, *Comme si la lutte entière*, Paris, 1946, pp. 117–20.
39. See I. Galster, *Sartre, Vichy et les intellectuels*, Paris, 2001, p. 54.
40. See e.g., D. Peschanski, *Des Etrangers dans la résistance*, Paris, 2002; E. and Y. Brès, *Un Maquis d'antifascistes allemands en France (1942–1944)*, Montpellier, 1987.
41. Cohen-Solal, *Sartre*, pp. 308–12; *Force*, pp. 504–11.
42. *Force*, p. 514.
43. S. de Beauvoir, J.-L. Bost and J. Pouillon, 'Les Philosophes sous l'occupation', *Le Monde*, 26 July 1985.
44. *Force*, p. 514.
45. *Adieux*, p. 322.
46. *Le Monde*, 26 July 1985.
47. G. Joseph, *Une si douce occupation*, Paris, 1991.
48. There is an eloquent refutation of this position by Dominique Desanti, a Resister who was a member of *Socialisme et liberté* and then of the PCF, in Galster, ed., *Naissance*, pp. 344–46.
49. Galster, *Sartre, Vichy*, pp. 1–121; see also J. Lecarme, 'Sartre et la question antisémite', *TM* No. 609, June–July–August 2000, pp. 23–40; *L'Année sartrienne* No. 15, Paris, June 2001, pp. 215–16.
50. An exception to this is Vladimir Jankélévitch, who in 1948 in *Les Temps modernes* denounced those who had been inactive during the Occupation, and in 1985 directed this criticism much more specifically at Sartre. See Galster, *Sartre, Vichy*, pp. 118–19, 151.
51. Gerassi, *Jean-Paul Sartre*, p. 179.
52. *Lettres françaises*, No. 15, April 1944; reprinted *TM* No. 609, June–August 2000, pp. 1–22.
53. *Force*, p. 551.
54. She does not appear in Maitron and Pennetier's list of prewar Trotskyists (see Chapter 2), and I know of no reference to her activity as a Trotskyist.
55. See Y. Craipeau, *Contre vents et marées*, Paris, 1977; J. Pluet-Despatin, *Les Trotskystes et la guerre*, Paris, 1980; I. Birchall, 'With the Masses, Against the Stream', *Revolutionary History* Vol. 1, No. 4 (1988), pp. 34–38.
56. See P. Broué and R. Vacheron, *Meurtres au maquis*, Paris, 1997.
57. Gerassi, *Jean-Paul Sartre*, p. 183.
58. See L. Trotsky, *Against Individual Terrorism*, New York, 1974.
59. *Verger* Vol. I, No. 5 (1948); *TDS*, pp. 231–32.
60. *Carrefour*, 9 September 1944; *TDS*, p. 225.
61. Gerassi, *Jean-Paul Sartre*, p. 184.
62. K. Marx and F. Engels, *Collected Works*, London and Moscow, 1975–2001, 20:14.

PART II

Postwar Choices

Chapter 5

THE BETTER CHOICE

When his friend Merleau-Ponty died in 1961, Sartre wrote a long tribute to him, which contained a detailed account of the magazine they had launched together in 1945, *Les Temps modernes*. It also contained a frank assessment by Sartre of the choices available at the Liberation:

> In 1945 it was possible to choose between two positions. Just two, no more. The first and better one was to address the Marxists, and them alone, and to denounce the aborted revolution, the murdered Resistance, and the fragmentation of the left. Some periodicals courageously took up this position and vanished unheard: those were the happy days when people had ears so as not to hear and eyes so as not to see. Far from believing that such ventures were proven wrong by their failures, I claim we could have imitated them without going down: the strength and weakness of these reviews was that they confined themselves to the purely political field; our journal published novels, literary essays, eye-witness reports and documents: these floats prevented it from sinking. But to denounce the revolution betrayed, you first had to be a revolutionary: Merleau was not one, and I was not one as yet. We didn't even have the right to declare ourselves to be Marxists, despite our sympathies for Marx. Now revolution is not a state of mind: it is a day-to-day practice illuminated by a theory. And if it is not enough to have read Marx to make you a revolutionary, when you actively promote revolution you sooner or later meet up with him. The consequence is obvious: only people formed by this discipline could criticise the left effectively; at the time that meant that they had to belong more or less closely to Trotskyist circles; but such affiliation immediately disqualified them, although it was not their fault. In that mystified left dreaming of unity, they appeared as 'splitters'...

> The other attitude remained. We had no choice, it imposed itself. Having sprung from the middle classes, we tried to make a link between the intellectual petty bourgeoisie and the Communist intellectuals. This bourgeoisie had begotten us: we had inherited its culture and its values; but the Occupation and

---

Notes for this chapter begin on page 60.

Marxism had taught us that these could not be taken for granted. We asked our friends in the PCF for the tools necessary to take humanism out of the hands of the bourgeoisie.[1]

The period immediately after the Liberation was one of euphoria for the left. Fascism had been defeated and the right-wingers who had collaborated with it were for the moment largely discredited. The PCF had emerged from the Resistance with its reputation (and its vote) enormously enhanced; between September 1944 and May 1947 the Party served in almost every government. Moreover, it provided the effective leadership of the CGT, the main trade union federation with over five million members. Its members had undoubtedly shown enormous courage during the Occupation and it enjoyed good will in most quarters. To remind it of the Moscow Trials or the Hitler–Stalin Pact would have seemed tactless to most people.

And even in circles which were not directly influenced by the PCF, the idea of 'revolution' was enormously popular, even if – or rather precisely because – it was not clearly defined. There was a widespread acceptance that the world could not simply go back to the way it had been in the 1930s. At Notre-Dame in 1945, the theme for Lent was 'Christ and Revolution'.[2] In August 1944 Albert Camus described the fight for the liberation of Paris, and concluded: 'This terrible childbirth is that of a revolution'.[3] His paper, *Combat*, now a legal daily, carried the slogan: 'From the Resistance to the Revolution'. And he stressed the importance of the working class in liberated France: 'We believe in fact that any politics which separates itself from the working class is futile and that the France of tomorrow will be what its working class is'.[4]

Combat was not the only non-Communist paper to adopt a revolutionary stance. Georges Altman's *Franc-Tireur*, also a product of the Resistance, acquired a circulation among working-class readers to rival *L'Humanité*. Its staff included, alongside Communist supporters, journalists from the Trotskyist tradition such as Jean Rous (a Trotskyist from 1935 to 1939) and Pierre Rimbert.[5]

Edgar Morin, a PCF member who was to be expelled in 1951, described the atmosphere of the 1944–1946 period as follows:

> On the whole, the intelligentsia maintained relations of courtesy, deference and flirtatiousness towards Stalinist Communism. From the likes of Sartre, Malraux, Camus, no basic criticism was put forward. Naville, Rousset and the people around the *Revue internationale* did not cross swords. Only the Trotskyists, persecuted by everyone including those who were themselves persecuted, maintained their criticisms, but they were outside, below us.[6]

David Rousset, a leading Trotskyist since 1933, who had cooperated with *Socialisme et liberté*, tried unsuccessfully to persuade the Trotskyist movement that Stalinism had again become a progressive force: 'The Soviet bureaucracy is today obliged... to put forward and carry through the revolution abroad... In the new phase we have entered, Soviet economic forces represent the only effective guarantee of the socialist revolution in the world'.[7]

It seemed widely accepted that it was not possible to launch an open attack on the PCF. Camus, later perceived by many as a symbol of anti-Communist opposition to Sartre, wrote in 1944 in defence of the slogan: 'Anti-Communism is the beginning of dictatorship': 'If we do not agree with Communist philosophy nor with its practical morality, we vigorously reject political anti-Communism, because we know where it gets its inspiration and what its undeclared aims are'.[8]

Thus it was not only the fellow-travellers with Communism, but a large part of the anti-Stalinist left which hesitated to seek a head-on confrontation with the PCF. Victor Serge is often quoted by critics of Sartre such as Tony Judt and Bernard-Henri Lévy[9] as an example of a leftist who, in contrast to Sartre, took an uncompromisingly anti-Stalinist line. And it is true that Serge, who suffered terrible persecution from Stalinism, never capitulated to the forces of reaction and repression, East or West. It is therefore worth recalling what Serge wrote in 1946 to René Lefeuvre, the editor of *Masses.* He was sharply critical of reports by W. White published in *Masses* about conditions in the USSR because they were inadequately documented and did not put the situation in a proper context, and he warned against allowing a left-wing journal to be conscripted into a pro-American and anti-Russian campaign; 'if the Soviet regime must be criticised, let it be from a working-class and socialist point of view'. He went on to add:

> The PCF still has an influence on a large part of the working class. We must be able to win to our cause elements who today are following the Stalinists... We cannot adopt a purely negative attitude towards the PCF. We shall get nowhere if we seem more concerned with criticising Stalinism than with defending the working class. The threat of reaction is still there and in practice we shall often have to work alongside Communists.[10]

His argument is remarkably similar to that used by Sartre over the next few years.

In this atmosphere there was a pervasive use of Marxist concepts and language. Although Sartre did not as yet see himself as a Marxist, he certainly used many ideas borrowed from Marxism. In *Réflexions sur la question juive* (1946) he traced the roots of anti-Semitism to class society; indeed he rather naively argued that anti-Semitism scarcely occurred in the working class. And he concluded by asserting that the only answer to anti-Semitism was socialist revolution: 'the socialist revolution is necessary and sufficient to suppress the anti-Semite; we shall *also* make the revolution for the Jews'.[11] While the book excited debate on other grounds, nobody at the time seems to have taken exception to this conclusion; it was part of the common sense of the epoch.

It was in this climate that Sartre and Merleau-Ponty decided to launch *Les Temps modernes* in October 1945. In the first year or so both personnel and politics were fairly fluid, before the postwar political line-up had completely stabilised.[12] Though the initial print-run was just 3,500[13] it rapidly acquired an influence and reputation out of proportion to its readership. Many items first published in its pages later appeared in book form, and extracts often appeared in the daily and weekly press. It was to form an integral part of Sartre's political project of fighting for left-wing ideas in the intellectual milieu.

The immediate postwar period was, in a sense, a honeymoon period between the PCF and the non-Communist left. But it was a honeymoon racked with latent tensions, a brief prelude to a long conflictual relationship.

As Sartre acquired rapid celebrity in the immediate post-Liberation period, the PCF seems to have been, initially, somewhat confused as to how to respond to him. He was invited to collaborate with *Action*, a weekly under PCF control but which maintained a degree of intellectual openness. Jean Kanapa, now a PCF member, contributed an article to an early issue of *Les Temps modernes* on contemporary painting. But he began the article by distinguishing the authentic humanism of the Communists from the alleged humanism of existentialism, and making it clear that his article should not be seen as endorsing the latter. However, he did note that the fact of his article's publication could be attributed to the 'tolerance of J.-P. Sartre', showing a courtesy which was to prove short-lived.[14] At around this time Kanapa invited Sartre to meet some PCF intellectuals. But when Sartre turned up, he was insulted by Roger Garaudy.[15] In 1946 the PCF's leading philosopher, Henri Lefebvre, devoted a whole volume (*L'Existentialisme*) to a critical treatment of Sartre and his philosophy.

But despite such manifestations of hostility it took some time for all-out war to be declared. In the first months of 1946 *Action* ran a symposium, with contributions from well-known personalities and from its readers, on the provocative question: 'Should we burn Kafka?' An examination of the debate shows that Kafka was merely a pretext; the real issue at stake was the attitude to be taken towards 'gloomy literature' (*littérature noire*), that is, the allegedly pessimistic writings of Sartre, Camus, de Beauvoir etc. Yet the debate was reasonably open and showed that the PCF's intellectual periphery had not yet made up their minds about Sartre. As late as November 1946 Pol Gaillard wrote a favourable review of Sartre's plays *Morts sans sépulture* and *La Putain respectueuse* in a pro-Communist paper. The joint performance was described as 'not to be missed', though Gaillard concluded by urging Sartre to abandon writing philosophy and novels and to concentrate on the theatre.[16]

Initially Sartre was quite happy to cooperate with the PCF. He recognised that the majority of French workers felt an allegiance to the Communist Party, and considered that the USSR, whatever its weaknesses, still at least aspired towards socialism. But differences rapidly emerged as the PCF settled in to its new-found governmental role. The outbreak of war in Indo-China produced a sharp response from *Les Temps modernes*, which devoted an editorial to the call for withdrawal of French troops, and followed this up with a number of other pieces devoted to opposition to the war, although independence was not explicitly demanded.[17] At the time the PCF ministers in government were voting war credits for Indo-China, while the Party's deputies merely abstained. The dividing line between Sartre and the PCF, which was to become much more pronounced during the Algerian War, was already visible.

By the time he wrote *Qu'est-ce que la littérature?* in the first half of 1947, Sartre had developed some more fundamental criticisms of Stalinism, though they were still couched in relatively moderate terms: 'The PCF aligns its policy on that of Soviet Russia because it is in that country alone that we find the outline of socialist organisation. But if it is true that Russia initiated the Social Revolution, it is also true that it has not completed it'. He was somewhat harsher about the PCF's domestic policies:

> To reassure the bourgeoisie without losing the confidence of the masses, to allow it to rule while preserving the outward appearance of being on the attack, to occupy positions of command without letting itself be compromised: that is the policy of the Communist Party. Between 1939 and 1940 we were witnesses and victims of the decay of a war; at present we are observing the decay of a revolutionary situation.[18]

In the autumn of 1947 the *Temps modernes* team made a series of six radio broadcasts. The second of these, on 27 October 1947, was devoted to 'Communism and anti-Communism'. While Sartre and his colleagues clearly differentiated themselves from the anti-Communism of de Gaulle, and made it clear they were on the side of the working class, they were also highly critical of both the USSR and the PCF. They pointed to the high income differentials in the USSR and argued that the regime was based on a 'concentration-camp system' (*système concentrationnaire*). Sartre delivered a sharp critique of the postwar strategy and tactics of the PCF:

> The PCF since the Liberation has throughout shown the greatest hesitancy. It began with a policy of class collaboration and to this end demanded sacrifices from the proletariat. The aim of this policy was to enable the PCF to win positions in the administration and in the government. It did not make it clear to the workers that this was what it was aiming at, and on many points it abandoned its theories and its demands. One fine day it noticed that it was running the risk of the masses becoming disaffected, it was afraid of being outflanked on its left; so what did it do? It immediately left the government and took refuge in the opposition.[19]

Léopold Durand in *L'Humanité* responded by calling Sartre a 'servile voice', guilty of 'Gaullist-style anti-Sovietism, Blum-style anti-Communism'. The attack was directed at Sartre personally rather than *Les Temps modernes*, which was not mentioned. Clearly Durand did not want to name Sartre's magazine, for fear of giving it a free advertisement.[20]

Sartre did not hide his criticisms of the PCF, and he might well have expected some vigorous political debate from the PCF. What he got, throughout the late 1940s, was a flood of books, pamphlets and articles which denounced him in terms of pure abuse. It would be wearisome to refer to more than a very small percentage of this output, but it certainly raises questions for the likes of Judt and Burnier, who have claimed that Sartre was serving the interest of Stalinism. If he was, why should he be subjected to such vilification?

When the PCF launched *La Nouvelle critique*, supposedly a journal aimed at 'intellectuals', in 1948, Sartre was listed, along with Mauriac, Malraux and Rousset, and politicians such as Truman, Blum, Moch and Bidault, as 'following the lead of the American industrialists'. The editorial (anonymous but probably written by the editor, Jean Kanapa) explicitly rejected concepts such as 'unconscious ideological distortion' and 'mystification' deployed by more subtle Marxists, and insisted that Sartre and friends were conscious agents of reaction: 'The orders they carry out are clear to them, the intentions they serve are well-known to them. They are not the slightest bit mystified. *They are lying.* And they know they are lying'.[21]

It was Kanapa who produced the most virulent of all the criticisms. In a short book he denounced Sartre, *Les Temps modernes* – with its 'little fanatics sympathetic to Trotskyism' – and anything else that came within range. Thus Camus's *Combat* was described as 'neo-fascist' and *Partisan Review* (which had devoted a special issue to existentialism) as 'anti-Communist and antidemocratic in an unimaginable fashion'. Sartre's alleged links with Heidegger were invoked to show that he was on the road to fascism – even if it was necessary to cite an article from *Les Temps modernes* to substantiate the point.[22]

Kanapa's grotesque hostility to Sartre undoubtedly had personal roots in an Oedipal revolt against his former teacher and mentor. In her autobiographical novel *La Nostalgie de l'espérance*, Jeannette Colombel (a friend of Sartre who left the PCF in 1968) recounted a dialogue between her Communist heroine and Kanapa, who appeared under his own name. Asked why he was so hostile to Sartre, Kanapa responded:

> 'You aren't the daughter of a banker, even one who went bankrupt. To rid myself of the old man [a common term in the PCF for breaking with bourgeois culture] is first of all, for me, ridding myself of Sartre: individual thought must be integrated into the struggles of the working class. Now, however great my efforts, I shall never get out of this crucible. I must be vigilant, and hence ruthless... Sartre, precisely because he is the closest to us, is the most dangerous... "a potential traitor", that is what he is, that is what each of us risks becoming if we do not adjust our lives and thought to the Party'.[23]

Kanapa was also showing gross ingratitude (Sartre had helped to pay his sanatorium expenses when he was suffering from tuberculosis). But it will not suffice to see Kanapa as mentally unbalanced (though he undoubtedly was). He was personally congratulated on the book by no less than Maurice Thorez, the PCF's leader, who wrote of his 'excellent work on, or rather against, the existentialist putrescence'.[24] Quite a compliment for a 26-year-old.

Kanapa, with all the frankness of a man out of his depth, had grasped the essence of the ferocity of the PCF's attacks on Sartre in the phrase 'precisely because he is the closest to us'. The logic of Stalinist sectarianism has rarely been so succinctly expressed. While Communist Parties might employ the slogan 'no enemies on the left', the real meaning was 'no enemies on the right'. PCF ministers could cheerily sit in cabinets alongside de Gaulle or Bidault, but they could not tolerate anyone appearing to outflank them on the left, especially while they were still in government (hence their extreme sensitivity to the Trotskyist-led Renault strike in the spring of 1947). And although Sartre did not at this stage have a coherent and structured critique of the PCF, he could easily be perceived as a left critic in some respects.

Garaudy's attack on the 'gravediggers of literature' – Sartre, Mauriac, Malraux and Koestler – was marginally more serious. Sartre responded to the title with one of his best witticisms (his talents as a humorist are often underestimated). 'Gravediggers are decent people, certainly trade unionists, perhaps Communists. I would rather be a gravedigger than a lackey'.[25]

But in trying to follow Sartre onto the terrain of philosophy, Garaudy ended up exposing himself as a buffoon in a remarkable passage in which he attempted to deny his own free will:

I AM A COMMUNIST WITHOUT ANGUISH

First of all because I didn't choose to be a Communist. I didn't choose it because it is not for me to deny the reality of the internal contradictions of capitalism, of its crises and of the class struggle which is the motor of its development. Since the day when the analyses of *Capital* taught me the dialectic of history, I have found myself faced by a compelling force. And at no moment have I the choice between Marxism and those who deny it. I should gladly say, as Luther did to his judges: 'Here I stand; I can do no other'.[26]

As Garaudy showed by the final sentence, he was a lot closer to divine grace than to historical materialism. Fifty years on, one can only wonder what process of ineluctable historical logic took Garaudy from orthodox to dissident Communism, and thence to Catholicism and Islam. There is a long history of Marxist discussion on the scope and limits of the individual within the historical process, but Garaudy threw it all aside in the interest of polemic. Small wonder that Sartre felt obliged to reopen the issue in his existential biographies.

It appeared that Sartre was such a threat that the talents of Garaudy and Kanapa did not suffice. The veteran Hungarian Marxist philosopher Georg Lukács was brought in to write a book-length polemic against Sartre.[27] Though strongly polemical, it was a more serious treatment than Kanapa or

Garaudy were capable of. This in turn led to a heated polemic in the pages of *Combat* in which Sartre accused Lukács of not being a Marxist.[28]

Yet how much of a threat was Sartre? Ariane Chebel d'Appollonia quoted Garaudy as telling Sartre 'You're preventing people coming over to us'[29] and commented: 'This explanation, flattering for Sartre, is scarcely satisfactory since the little Sartrean division did not shine bright in comparison with the Communist armada'.[30]

True, the PCF had massive working-class support through the CGT, and it can scarcely have feared that factory workers across France would throw aside *L'Humanité* in order to debate the relation of the *en-soi* to the *pour-soi*. But the Party also knew that students, teachers and other intellectuals constituted a significant, if secondary, section of its membership, and here Sartrean ideas did constitute a threat which the bureaucracy could not ignore. As the RDR was to show in 1948, that threat could take on a concrete form. Thus Garaudy complained that 'Sartre is leading our students into a dead end'. (It is not clear if 'our' refers to the PCF or the French nation; doubtless formally the latter, but in practice the former.) Yet he went on to undermine his own argument by saying:

> This way of thought [existentialism], cut off from reality, has no hold over the working class which today is the guardian of the golden rule of philosophy: thought is born of action, is action, serves action. At most what we have is an itch, a mild fever affecting a few intellectuals who think they are 'demobilised' now that the Resistance is over.[31]

But if Sartre was so insignificant, then what need for such passionate indignation; why bother writing books against him – especially at a time of serious paper shortage? In any case, if historical laws were inevitable and the truth of Marxism was inescapable, what harm could a Sartre do, however malevolent he might be? Garaudy's leaps from historical fatalism to bureaucratic voluntarism were indeed bewildering; it is no surprise that Sartre began to feel that he had a mission to 'reform' Marxism.

The PCF was also under some pressure from Moscow to attack Sartre. *Pravda* published an article by one D. Zaslavsky attacking the 'nauseous putrid concoctions' of existentialist literature and claiming that existentialism taught that 'any historical process is absurd and fortuitous, any morality a lie. It is the doctrine of the spiritual vacuum'.[32] Stalinist dialectics could apparently accommodate the contradictions of any paradox, however gross; here we have the spectacle of a Marxist materialist denouncing existentialism for its lack of spirituality.[33] And Zhdanov himself, Stalin's top cultural and philosophical hit-man, found time to denounce Sartre and the *Temps modernes*.[34] Obviously the likes of Kanapa and Garaudy were only obeying their master's voice.

For Sartre, the Stalinist vilification posed a problem, which was to remain with him for many years. The PCF had the political allegiance of a good part of the working class and could not be ignored, yet at the same time its political line and its sheer dishonesty made cooperation impossible:

But we should not hesitate to state that the fate of literature is linked to that of the working class…

Unfortunately, in our country, we are separated from these people, to whom we *must* speak, by an iron curtain: they will not hear a word we speak to them. The majority of the proletariat, corseted by a single party, encircled by propaganda which isolates it, forms a closed society with no doors or windows. Only one way in, and a very narrow one – the Communist Party.[35]

Sartre recognised this situation as specifically French. In a series of seven articles written for *Combat* in 1945 on the working class in the United States, Sartre depicted a very different situation, where the mediation of the Communist Party was not needed to establish contact with the working class.[36]

Sartre would have undoubtedly welcomed a lively but fraternal exchange of views with the PCF; after all, that would have helped him reach his target audience. But as he pointed out, the PCF style of argument could not tolerate any such thing: 'They never reply to their opponents: they discredit them – they are said to belong to the police, the Intelligence Service, to be fascists. As for evidence, they never produce it, because it is terrible and would implicate too many people'.[37]

Sartre was doubtless thinking here in particular of the PCF's slanders of Nizan. But his general point was clearly valid. The style of Garaudy and Kanapa was not conducive to serious argument; indeed, one might well imagine that anyone seriously wavering between Sartre and the PCF would be repelled rather than attracted by such diatribes.[38] (As the PCF membership declined steadily after 1947,[39] such would be a reasonable conclusion to draw.)

Such complaints were a recurrent grievance of Sartre in this period; obviously he found the refusal of the PCF to debate seriously a severe frustration. In his 1946 lecture 'Forgers of Myths' he compared the use of character in dramatic composition to the way in which political arguments were trivialised by presenting them in terms of personalities: 'We must replace the conflicts of characters by the representation of conflicts of rights. There was no question of opposition of character between a Stalinist and a Trotskyist'.[40] In other words, Sartre was quite amenable to being persuaded that 'socialism in one country' was a correct strategy; but he did not feel the argument was assisted by the claim that Trotsky was a Gestapo agent.

That Sartre was from time to time accused of Trotskyism was the least of his worries. Obviously he was not a Trotskyist, had no connections with any Trotskyist organisation and had a relatively limited grasp of Trotskyist theory, as was shown by some rather erratic uses of the term 'permanent revolution'.[41] But for Stalinist witch-hunters there was a short step between wanting to take Trotskyism seriously and being a Trotskyist.

In the face of such attacks Sartre could count on a certain amount of sympathy from those formed in the traditions of the Left Opposition. Thus

Maurice Nadeau wrote a defence of Sartre in *Gavroche*, making clear that differences were a matter for rational debate, not abuse. Existentialism was compared to the blossoming of surrealism after the First World War (quite a compliment from Nadeau, who was to be a distinguished historian of surrealism). He noted that existentialism was being attacked

> from the standpoint of morality, literature and above all social conservatism. If for our part we have reservations about its intentions to become a morality and a politics, because it seems to us that what has been revealed to us of this morality and politics has nothing essentially new about it, we shall be the first to denounce the reactionary critics snapping at the heels of Sartre and his friends.[42]

In those hectic years after the Liberation Sartre rapidly became an international figure; in addition to his contacts with the French left he also underwent the influence of North American anti-Stalinism. The four months he spent in the United States in 1945 allowed him to get at least a nodding acquaintance with the left in a country with very different traditions from France. He certainly made a number of significant observations; thus his play *La Putain respectueuse* (1946) was criticised at the time for anti-Americanism,[43] but in fact he showed a prescient recognition that the racial question would play a major role in the U.S.A.'s future. While he had profound reservations about U.S. society, he did not collapse into the crude anti-Americanism with which the PCF responded to anti-Communism.

Sartre's position was reflected in the deeper and more extensive study of the U.S.A. by Daniel Guérin, who spent the years 1946 to 1949 there, studying U.S. society and especially racial oppression and the labour movement. *Les Temps modernes* published a number of Guérin's articles, and was indeed their natural home, for few other French publications would have accepted them, since they fitted the stereotypes of neither the Stalinists nor the anti-Communists. Guérin concluded a series of articles on the U.S. labour movement by declaring: 'I maintain an unshakeable confidence in the future of the American people. They must not be confused with the few monopolies who dishonour them in the eyes of the world'.[44]

While in the United States Sartre made contact with the team of writers around *Partisan Review*. But despite *Partisan Review*'s allegedly Trotskyist roots the journal had become strongly anti-Communist. In 1946 it had shown some enthusiasm for the existentialist milieu, publishing texts by Sartre, Genet and Camus. But it also carried a piece by William Barrett called 'Talent and Career of Jean-Paul Sartre',[45] which, while not denying the talent, was ferociously anti-Communist, and accused Sartre of being 'well along the road to Stalinism'. This was on the basis of the rather questionable assessment that Brunet is shown as 'the 'noblest character' in *L'Age de raison*, when in fact he is 'a poor boob who has let himself become a tool of the enemy of mankind, and by his participation in a party of gangsters and assassins becomes himself an assassin and gangster'. (Two years later de Beauvoir was to be sharply critical of *Partisan Review*, which she called a 'wretched rag' and 'trash'.)[46]

Sartre was more sympathetic to *Politics*,[47] edited by Dwight Macdonald, which in 1947 published articles by Sartre, de Beauvoir and Merleau-Ponty. Macdonald, a former Trotskyist and member of the Workers' Party (formed by Shachtman in 1940 after he rejected Trotsky's demand for 'unconditional defence of the USSR' in the Second World War) had been involved with *Partisan Review*, but had developed disagreements in the course of the war, when he had argued for revolutionary defeatism. Like Shachtman he held that Russia was a 'bureaucratic collectivist' society, neither capitalist nor socialist. In February 1944 he broke from *Partisan Review* to launch his own journal *Politics*, which proclaimed itself to be 'Marxist' and 'partisan to those at the bottom of society – the Negroes, the colonial peoples, and the vast majority of common people everywhere, including the Soviet Union'. Although his radicalism waned in the late 1940s, it is interesting that it was with this current of dissident Trotskyism that Sartre and de Beauvoir felt most at home.[48] As de Beauvoir summed it up, *Partisan Review* 'ended up sliding to the right and more or less adapting to American imperialism, which was one of the reasons for the split with *Politics*, which remains much more loyal to the ideal of permanent revolution'.[49]

But the most important American contact Sartre had with the U.S. left was Richard Wright. Wright had been a member of the Communist Party of the U.S.A.; he described his experiences and reasons for leaving in an article for *Les Temps modernes* in 1949.[50] This article was to appear the following year in the celebrated Cold War anthology *The God that Failed*.[51] The fact that *Les Temps modernes* published this text should be an ample refutation of the claim that the journal or its editors were 'soft on Communism' in 1949.

Wright, as a black ex-Communist, understood the realities of both U.S. racism and Stalinism, and in a moving speech in Paris in December 1948 he set out clearly the bases of a politics independent of both Washington and Moscow: 'The American state of Mississippi gave me my body; the Russian October Revolution gave me my heart. But today these two giant nations – symbols of the nationalist plague of our time – are outdoing each other in efforts to establish plans to brutalise the human spirit'.[52]

Such sentiments provided the basis for an authentically independent 'third camp' politics, rejecting both U.S. imperialism and Russian Stalinism. Sartre's contact with such nonalignment, both in France and the U.S., provided him with an alternative point of reference during the heated and often vicious debates of the late 1940s. Moreover, Sartre would find that those coming from the anti-Stalinist tradition were more willing to give him a serious hearing, and to polemicise with him on his own terms.

Notes

1. *Sit* IV, pp. 218–20.
2. J. Kergoat, *Le Parti socialiste*, Paris, 1983, p. 161.
3. A. Camus, 'Le sang de la liberté', *Combat*, 24 August 1944.
4. *Combat*, 1 October 1944.
5. J. Ferniot, *Je recommencerais bien*, Paris, 1991, p. 161.
6. E. Morin, *Autocritique*, Paris, 1959, p. 77.
7. Cited in J.-J. Marie, *Trotsky, le trotskysme et la IVe internationale*, Paris, 1980, p. 104.
8. *Combat*, 7 October 1944.
9. B.-H. Lévy, *Le Siècle de Sartre*, Paris, 2000, pp. 497, 499.
10. V Serge, *16 Fusillés à Moscou*, Paris, 1984, pp. 123–25.
11. J.-P. Sartre, *Réflexions sur la question juive*, Paris, 1954, pp. 40–41, 182.
12. See C. Martin, 'A la naissance des *Temps modernes*', *La Revue des revues* No. 26, 1999, pp. 3–28.
13. H. Davies, *Sartre and 'Les Temps modernes'*, Cambridge, 1987, p. 217.
14. 'Absence de l'homme', *TM*, January 1946, pp. 730–36, especially pp. 730–31.
15. *Choses*, pp. 19, 55–56.
16. P. Gaillard, 'Bourreaux et victimes', *Les Lettres françaises*, 22 November 1946.
17. For a full account see D. Drake, '*Les Temps modernes* and the French War in Indochina', *Journal of European Studies*, XXVIII (1998), pp. 25–41. See also N. Lamouchi, *Jean-Paul Sartre et le tiers monde*, Paris, 1996, pp. 51–53.
18. *Sit* II, pp. 277, 279–80.
19. The text of this quotation is taken from Serge Halimi: *Sisyphe est fatigué*, Paris, 1993, pp. 342–43. This is not a precise transcription of the programme as recorded, but it does not betray the sense.
20. L. Durand, 'Le Laquais de service', *L'Humanité*, 28 October 1947.
21. Editorial in *Nouvelle critique* No. 1, 1948, p. 1ff. This was unsigned but almost certainly written by Kanapa.
22. J. Kanapa, *L'Existentialisme n'est pas un humanisme*, Paris, 1947, pp. 19–25, 53, 57–58.
23. J. Colombel, *La Nostalgie de l'espérance*, Paris, 1997, p. 224.
24. G. Streiff, *Jean Kanapa*, Paris, 1998, pp. 37, 62.
25. *Sit* II, p. 287.
26. R. Garaudy, *Les Fossoyeurs de la littérature*, Paris, 1947, p. 79.
27. G. Lukács, *Existentialisme ou marxisme?* Paris, 1948.
28. Interviews by François Erval with Lukács (*Combat*, 13 January and 3 February 1949) and with Sartre (*Combat*, 20 January and 3 February 1949).
29. *Choses*, p. 146.
30. A. Chebel d'Appollonia, *Histoire politique des intellectuels en France*, 2 vols, Brussels, 1991, 1: 128.
31. Garaudy, *Les Fossoyeurs*, pp. 22–23.
32. *Pravda*, 24 January 1947, reproduced *TM*, May 1947, pp. 1531–36. For Sartre's response, see *C&R*, pp. 161–62, 677–79.
33. Someone on the *Temps modernes* team knew their Lenin well enough to dig up what he had written about the 'blackmailing, venal pens' of the likes of Zaslavsky when he had been a Menshevik, some thirty years earlier. See 'Political Blackmail', V.I. Lenin, *Collected Works*, 45 vols., Moscow and London, 1960, 25: 257–60. The journal commented: 'This type of man doesn't change much, even when he changes sides. The question is why *Pravda* employs such people', *TM*, December 1947, pp. 1138–40.
34. 1947 speech 'On Philosophy' in A.A. Zhdanov, *On Literature, Music and Philosophy*, London, 1950, p. 109.
35. *Sit* II, p. 277.

36. *Combat*, 6, 7, 9, 10–11, 12, 14, 30 June 1945. See *Sartre Studies International*, Vol. 6, No. 1 (2000), pp. 1–22.
37. *Sit* II, p. 280.
38. One Stalinist term of abuse which Sartre seems to have found amusing was '*rat visqueux*'. On 2 February 1949 *Le Monde* reported the use of the term in *Pravda* by one Simonov, and noted it as a new term of abuse. As Sartre defined it: 'The viscous rat has not betrayed. But the Party is sure he would have done if he had had the opportunity', *Sit* VI, p. 88. The term 'viscous rat' reads oddly in English, with its connotations of Sartre's philosophical concept of viscosity, and also the suggested rhyme with 'whiskers'. Slimy rat, or simply sewer rat (a term with an honourable tradition in Stalinist invective) would be better. (Irene Clephane's translation of *The Communists and Peace*, London, 1969, p. 5, renders it as 'slimy rat'.) In fact the term 'rat visqueux' can already be found in a 1934 text by Paul Nizan on a provincial French town; he described the Catholic laity as 'fleeing like rats, weasels, dark little animals, slimy (*visqueux*) from having passed through drains and sewers'. *Paul Nizan intellectuel communiste*, 1: 160.
39. A. Kriegel, *Les Communistes*, Paris, 1968, p. 31.
40. *TDS*, p. 60.
41. For example, *Sit* II, pp. 130, 186.
42. M. Nadeau, 'En Clignant des yeux', *Gavroche*, 3 January 1946.
43. *TDS*, p. 243.
44. D. Guérin, 'Où va le peuple américain? – III', *TM*, March 1950, p. 1667.
45. *Partisan Review* Vol. XIII, No. 2 (Spring 1946), pp. 237–46.
46. De Beauvoir, *Lettres à Sartre*, Paris, 1990, 2: 296.
47. De Beauvoir, *Lettres à Sartre*, 2: 311, 347.
48. See A. Wald, *The New York Intellectuals*, Chapel Hill, 1987, pp. 200–10; J. Newsinger, *Orwell's Politics*, Basingstoke, 1999, pp. 99–100, 147–48.
49. S. de Beauvoir, *L'Amérique au jour le jour*, Paris, 1948, pp. 346–47.
50. R. Wright, 'J'ai essayé d'être communiste', *TM*, July 1949, pp. 1–45.
51. R. Crossman, ed., *The God that Failed*, London, 1950, pp. 121–66.
52. *Franc-Tireur*, 16 December 1948.

Chapter 6

MATERIALISM OR REVOLUTION?

On 28 October 1945 at the Club Maintenant, Sartre gave the famous lecture known under the title *L'Existentialisme est un humanisme*. Maurice Nadeau, in an article that was sympathetic but not without irony, described the huge crowd that turned up: 'Those present are now gripped by an anguish which is not existential. We are going to die of suffocation'.[1]

The hall was so packed that no discussion was possible; as a result the lecture was repeated in private to enable debate to take place. Among those who attended this second lecture it was Pierre Naville who made an extended critique of Sartre's positions from a Marxist point of view, a critique included when the lecture was published in book form by Nagel in March 1946.[2] (Naville's contribution made up about twenty-eight pages out of a total of 133 pages of text, something in excess of 20 percent. We must assume that Sartre approved of Naville getting such prominence in a book that appeared under Sartre's name.)

Naville's contribution attempted a critique of Sartre's views of the human condition, history, commitment and causality, and concluded that existentialism could not offer a political direction of a collective nature. Naville was quite harsh towards Sartre, accusing his philosophy of being 'the resurrection of Radicalism', saying that the world social crisis no longer permitted liberalism of the traditional kind, but required a 'tortured, anguished liberalism'; Sartre was thus identified with the politics of the Radical Party which looked back to the republicanism of the nineteenth century. He was, moreover, said to be returning to a concept of 'human nature as it was defined in the eighteenth century'.[3] Yet the difference in tone between Naville's response and the attacks by Kanapa and Garaudy was obvious in every sentence. Kanapa and Garaudy brawled like petty street criminals defending their patch from encroachment; Naville, with no territory at stake, was able to give a calm and reasoned defence of the principles of Marxist philosophy.

His claim that 'today, taking up again, in whatever form, a position prior to Marxism is what I call returning to Radicalism' clearly had some effect on Sartre. At the time Sartre responded that his position was subsequent to Marxism, not prior to it.[4] But fifteen years later, in the *Critique de la raison dialectique*, Sartre came to adopt Naville's position.

The significance of this confrontation between Sartre and Naville has often been misunderstood by commentators who are unaware that Naville's Marxism was many miles distant from that of the PCF. In fact the exchange after Sartre's lecture was only a small part of a much broader debate going on within the French left after the Liberation.

Pierre Naville had been a revolutionary militant for many years. At a time when for Sartre the 'heavy presence... of the working-class masses' was still on the horizon,[5] Naville already had a long experience of the proletariat. He was part of the surrealist group, but became a Communist in 1925. While André Breton, during his short period in the PCF, felt himself 'unable' to speak to a meeting of the gasworkers' cell about the situation in Mussolini's Italy,[6] Naville was enthusiastically active in the cell of workers from the Farman factory; an experience of which, towards the end of his life, he still retained a 'magical memory'. At this time intellectuals in the PCF were not put in separate cells, as later on, but were attached to factory cells to do the jobs that workers themselves could not do for fear of victimisation. This involved leafleting, holding meetings at factory gates and in working-class cafés, and selling papers at tube stations.[7] Sartre was only to know such activities after 1968.

Naville had met Trotsky in Moscow in 1927, and he visited him in Prinkipo in 1929 together with Gérard Rosenthal. Trotsky tended to be somewhat distrustful of Naville as being too intellectual, but Marguerite Rosmer wrote to Trotsky that Naville and Rosenthal were becoming good militants: 'They go and sell papers at 6.00 a.m., give out leaflets outside factories, are always ready for any practical task; that is thoroughly deintellectualising them, I assure you'.[8]

Naville took charge of the practical aspects of the organisation of the founding conference of the Fourth International in 1938. With the outbreak of war, he left the Trotskyist movement, while not abandoning his revolutionary ideas. At the very time that Sartre was facing the necessity of political commitment for the first time, Naville returned to a life of study.

Naville had been a materialist since the beginning of his political evolution. As a surrealist, he had aligned himself with Artaud, for whom surrealism had to break its shackles 'if necessary with material hammers'.[9] In his 1926 pamphlet on revolution and intellectuals, he asked the surrealists the question: 'Do they believe in a liberation of the spirit prior to the abolition of the bourgeois conditions of material life, or do they consider that a revolutionary spirit can be created only as a result of the accomplishment of the revolution?'[10]

During the Occupation Naville published two books defending materialism. One was devoted to the baron D'Holbach and scientific thought during the eighteenth century.[11] Here Naville was polemicising indirectly against the domination of clerical and idealist notions under Vichy. But the book also revealed another preoccupation – a deep hostility to Hegelian Marxism; in the preface to the second edition Naville was to claim explicitly that Marxism owed more to D'Holbach than it did to Hegel, and that it was a Hegelianised Marxism that served as a conservative philosophy in China and the USSR.[12]

Naville's other book was devoted to the psychology of behaviour.[13] This was essentially an exposition of the behaviourist psychology of the American John Watson; it was published in 1942, one year before Sartre's *L'Être et le néant*. At first sight there was a striking contrast between the two works; the two men seemed to start from totally opposed premises and to reach wholly different views of the world. But a careful analysis reveals not only differences but certain shared concerns and points of convergence.

For Sartre, the starting point of any discussion of human action was freedom: 'either man is entirely determined (which is unacceptable, particularly since a consciousness which is determined, that is, motivated in exteriority, becomes itself pure exteriority and ceases to be consciousness) or else man is entirely free'.[14] Sartre did not reject determinism in the physical world, but he insisted that determinism did not apply to the facts of consciousness.[15]

For Naville, on the other hand, human psychology must use the same methods as the natural sciences: 'The methods of the physical and natural sciences centred on the "behaviour" of objects. Why should not the so-called sciences of the "mind" do the same?'[16]

We find exactly the same positions in the debate about *L'Existentialisme est un humanisme*. For Naville, 'there are laws of functioning for man as for any other object of science, which, in the strong sense of the word, constitute his nature'. For Sartre, on the other hand, 'the sciences are abstract, they study the variations of factors which are likewise abstract, and not true causality… Whereas in Marxism, we are dealing with the study of a unique totality within which we are seeking a causality. It is not at all the same thing as a scientific causality'.[17]

For Sartre, consciousness and freedom were inextricably linked: 'it is in anguish that man becomes aware of his freedom'.[18] Naville, on the other hand, defended Watson, for whom 'consciousness is a concept which is neither defined nor usable'.[19]

Nonetheless, Sartre and Naville had certain features in common. Naville was a longstanding revolutionary socialist; if he had developed an interest in behaviourism, it was within the context of a political project. 'The behaviourist does not claim to be a pure spectator of human activity; he wants to direct and control it.[20] On 20 October 1940 he had noted in his diary:

As for man, and his future, there are only two attitudes: 1) Gobineau: 'We must recognise that, for a very large number of human beings, it has been impossible and will always remain impossible to take even the first step towards civilisation... ' And 2) Watson: 'I have an unfailing respect for all that can be done with this malleable mass, the human child... *Give me the baby*'.[21]

While Sartre was not yet a Marxist, he shared Naville's ultimate purpose; the very essence of his philosophy was that human beings could and must change the world.

And in this task both also recognised that the question of the individual within the framework of Marxist theory had not as yet been resolved. For Sartre that problem was to lead him to his existential biographies of Genet and Flaubert, where he attempted to comprehend an individual within a historical context. Naville also perceived a lacuna in Marxism. Neither Marx nor Engels 'took a direct interest in psychology in the strict sense.... [Marx and Engels] have left to others the scientific study of the individual processes of behaviour'.[22]

It was scarcely surprising that two thinkers like Sartre and Naville should address this problem of the role of the individual in Marxism. Neither of them had the naivety – or the bad faith – of a Garaudy with his invocation of historical necessity. For those who were prepared to look reality in the face in the century of those enigmatic individuals Hitler and Stalin, it was clear that historical necessity had not delivered the results expected of it. Thus Sartre turned to phenomenology, Naville to behaviourism, in an attempt to resolve these problems.

Both rejected the notion of a 'human nature'. For Sartre human existence preceded essence; for Naville the behaviourist theory of milieu

destroys the notion of the biological inheritance of 'mental' characteristics... There are no more born criminals, born intellectuals, born proletarians, born blacks; there are only criminals, intellectuals, proletarians and blacks, whose situation is in no way unchangeable, but depends on the social conditions which have seen them be born and grow, conditions which it is in our power to modify within certain limits.[23]

By thus making human beings responsible for their own destiny, Naville came close to Sartre's positions – indeed some phrases from the paragraph just quoted might have been written by Sartre.

It can hardly be denied that Sartre and Naville had conceptions of consciousness which were diametrically opposed, and that Naville could be legitimately criticised for neglecting the role of subjectivity. But they were both facing the same problem: both wanted to get rid of the last remnants of the theological notion of an immaterial and immortal soul; both wanted to transcend the Cartesian dualism of mind and body. Hence for Naville consciousness did not exist, or was at best a secondary product of language; for Sartre consciousness was a nothingness.

Like Sartre, Naville had a somewhat ambiguous attitude towards Freud, but on the subject of Freud's theories he commented: 'Man does not suddenly appear between his fifteenth and twentieth year with all his instincts and reflex mechanisms, as if they came out of nowhere'.[24] This was to be later echoed by Sartre in the *Critique de la raison dialectique*: 'Marxists today are concerned only with adults; to read them you would imagine that we are born at the age we earn our first wage'.[25]

If Sartre and Naville conceived the relations between language and consciousness in very different ways, they nonetheless converged in the belief that language was a form of action. Naville recalled that 'for Watson, speech is an action like any other',[26] while for Sartre 'to speak is to act'.[27]

But there was also a point of difference which underlay the whole debate. For Naville 'there is no Marxist philosophy, for in Marx's eyes philosophy had had its time'.[28] As could be expected of a veteran of the struggles of the Left Opposition, his critique of Stalinism was above all a *political* critique. Sartre, on the other hand, had perfected his criticisms of Stalinism on a philosophical level before entering the political arena.

Naville developed his position in a book written in 1946, *Les Conditions de la liberté*. Here he had much to say about Sartre. For Naville, materialism was not juxtaposed to action; on the contrary, it was only within a materialist framework that action could find any meaning:

> How can it be denied that the merchants of anguish [*angoissistes*] are irresolute, unstable people, often defined by having chosen to belong to the milieu of the intellectual petty bourgeoisie? Men who work now need a directed will, a certain activity, a plan of action and a programme for struggle. Abstract activism proliferates in all directions, and it produces what concrete historical determinations impose on it: the fascist as well as the communist, and also the gangster, the careerist, the pedant... Philosophy which does not help to illuminate the process of the liberation of the oppressed should be rejected.[29]

He made fun of Sartre's adoption of the term humanist: 'Who is not a humanist nowadays? Mr Truman is a humanist, M Sartre is a humanist, the Pope is a humanist. But if materialists are humanists, they do not give the word the same meaning. It is futile to proclaim oneself a humanist in inhuman social conditions. M Sartre himself agrees'.[30]

At around the same time Naville wrote a long article called 'Marx or Husserl?'. This was primarily aimed at the phenomenologist Domarchi, Tran Duc Thao (a Vietnamese philosopher associated with Sartre and the *Temps modernes* group) and the Heidegger scholar Beaufret; but Naville was doubtless also thinking of Sartre and the *Temps modernes* team, who were attempting to use phenomenology in the service of a revolutionary view of the world. In the course of his polemic Naville cited Marx's 'Theses on Feuerbach'.[31] Unfortunately he did not cite the third thesis on Feuerbach, which contained a more lucid critique of behaviourism than any of Sartre's:

The materialist doctrine that men are products of circumstances and upbringing, and that, therefore, changed men are products of other circumstances and
changed upbringing, forgets that it is men who change circumstances and that
the educator must himself be educated. Hence this doctrine is bound to divide
society into two parts – one of which is superior to society (in Robert Owen, for
example).

The coincidence of the change of circumstances and of human activity can be
conceived and rationally understood only as revolutionising practice.[32]

For while Watson had much to say about modifying human beings, he
never explained *who* would be doing the modifying, unless it were to be
some sort of benevolent dictator after the fashion of Robert Owen, who
would stand outside of humanity and therefore be exempt from the determinism that affected other human beings.

Though Naville had broken with organised Trotskyism at the outbreak
of the Second World War, he had not abandoned the attempt to build some
kind of Marxist collective. Hence the encounter between Sartre and Naville was not simply a debate between individuals. While Sartre was the
leading figure in the *Temps modernes* team, Naville was the principal ani-
mator of one of its main rivals, *La Revue internationale*. When Sartre, in his
obituary of Merleau-Ponty cited in the previous chapter, wrote of those
journals at the Liberation which had taken a 'better' choice, he named no
names, but *La Revue internationale* largely fitted the description.

In many ways the *Revue* was a parallel enterprise to that of the *Temps
modernes*. If its team did not include any stars as famous as Sartre, its editorial committee contained a certain number of people who would become
well known in the postwar left – Charles Bettelheim, Gilles Martinet, Maurice Nadeau, and a little later David Rousset and Gérard Rosenthal. Like
Les Temps modernes it sought to address a wide range of political and cultural topics. As well as politics, economics and literature, it gave coverage
to the natural sciences (something which got less attention from *Les Temps
modernes*). The first issue, which appeared in December 1945, contained
David Rousset on the world of the concentration camp, Jean Rostand on
embryology and evolution, and poems by Jacques Prévert. The following
issue contained articles by the distinguished historian of the French Revolution Georges Lefebvre, Tran Duc Thao and Maurice Nadeau; other contributors included former surrealist Ferdinand Alquié and Daniel Guérin.

In the Introduction to the new journal printed in this first issue, the
Revue declared itself explicitly Marxist, but at the same time pronounced
itself in favour of open debate. 'The ideas which inspire the founders of
this review are those of dialectical materialism; it is only honest on our part
to declare this from the very start. But we do not intend this description to
refer to a dogma which is as sterile as any other'.[33] In fact, several of the
leading figures involved in the venture – Naville, Rousset, Rosenthal,
Nadeau – were veterans of the Trotskyist movement who had now broken
their connections with organised Trotskyism but who remained attached

to the principles of anti-Stalinist Marxism. Yet in a political sense *La Revue internationale* was in no way a Trotskyist review. The political line was fairly eclectic, and there was little criticism of the PCF. A range of different points of view on the situation in the USSR and the emerging People's Democracies in Eastern Europe were presented – some sympathetic, some rather less so, though there was little that was strongly anti-Stalinist. Thus Jacques Charrière welcomed nationalisations in Czechoslovakia, but argued that in themselves they were insufficient to transform a bourgeois state into a proletarian state.[34] However, in one piece the former Trotskyist Raya Dunayevskaya put forward the position that the Soviet economy 'uses almost all the mechanisms of a capitalist type'.[35] At this time Naville himself was active in the *Mouvement socialiste unitaire et démocratique* (later to become the *Parti socialiste unitaire*), which was quite close to the PCF, though this was probably conceived as a form of 'entrism', since he had not abandoned his basic Trotskyist convictions.

Les Temps modernes and *La Revue internationale* had different roots and different political agendas. But in the relatively open climate of the early years after the Liberation there were quite fraternal relations between them. *La Revue internationale* carried a number of articles in which phenomenology was vigorously attacked, but it opened its pages to Merleau-Ponty to reply to these criticisms and defend his own view of Marxism.[36] The reviews of Sartre's books were sometimes sharply critical, but never malicious in the way that those in PCF publications were. Sartre and de Beauvoir were readers of the *Revue internationale*.[37]

But there was one essential difference between the two journals. Sartre was now a 'star', and, despite what appears to have been his own natural modesty, all his political interventions from now until the end of his life were made in this capacity. *Les Temps modernes* thus had sufficient notoriety to keep its head above the waters of the market. Without stars, *La Revue internationale* was subject to constant financial difficulties. It appeared monthly until February 1948, then suspended publication. It made a brief reappearance in 1950 as a quarterly, but the following year it disappeared for ever.

Of those involved with *La Revue internationale*, Pierre Naville and David Rousset would cross Sartre's path again. And the debate with Naville certainly left important traces in his memory, above all because it was a real debate, and not the ritual exchange of abuse into which any discussion with the PCF soon degenerated. Yet this encounter has largely been ignored by commentators on Sartre. (Naville does not appear in the index of Cohen-Solal's biography, and he is not among the list of well over two hundred people she acknowledged as having helped her.)

Sartre developed his side of the argument further in a long essay called 'Matérialisme et révolution', written in early 1946. This was a more serious piece of work than *L'existentialisme est un humanisme* and represented Sartre's most substantial philosophical attack on Marxism, and an attempt to propose existentialism as an alternative theoretical basis for a revolutionary movement.

In a footnote added in 1949 he stated that its target was 'Stalinist neo-Marxism' rather than Marx himself.[38] Yet a careful reading of the essay shows that this was not wholly true. Sartre did indeed attack such PCF thinkers as Garaudy, but exposing the contradictions and crudities in Garaudy's version of Stalinist Marxism was an easy task. Naville was a more serious target, and he received several mentions in the text.[39] In fact Sartre began his argument by citing Naville's definition of dialectical materialism as being 'the expression of a progressive discovery of the interactions in the world, a discovery which is in no way passive, but implies the activity of the one who discovers, seeks and struggles'.[40]

Sartre noted that the PCF was having difficulty in attracting radicalised students because of its dogmatic philosophy.[41] After a rather uncomfortable discussion of the natural sciences, he attacked the crude reductionism to which the materialist method could lead, citing as an example the historian who saw Spinoza's philosophy as a 'reflection' of the Dutch grain trade.[42]

That this method could have grave political consequences was shown in his discussion of the way in which Stalinist writers used the concept of 'objectivity'. By beginning with the premise that anyone opposed to them was 'objectively' serving bourgeois interests, their logic led remorselessly to the proposition that 'Trotskyists are police spies'. He added: 'I am summarising here conversations about Trotskyism that I have had on many occasions with Communist intellectuals, including some of the most important. In every case they have developed as I have indicated'.[43]

Sartre showed just how much he had in common with Marxism when he stated: 'I know that there is no other salvation for mankind than the liberation of the working class'.[44] And, like Naville, he found himself confronting the early Marx. In 1949 Sartre added a footnote to 'Matérialisme et révolution' where he referred to the *Theses on Feuerbach*, citing Marx's term 'practical materialism'[45] but querying why it was necessary to call it 'materialism'.[46] It is interesting to see both Sartre and Naville turning to the young Marx in an attempt to resolve their problems. Both were trying to reestablish a socialist theory which could be genuinely scientific and at the same time hold a place for individual action. Both were trying to uncover the authentic Marxist tradition from beneath the debris deposited on it by Stalinism. (Unwisely, Sartre attempted to blame Marx's later development on his 'ill-fated encounter with Engels'.)[47]

In *L'existentialisme est un humanisme* Sartre had attempted to make humanism the basis of a morality; now he extended this to seeing it as the basis for a political strategy. Developing his argument that humanism rather than materialism was the philosophy of revolution, he asserted: 'The claim "We too are human beings" is at the foundation of every revolution'.[48]

This, he argued, would resolve the contradiction in the Communist attitude to morality – on the one hand a theory of rigorous determinism which showed the bourgeoisie as obeying laws of necessity, while on the other the PCF's propaganda cultivated 'moral indignation'.[49]

In a further attempt to undermine Naville, Sartre declared in a footnote that 'behaviourism is the philosophy of Taylorism'.[50] But it seems he had not read *La Psychologie du comportement* with sufficient care. Naville clearly differentiated himself from Taylorism, saying in a discussion of 'psychological tests':

> There is even a certain quackery attached to them. Trade and industry at first saw in them merely the opportunity to determine levels and forms of activity below which their wage earners were fit only for the scrapheap. Certain psychologists, following the example of engineers like Taylor, were above all interested in the employers' profits. Gradually, other psychologists came to see that human labour also responded to its own laws.[51]

Sartre argued that a rejection of materialism would mean that the PCF would have to regard its policy decisions, such as supporting the Hitler–Stalin Pact, as being choices taken with an awareness of risk and responsibility rather than as the product of historical inevitability.[52]

Sartre again argued a position very similar to that of the young Marx when he declared that 'it is by changing the world that we can know it'.[53] And insisting that there was no single predetermined path for human history, he elaborated on Rosa Luxemburg's slogan 'Socialism or Barbarism' by stating: 'But there can be many barbarisms and many socialisms, perhaps even a barbarous socialism'.[54]

At the end of the essay Sartre expressed his greatest anxiety: 'What would happen if one day materialism were to stifle the revolutionary project?'[55] His fears were understandable. For him the PCF was above all the representative of materialism, and he had before his eyes a Communist Party which, in the context of the 1945 division of the world into 'spheres of influence', was participating in a coalition with right-wing forces and was opposing all strikes. Yet to a man like Naville Sartre's anxieties must have appeared derisory. As a revolutionary militant for the last twenty years, he could know by 'introspection' that materialism was in no way an obstacle to tireless activity.

'Matérialisme et révolution' was a contradictory and sometimes a confused work; Sartre was still elaborating his own position. But he was clearly groping his way towards, rather than away from, Marxism, and he deserved fraternal debate rather than abuse. Sartre's Stalinist critics would have done well to remember Lenin's words: 'Intelligent idealism is closer to intelligent materialism than stupid materialism'.[56]

Notes

1. *Combat*, 30 October 1945.
2. *C&R*, p. 131; J.-P. Sartre, *L'Existentialisme est un humanisme*, Paris, 1966, pp. 105–41.
3. Sartre, *L'Existentialisme*, pp. 106–7, 109.
4. *Ibid.*, pp. 127, 131–32.
5. J.-P. Sartre, *Critique de la raison dialectique*, tome I, Paris, 1960, p. 23.
6. A. Breton, *Manifestes du surréalisme*, Paris, 1963, p. 99.
7. P. Naville, *La Révolution et les intellectuels*, Paris, 1975, pp. 43–44.
8. Letter of 19 March 1930, in A. and M. Rosmer, L.D. Trotsky, *Correspondance 1929–1939*, Paris, 1982, p. 131.
9. 'Déclaration du 27 janvier 1925', cited in M. Nadeau, *Histoire du surréalisme*, Paris, 1964, p. 68.
10. In Naville, *La Révolution*, p. 85.
11. P. Naville, *D'Holbach et la philosophie scientifique au XVIIIe siècle*, Paris, 1942.
12. Naville, *D'Holbach*, (2nd edition) Paris, 1967, pp. 15–16. De Beauvoir read this book in 1944, and rather unkindly judged that not only was Naville a *con*, but that D'Holbach had been one too. (S. de Beauvoir, *Lettres à Sartre*, 2 vols, Paris, 1990, 2: 249).
13. P. Naville, *La psychologie du comportement*, Paris, 1942 (references to 2nd edition, Paris, 1963).
14. J.-P. Sartre, *L'Être et le néant*, Paris, 1943, p. 518.
15. J.-P. Sartre, *L'Imaginaire*, Paris, 1966, p. 98.
16. Naville, *La Psychologie du comportement*, p. 13.
17. Sartre, *L'Existentialisme*, pp. 139–40.
18. Sartre, *L'Être et le néant*, p. 66.
19. Naville, *La Psychologie du comportement*, p. 15.
20. *Ibid.*, p. 30.
21. P. Naville, *Mémoires imparfaites*, Paris, 1987, pp. 191–92.
22. Naville, *La Psychologie du comportement*, pp. 370–71.
23. P. Naville, *Psychologie, marxisme, matérialisme*, Paris, 1948, p. 19.
24. Naville, *Psychologie, marxisme, matérialisme* p. 149.
25. Sartre, *Critique*, p. 47.
26. Naville, *La Psychologie du comportement*, p. 23.
27. *Sit* II, p. 72.
28. Naville, *La Psychologie du comportement*, p. 369.
29. P. Naville, *Les Conditions de la liberté*, Paris, 1947, pp. 60–61.
30. Naville, *Les Conditions*, p. 183.
31. P. Naville, 'Marx ou Husserl?', *Revue internationale*, March 1946, pp. 227–43, May 1946, pp. 445–54.
32. K. Marx and F. Engels, *Collected Works*, London & Moscow, 1975–2001, 5: 7.
33. *La Revue internationale*, December 1945, p. 3.
34. *La Revue internationale*, May 1946, pp. 471–78.
35. *La Revue internationale*, October 1946, pp. 231–35.
36. M. Merleau-Ponty, 'Marxisme et philosophie', *La Revue internationale*, June–July 1946, pp. 518–26.
37. *Choses*, p. 162.
38. *Sit* III, p. 135.
39. De Beauvoir's *Pour une morale de l'ambiguïté*, Paris, 1947 was also conceived at least partly as a response to Naville, although he is not named in the text. See *Choses*, p. 79.
40. *Sit* III, pp. 138–39.
41. *Sit* III , p. 137.

42. *Sit* III, p. 158.

43. *Sit* III, p. 171.

44. *Sit* III, p. 172.

45. The phrase 'practical materialism' does not appear in the English translation of the *Theses on Feuerbach*; however, Marx does point to the limitations of '*contemplative* materialism, that is, materialism which does not comprehend sensuousness as practical activity'. (K. Marx and F. Engels, *Collected Works*, London & Moscow, 1975–2001, 5: 8).

46. *Sit* III, p. 184.

47. *Sit* III, p. 213. For a critique of the widespread claim that Engels was in some sense a precursor of Stalinism, see J. Rees, 'Engels' Marxism', *International Socialism* 65 (1994), pp. 47–82.

48. *Sit* III, pp. 188–89.

49. *Sit* III, p. 193.

50. *Sit* III, p. 206. Sartre's distrust of the dehumanising logic of Taylorism was wholly justified. F.W. Taylor, the pioneer of 'scientific management', summed up his philosophy in the words: 'One of the very first requirements for a man who is fit to handle pig iron as a regular occupation is that he shall be so stupid and so phlegmatic that he more nearly resembles in his mental make-up the ox than any other type'. See T. Cliff, *The Employers' Offensive*, London, 1970, p. 104. When 'Matérialisme et révolution' first appeared in *Les Temps modernes*, Sartre's footnote was the much more open-minded: 'A curious parallel could be drawn between behaviourism and Taylorism' (*TM*, July 1946, p. 20). By the time it was reprinted in *Situations III* in 1949, Sartre had opted for a more aggressive formulation.

51. Naville, *La Psychologie du comportement*, p. 324.

52. *Sit* III, p. 214.

53. *Sit* III, p. 220.

54. *Sit* III, p. 221.

55. *Sit* III, p. 225.

56. V.I. Lenin, *Collected Works*, Moscow and London, 1960, 38: 276.

Chapter 7

The Spectre of Trotsky

After completing 'Matérialisme et révolution', Sartre's quest continued. Philosophically and politically dissatisfied with the PCF, he wished to establish a revolutionary alternative. Yet Naville's anti-Stalinist materialism was clearly not what he was looking for. In this context a major influence was his fellow-editor of *Les Temps modernes*, Maurice Merleau-Ponty, who was usually the author of editorial statements signed 'T.M'., to which Sartre gave his consent,[1] apparently recognising that Merleau-Ponty was more politically sophisticated than he was. Merleau-Ponty was not a Trotskyist, but he had had a number of friends and contacts in the Trotskyist movement since before the war.[2]

And in Merleau-Ponty's postwar strategy it was possible to detect that his Trotskyist contacts had had some influence. In his obituary Sartre argued that Merleau-Ponty's 'resolute stance' contained an echo of Trotskyist thought: 'if the USSR is attacked, said Trotsky, we must defend the foundations of socialism; as for the Stalinist bureaucracy, it is not for capitalism to settle accounts with it, the Russian proletariat will deal with that'.[3]

It is an interesting analogy, and one that might be applied to Sartre's own thinking at certain stages of his career, but the comparison should not be stretched too far. In a text of 1946 Merleau-Ponty set out a position which he attributed to Trotskyists in a series of rhetorical questions:

> Is it not enough to make manifest what is latent, and to apply to the present the classic schemas of Marxism for the parties to regroup, and for political life to become once again transparent, and for political choice and loyalty to become easy again?… Is it not enough to rediscover the Marxist inspiration which originally motivated the Socialist Party as well as the Communist Party in order for all Machiavellianism to disappear and with it the hesitations of the scrupulous intellectual?

Notes for this chapter begin on page 90.

Merleau-Ponty dismissed this as an 'abstract and naive solution',[4] show-ing that he had no sympathy with the strategy and tactics of organised Trotskyism.

But what cannot be denied is that, through his friendships and his read-ing, Merleau-Ponty knew his Trotskyism. In an article of July 1948 he referred to the denial by Trotsky's widow that André Malraux had ever been a Trotskyist, to a letter written to Malraux by Victor Serge shortly before his death, and to the claim by *France-Dimanche* that Trotsky had left a testament saying he would unite with anti-Communists against Stalin-ism. In his reply Merleau-Ponty showed considerable sympathy for Trot-sky, whom he distinguished from dogmatists and 'sacristans of Marxism'. He cited not only Trotsky's *In Defence of Marxism,* and a letter from his widow Natalia Sedova, but some relatively obscure Trotskyist publica-tions – not only the *New International* but a 'roneoed statement from the International Secretariat of the Fourth International'. He also showed awareness of Trotsky's disagreements with Burnham and Shachtman (who had rejected the argument that Russia was a workers' state), though like many others on the left he was unable to spell the latter name. And in the tone of one proclaiming 'what every schoolboy knows' he declared that 'Everybody knows… that Victor Serge had ceased to be a Trotskyist some years ago'.[5]

Merleau-Ponty was also in contact with various dissident Trotskyists who were developing new ideas about the nature of Russian society and in particular were arguing that it was a state capitalist society. Among these were his protégé on the editorial board of *Les Temps modernes,* Claude Lefort.

Merleau-Ponty tried to set out his thinking on the question of Stalinism in his book *Humanisme et terreur* (1947), expanded from articles in *Les Temps modernes.* This pleased nobody. Anti-Communists saw it as a defence of Stalinist repression, while Stalinists, even if they recognised that they were being defended, found the terms of the defence quite unac-ceptable. Merleau-Ponty had largely himself to blame, since he wrote in a convoluted style which reflected a contradictory and incomplete process of thought. Certainly the book did not justify the Moscow Trials; Merleau-Ponty made clear that not even the victories of the Second World War could legitimate them.[6] And, like Sartre, he had no sympathy for the Stal-inist practice of evading political debate by depicting political enemies as traitors and spies.[7] But he detached himself from the traditions of the Left Opposition by insisting that 'between the Leninist course and the Stalinist course, there is no *absolute* difference. Nothing enables us to say with pre-cision: here Marxist politics ends and here counterrevolution begins'.[8]

Merleau-Ponty's bleak conclusion was that he found himself in a hope-lessly entangled situation. 'You can't be an anti-Communist, and you can't be a Communist'.[9] It was a perceptive analysis of the political contradic-tions of the period, but it also laid Merleau-Ponty open to the same criticism that Naville had directed against Sartre, that his philosophy failed 'to give directions, to say whether, in 1945, we should join the UDSR [a small social democratic party], the SFIO or the PCF or something else'.[10]

Sartre continued to rely on Merleau-Ponty's political judgement, and undoubtedly gained from him insights into the alternatives within the Marxist tradition. But Merleau-Ponty could not help him resolve the basic philosophical dilemmas he still faced. The revolutionary humanism which Sartre had advocated in 'Matérialisme et révolution' pointed back to the problem of morality, a problem which he believed the PCF's materialism could not resolve. The question of morality always held central importance for Sartre. On the one hand, he saw a world without God, in which there could be no values prior to or beyond those that human beings created for themselves. Yet at the same time, humanity lived in a world in which it could not refrain from interacting with other human beings; hence it was constantly required to make moral choices. Morality was simultaneously impossible and necessary. Hence Sartre's unfulfilled promise at the end of L'Être et le néant to write a sequel in which the question of morality would be confronted.[11] In the period 1947 to 1948 he wrote extensive notes for this sequel, notes which would be published only after his death.[12]

It was this concern with morality that caused Sartre so much difficulty when he attempted to confront Marxism. For him, politics was the extension of morality – how should we act in society? How should society be changed for the better? 'Morality *today* must be revolutionary socialist'.[13] Yet Marxism in its Stalinist guise had great difficulty with morality. The economic determinism that passed for 'dialectical materialism' left no place for morality other than as the ideology of a repressive order.

As Sartre had already noted in 'Matérialisme et révolution', this meant that in practice the PCF had an esoteric and an exoteric doctrine. In the manuals of Marxist theory capitalists acted according to immutable historical and economic laws; but in the pages of L'Humanité employers were 'wicked' and greedy.[14] Materialism ought to prevent Communists from making judgements on their opponents: 'a bourgeois is merely the product of a rigorous necessity. Yet the climate of L'Humanité is moral indignation'.[15] In particular, two questions of political morality were to acquire particular importance for Sartre: the debate about means and ends and the problem of oppression.

For Sartre, any formulation based on the principle that the 'end justifies the means' was inadequate, since it implied a view of history in which the end was already given and the means were simply the quickest route to attaining it. If socialism was something already clearly defined and unproblematic, then any means – from poison gas to the ballot box – that would get us there quickly should be unhesitatingly accepted. But if the end just as much as the means were the product of human choice, the means and ends became inseparable parts of a single dialectical process:

If the end is *still to be made*, if it is a choice and a risk for man, then it can be corrupted by the means, for it is what we *make* it and it is transformed at the same time as man transforms himself by the use he makes of the means. But if the end is to be *reached*, if in a sense it has a sufficiency of being, then it is independent of the means. In that case one can choose any means to achieve it.[16]

Thus Sartre obviously found it of great interest to discover that there was an alternative tradition of Marxism which posed the question of ends and means in similar terms to those he himself was exploring. In his notes on morality he devoted some eight-and-a-half pages to a detailed examination of Trotsky's *Their Morals and Ours* (1938), described as 'strong but short'.[17] Such a serious examination of Trotsky's text would have been quite alien to the Stalinist tradition.[18]

Sartre was not uncritical of Trotsky's exposition – which in any case was a polemical pamphlet dealing with certain debates about the relations of Leninism and Stalinism rather than being intended as a comprehensive Marxist account of the problem of morality. Thus he began by quoting Trotsky's account of the place of morality in Lenin's thought: 'The "amoralism" of Lenin, that is, his rejection of supra-class morals, did not hinder him from remaining faithful to one and the same ideal throughout his whole life; from devoting his whole being to the cause of the oppressed'.[19]

For Sartre, this involved using 'bourgeois criteria'. Any 'bourgeois democrat' could use similar terms; the only difference would be in the concept of oppression, which would be seen as a purely individual question.[20] He went on to quote Trotsky on lying: 'Nevertheless, lying and violence "in themselves" warrant condemnation? Of course, even as does the class society which generates them. A society without social contradictions will naturally be a society without lies and violence. However, there is no way of building a bridge to that society save by revolutionary, that is, by class means'.[21]

Here Sartre detected a contradiction in Trotsky's thought; on the one hand a view of the 'dialectical process' in which 'every end becomes a means', and on the other hand the depiction of an 'absolute end'. Beyond the class struggle there was a final end, the collectivist organisation of society.[22]

For Trotsky the question was set out as follows: 'A means can be justified only by its end. But the end in its turn needs to be justified. From the Marxist point of view, which expresses the historical interests of the proletariat, the end is justified if it leads to increasing the power of man over nature and to the abolition of the power of man over man'.[23]

On this Sartre commented: 'Here then is an absolute end: social antagonisms are suppressed and man becomes an end for man, lies and violence are banished, all the strength of the human species is directed towards nature which man undertakes to conquer. Here I discover a Kantian ideal: it is the city of ends'.[24]

Sartre then tried to apply the principles in practice, with a consideration of contemporary political issues, which in many ways anticipated some of the tactical and strategic arguments he was to develop in the early 1950s. Thus he argued that in France in 1947 the PCF was corrupting the working class and destroying its self-confidence. Was it therefore legitimate to use 'all means' to defeat Stalinism, as Koestler believed, including alliance with reactionary forces such as the U.S.A. and Gaullism? Sartre responded that 'the triumph of these forces would not mean simply the liquidation of the PCF but a reinforcement of the oppression of workers and a total loss of the confidence that this class has in itself'.[25]

In other words, by setting the end in a broader context, we see the con-tradictory effects of the means. Unlike Koestler, a Trotskyist would refuse to ally with reactionary groupings. But since the vast majority of the work-ing class supported the PCF, the Trotskyist position became idealist, because it was unable to have any direct impact on the struggle. Sartre did not condemn this position, and admitted it might be the only possible course; nonetheless it was 'moral and abstract'. Only if Trotskyism had mass support could its position become a 'concrete morality'. Sartre went on to distinguish his view of oppression, founded on the concept of human freedom, from the Trotskyist view of the future society which defined oppression.[26]

Sartre then cited Trotsky's self-defence from criticism over the question of the 1919 decree on hostages: 'Only in the historical content of the strug-gle lies the justification of the decree as in general the justification of the whole civil war'.[27] Sartre commented that the struggle itself required jus-tification, and that this could only be in terms of the future society being struggled for. 'Thus the notions of value and, in a sense, liberty, are present in Trotskyism'.[28] And he concluded: 'A necessary future sends you back… to Machiavellianism: every means is justified since it is the future itself which makes it appear. When Trotsky rejects certain means he posits thereby the existence of values and of liberty'.[29]

In a sense, then, Sartre found the same dualism – between moralism and a necessary historical process – in Trotsky that he found in Stalinism. Yet the argument was conducted on quite a different level. Whereas he had seen Stalinist moralism as dishonest and manipulative, with Trotsky he was clearly dealing with a thinker he respected even where he disagreed with him; he was using Trotsky's argument as a means of clarifying and sharpening his own position. (That this was not just a passing interest in shown by the fact that Sartre returned to a discussion of Trotsky's essay in his lecture on Marxist ethics to the Gramsci Institute in Rome in May 1964.)[30]

Moreover, on one fundamental point his thought was very similar to Trotsky's; any formulation in which ends and means are neatly separated and juxtaposed, so that the former can 'justify' the latter, will not do. Only a recognition that there is a historical process in which ends and means form part of the same totality and thus interact on each other gives us a basis for deciding which means are 'permissible'.

Although Sartre did not regard his thoughts on morality as being definitive enough to justify publication, the preoccupation with ends and means would be visible in his political preoccupations over the coming years. Thus the founding appeal for the RDR in 1948 stated: 'For us, the means are as important as the end. And the socialist end will not tolerate the use of no matter what means'.[31] In his 1949 polemic with Lukács he used a similar formulation: 'We consider that means are valid to achieve an end, provided they do not destroy that end'.[32] The argument in *Les Jours de notre vie* in 1950, that the existence of labour camps on a massive scale called into question the socialist nature of the USSR, followed exactly the same logic.[33]

The question of oppression also raised a number of problems. In the orthodoxy of Stalinist Marxism, there was little place for a serious analysis of oppression, be it racial or sexual. On the one hand, the PCF's theory reduced all questions of oppression to a mechanical model of class; at the same time, in practice the PCF often capitulated to the most backward prejudices of its proletarian membership, for example on such questions as women's rights or racism.

For Sartre oppression was to be defined in existential terms. Oppression was essentially a relation between two freedoms – the oppressor and the oppressed. (I cannot oppress a stone – and nor can I be oppressed by one.) From this Sartre deduced that there was 'a complicity between the oppressor and the oppressed'.[34] At first sight it might seem that he was thus arguing that the oppressed are, at least in part, to blame for their own oppression. But a much more important point was at stake. For if oppression is something which is entirely externally imposed, if the oppressed are not in some way responsible for their own oppression, then liberation too must be something external; the oppressed could never liberate themselves. In this sense Sartre's view of oppression was the necessary precondition for Marx's insistence that 'the emancipation of the working classes must be conquered by the working classes themselves'.[35]

Merleau-Ponty rather sourly observed that 'for Sartre, as for the anarchists, the idea of oppression is always predominant over that of exploitation'.[36] On a superficial level he was correct. Sartre came to politics through morality, and there is no evidence that he ever took much interest in the purely economic aspects of Marxist theory. But that is to look at the question ahistorically. At the time of the founding of the Communist International, Lenin and Trotsky recognised that anti-authoritarian anarchists and syndicalists like Victor Serge and Alfred Rosmer – those who, in Trotsky's words, 'really wanted to tear the head off capitalism' – were much better revolutionaries than the Kautskys and Scheidemanns who had inherited the Marxist orthodoxy of the Second International in the form of an abstract historical determinism. Thirty years on, Stalinism had again transformed Marxism from a living theory of revolution into a set of mechanical dogmas. In that context, Sartre's insistence on the struggle against oppression could be a valuable revivifying factor.

For Sartre racism, and the associated phenomena of fascism, colonialism and imperialism, were a central concern from his earliest works to the very end of his life. On the one hand, racism was the most clear-cut example of 'bad faith' and why it was bad – it meant denying the human status of certain persons on the grounds of accidental and irrelevant physical features. At the same time racism was at the heart of most of the major political conflicts of Sartre's lifetime – from the rise of Hitler to the Vietnam War. Racism was not simply an obsession with Sartre, it was a key element which provided the bridge between writing and action. It is surprising how few commentators have pointed to the centrality of this theme in his work; yet to fail to do so deprives us of a central element giving coherence to the whole course of his development.

In *Réflexions sur la question juive* Sartre made his fullest analysis of the roots of racist oppression; at the same time he linked it to class and argued that only the triumph of the working class and the establishment of socialism could put an end to anti-Semitism.[37] Reporting on the racial question in the U.S.A., Sartre saw it as inseparably linked to class. He expressed some sympathy with the view that blacks formed the 'true American proletariat' and that 'the prosperity of white workers is based on the semi-slavery of the black population'. But he saw this as an exaggeration, since thirteen million blacks could not guarantee the prosperity of 122 million whites. He went on to argue:

> The fact remains that the black problem is neither a political problem nor a cultural problem: the blacks belong to the American proletariat and their cause is the same as that of the white workers. Within a capitalist framework, even in the most optimistic hypothesis, they can only hope for a certain improvement in their condition, but not for equality with whites.... It seems there is only one solution to the black problem – and it is a long way off: when the American proletariat – black and white – has recognised the identity of its interests in face of the employing class, the Negroes will struggle with white workers and on an equal footing with them for the recognition of their rights. It is from the workers' organisations, and from them alone, that blacks can hope for effective assistance.[38]

Sartre was attempting to understand the complex interactions of race and class. But this was too subtle for his opponents in the PCF. When Sartre published *Orphée noir* – his preface to Senghor's anthology of African and Caribbean poetry – he was promptly and vigorously denounced by Gabriel d'Arbousier in a PCF publication for having strayed from the clichés of Stalinist rhetoric: 'In all this rubbish, all we hear about is consciousness, subconsciousness, state of mind, metaphysics. Race is a concrete notion, but that of class is only abstract although universal, and

Sartre only alludes furtively to the most concrete reality which dominates and determines all the notions he mentions, namely colonisation, the daughter of imperialism.' To oppose Sartre, d'Arbousier invoked some of the mechanical platitudes to which Stalinism reduced the complexities of reality: 'And thus every day the black peasant and the white worker grasp more perfectly, not the fact that their interests are identical, but their solidarity in the struggle against imperialism which divides them only in order to oppress them the better'.

As the Algerian War was to show, things were not so simple. Sartre's position, whatever its weaknesses, was better fitted to confront the real contradictions of anti-imperialist struggle.

D'Arbousier then pointed out that 'we have repeatedly warned Alioune Diop (of *Présence africaine*)[39] and Senghor against the use which could be made of their position and their publications', and accused Sartre of being 'on the look-out for anything which he can use in his demoralising activity'.[40]

Clearly it was not so much theory as political hegemony which concerned the PCF. Just as it had feared that Sartre might undermine its support among left-wing students, so now it saw Sartre as challenging its hegemony among the black students and intelligentsia in Paris. Some of these – like Senghor himself (later first President of independent Senegal) or Aimé Césaire – were to play an important role in the political evolution of their countries over the next two decades. So the danger of the emergence of a tendency to black nationalism developing away from the influence of Communism was not just a matter for the PCF, but also for Moscow, which was concerned to exercise influence in postcolonial Africa.

As for feminism, the French left had kept it at arm's length for two centuries. In the course of the French Revolution there had been an explosion of feminism, with the creation of women's clubs. The Jacobins could not tolerate this, and the clubs were closed. Jacobinism was rooted among small artisans, for whom the family was an integral part of the productive process; women were needed at home, and could not be allowed to engage in politics.

This distrust of women remained integral to the Republican tradition in France, and, through the Popular Front, infected also the PCF – hence the fact that women obtained the vote so much later in France than in many European countries. The excuse commonly given was that women were under the influence of the Church, and if allowed to vote would support candidates of the right; yet the left's neglect of women's interests precisely had the result of thrusting women into the arms of the Church.

As late as the mid-1950s the PCF could quite openly declare itself opposed to birth control (illegal in France until 1967): 'the Communists condemn the reactionary ideas of those who advocate the limitation of births and thus seek to divert workers from their battle for bread and socialism'.[41] This was qualified only with rather vague criticisms of the repressive state laws on abortion. When Colette Audry attempted to develop a campaign in favour of birth control, she was told by Jeannette Vermeersch, wife of Maurice Thorez and herself a powerful figure in the PCF, that 'you want to strip love of its poetry!'[42] That the denunciation of 'Malthusianism' was made a major issue at the PCF Fourteenth Congress in 1956 was seen by many delegates as an attempt to divert attention from the Khrushchev 'secret speech' and the Algerian War.[43] Rather than defending women's right to control their own bodies, the PCF's women's paper, *Heures claires des femmes françaises*, devoted at least half of every issue to knitting, embroidery and similar crafts, and in a feature on happy Russian women assured its readers that 'of course, Soviet women knit'.[44]

Hence it had only been in the marginalised organisations of the far left that the demand for genuine equality for women had been able to develop. As we have seen, it was Colette Audry in the 1930s who repeatedly argued to a sceptical de Beauvoir that a book should be written which would inspire women to reject their oppression.

It would not be plausible to present Sartre as a paragon ally of feminism or a complete 'new man'. Indeed, for much of his life he took women's oppression rather less seriously than racism or homophobia, and he was guilty of lapses into sexism, as when he told an interviewer – appropriately enough from *Playboy* – that 'female ugliness upsets me'.[45] Yet de Beauvoir, in a 1975 interview, even while berating Sartre for 'machismo' and 'phallocracy', conceded that Sartre had 'strongly encouraged' her to write *Le Deuxième Sexe*.[46]

When set against the background of the contemporary positions of the PCF, it becomes clear what a profoundly original and courageous work *Le Deuxième Sexe* was.[47] Whatever legitimate criticisms may have been made of it subsequently, it nonetheless marked a major turning point in the understanding of women's oppression, and both Sartre and Colette Audry deserve credit for their role in inspiring it.

Le Deuxième Sexe, not surprisingly, got a hostile reception, not only from the conservative right, but from publications effectively dominated by the PCF. In *Les Lettres françaises* Marie-Louise Barron linked de Beauvoir to the Kinsey report (automatically denounced because it was American), and showed that she had not read much of the book by claiming that de Beauvoir wanted to 'limit the problem of women's liberation... to the – distorted – knowledge of one's genital organs'.[48] The unsigned review in *Action* failed to consider the main themes of the book and concentrated on sneering at de Beauvoir's philosophical language;[49] it illustrated its critical article with a picture of a woman embracing an ape.[50] In *La Nouvelle critique* Jeannette Prenant took de Beauvoir to task for her (in fact very limited) criticisms of the USSR, and accused her of reducing women's independence to a question of trousers and cigarettes. By stressing conflict between the sexes she was diverting women's discontent away from the real enemy, capitalism's drive towards war.[51]

The non-Stalinist left were less abusive, but nonetheless negative towards de Beauvoir's case. She was invited to lecture at a meeting organised by the *Ecole émancipée* (the left-wing teachers' paper for which Colette Audry had written in the 1930s), but was told that the problem would be resolved after the revolution.[52] Yet it was among the non-Stalinist left that de Beauvoir found some of her few supporters – notably Colette Audry in a survey of reviews in *Combat*. Audry stressed the book's 'burning relevance', and expressed surprise that the PCF press had been so hostile when in fact de Beauvoir had drawn heavily on Engels' *Origins of the Family*.[53]

Since the 1950s, and especially since 1968, the question of oppression has become far more central to socialist politics. Sartre's preoccupation with oppression can now be seen, not as it appeared to Merleau-Ponty, as an abandonment of Marxism, but rather as a pioneering effort to extend Marxism's scope. The Marxism of the PCF refused to recognise the reality or the significance of oppressions other than that of class. The danger was that those who rejected this would opt for a view in which all oppressions were autonomous and equal. Sartre was grappling with an analysis which would relate all oppressions to the fundamental core of class, without denying their specificity. Doubtless he did not succeed, but here, as elsewhere, he was important, not for the answers he gave, but for the crucial questions he asked when few others were asking them.

Sartre's tortuous political evolution in this period was paralleled by his development as a dramatic writer. Sartre's plays often showed him grappling with political dilemmas which had not yet resolved in real life. This was particularly the case with *Les Mains Sales* (1948), in which he dramatised his ambiguous relationship to the PCF. Here, too, he found himself coming up against the figure of Trotsky.

In an unnamed Eastern European country at the end of the Second World War a young Communist of bourgeois origin, Hugo, was sent by his party to assassinate Hoederer, one of the Party leaders who was alleged to be betraying the party by making a deal with right-wing politicians. Hugo found himself unable to carry out the job until Hoederer kissed Hugo's wife; Hugo then shot him out of jealousy when he could not do so for political reasons. The play centred around the conflict between the naive idealism of Hugo and the pragmatic realism of Hoederer.

Because of its dramatic ambiguity, the play acquired a logic of its own, quite independent of Sartre's own intentions, and was used in the interests of causes so alien to him that in the 1950s he banned its performance in several countries. Generations of English-speaking sixth formers and students learnt from the distinguished historian of French literature Geoffrey Brereton that the play was 'an indictment of Communism' which revealed 'the immorality… of a Party line which has to be unquestioningly accepted even when it changes direction' and which advised that 'moderates and progressives should *not* ally themselves with Communists'.[54] In January

1949 (i.e., during the blockade) a version of the play was staged in the British-occupied sector of Berlin in which Hoederer was played by an actor who closely resembled the East German leader Wilhelm Pieck. The Russian military authorities complained that it was a provocation, but the effect was somewhat spoiled by the actor playing Hugo, who performed like a 'neuropathic jack-in-the-box', diverting audience sympathy onto Hoederer.[55]

The fact that the play was so rich in ambiguities, and seemed so easily 'recuperable', can only be explained by the deep contradictions within Sartre's own political stance at the time he wrote it. Some of these become clearer if we examine the genesis of the play.

Simone de Beauvoir recounted that:

> The subject had been suggested to him by the murder of Trotsky. In New York I had known one of Trotsky's former secretaries; he had told me that the murderer, having succeeded in getting himself taken on as a secretary as well, had lived for some time alongside his victim, in a house which was very well guarded.[56]

Sartre himself later confirmed that Trotsky's murder had been one of his sources.[57]

The secretary in question was Bernard Wolfe, by then a writer and jazz musician, with whom de Beauvoir had become friendly with in the spring of 1947. She was apparently quite fond of him and spent several late nights in his company despite the fact that his 'good wife' was a 'bloody nuisance' (*emmerdeuse*); one night in a New York bar they sat up till 5.00 a.m. as he told her of the three years he spent as Trotsky's secretary. (De Beauvoir was profoundly annoyed at being told by her old friend Gerassi that she should not frequent 'Trotskyists'.)[58]

In fact Wolfe had been a junior member of Trotsky's secretarial staff, working on translation, news releases – and night guard duty – for just eight months in 1937 at the age of twenty-one. He had therefore left Coyoacán nearly three years before the assassination, and had no first-hand knowledge of it. However, he obviously had taken considerable interest in the event, since he later wrote a novel, loosely based on the events, called *The Great Prince Died*. And as his career as novelist and pornographer showed, he had a gift for narrative and was doubtless a vivid and convincing *raconteur*.[59] Hence it would seem reasonable to suppose that some accurate details of the assassination were conveyed. De Beauvoir returned to France and spent the summer with Sartre in Sweden; so she had ample time to pass on Wolfe's reminiscences. Sartre wrote the play towards the end of 1947, and completed it around the time of the launch of the RDR in early 1948.

Sartre was apparently fascinated by the fact that the assassin had lived under the same roof as his victim for some time. In fact Mercader, Trotsky's murderer, did not live in Trotsky's house, though he won Trotsky's confidence and was able to visit as he pleased.[60]

Dorothy McCall has drawn a number of parallels between the characters of Hugo and Mercader.[61] These included relatively trivial details, but also the fact that Mercader, when interrogated after the murder, stated that he had been worried that if he had postponed the act for too long, he might have 'allowed myself to be convinced by him'.[62] Likewise Hugo told Jessica: 'He didn't convince me. Nobody can convince me we should lie to the comrades. But if he had convinced me, it would be one more reason for killing him, because it would show that he will convince others'.[63]

Wolfe could doubtless testify to the amateurishness of the security at Coyoacán; Sartre's play has often been accused of lacking verisimilitude, but actually reflected aspects of the Trotsky assassination. Trotsky's household seem not to have displayed 'the degree of suspicion which is normal among underground totalitarian revolutionary groups', while the murderer used a forged passport in the name of 'Jacson', because the Russian police agents who forged it wanted him to have an inconspicuous name, but were too incompetent to spell it right.[64] After Mercader was jailed, he received a gift of chocolates from an unknown admirer. He gave them to the prison laboratory for analysis and they were found to contain a lethal dose of poison. This was widely reported by the Mexican press and was doubtless known to Wolfe.[65]

And perhaps most important of all, Mercader, in order not to reveal that he had acted as a Russian agent, was forced to refuse to give any information about his past 'self' or to acknowledge his family.[66] Such denial of the killer's own past and identity undoubtedly became one of the key themes of the play.

But if the Trotsky assassination inspired the psychological confrontation on which the play was based, what was its relevance to the politics of the play? If Hoederer was Trotsky, it was also the case that Sartre saw Hoederer as the true hero of the play (contrary to the anti-Communists who tried to steal the play by making the middle-class idealist Hugo into the hero). He told an interviewer in 1964: 'I am embodied in Hoederer. Ideally, of course; don't imagine that I claim to be Hoederer, but in a sense I feel much more fulfilled when I think of him. Hoederer is the man I should like to be if I were a revolutionary, hence I am Hoederer, even if only on a symbolic level.[67] (Ingrid Galster argues that Sartre only stressed his admiration for Hoederer after he had observed the play's hostile reception by the PCF.[68] But the clear identification of Hoederer with Trotsky shows this to be a more complex and contradictory gesture than she assumes.)

It was no secret that Sartre had long admired Trotsky as a revolutionary and as a thinker, whatever reservations he might have had about his followers. But Hoederer did not have Trotsky's politics; he was working for an alliance between the 'Proletarian Party' (created by a fusion of Communists and Social-Democrats) and the two main right-wing parties in Illyria – the fascist followers of the regent and the liberal nationalist 'Pentagon'.[69] In other words, he was advocating a popular front, and in this he stood clearly to the right of the faction which sent Hugo to kill him. (The idea of a popular front including fascists may seem bizarre, since the original popular fronts were anti-fascist, but in 1944 the Italian Communists had joined a government under the fascist Marshal Badoglio.) Trotsky had vigorously opposed the Comintern policy of the popular front, seeing it in particular as a cause of the defeat in the Spanish Civil War.

Why a right-wing, popular frontist Trotsky? There are two possible explanations. Firstly, that Sartre was thinking of the situation in Germany in 1932–33, when Trotsky had advocated a united front – if necessary 'with the devil and his grandmother' [70] – to prevent Hitler's accession to power, while the Stalinist German Communist Party had argued that Social Democrats were 'social fascists'. At that particular historical juncture Trotsky clearly did stand to the right of the Comintern's disastrous ultraleftism. Sartre seems never to have been quite clear about one of the crucial points in any Trotskyist critique of Stalinist strategy: the distinction between a united front (an alliance of workers' parties against fascism or for limited demands) and a popular front (in which Communists drop their specifically socialist programme in order to form a governmental combination with bourgeois parties).

Secondly, Sartre himself rather naively tried to explain the debate by referring to the authority of Lenin. In an interview with *Combat* he was asked whether the play referred to the argument about cooperation with bourgeois parties in the Resistance. He replied: 'That's right. But the problem is an even more general one. Lenin was the first to deal with it, in *Left-Wing Communism, an Infantile Disorder*. The same problem presented itself, before the war, to the Socialist Party which the Popular Front had brought to power'.[71] On this basis Hoederer's Leninism would be the 'healthy attitude' which Sartre supported against Hugo's 'ultraleftism'.[72]

It is not clear whether Sartre had actually read *Left-Wing Communism* or merely heard it quoted. For he would have been hard put to it to find any advocacy of popular frontism in it. *Left-Wing Communism* was written in 1920, at a time when the Communist International's main aim was to persuade the left-wing currents in Social Democratic parties to split away and affiliate to the Comintern. The 'ultralefts' whom Lenin was denouncing were those who refused to join trade unions or participate in parliamentary elections; the very idea of suspending socialist programmes in order to participate in governmental alliances would have been unthinkable to Lenin. True, Lenin did admit the necessity of compromise – people held up at gunpoint by bandits cannot refuse to compromise.[73] But this is rather different from making such compromise into a political strategy.

This context may help to explain one of the most striking paradoxes of the play. For most of the time Hugo was presented as the bourgeois idealist, while Hoederer was the political realist who understood what was possible in given concrete circumstances. But at one point when Hugo was arguing against Hoederer's policy of alliance, he seemed to go beyond his normal limitations in order to take on the argument on a concrete level:

> The party has a programme: the achievement of a socialist economy, and one means to achieve it: the use of the class struggle. You're going to use it to carry out a policy of class collaboration in the framework of a capitalist economy. For years you're going to lie, cheat and manoeuvre; you'll go from one compromise to another; you'll defend to our comrades reactionary measures taken by a government that you are part of. Nobody will understand: the hard ones will leave us, the others will lose the political education they've just acquired. We shall be contaminated, softened, disoriented; we shall become reformists and nationalists; in the end the bourgeois parties will only have to make the necessary effort in order to liquidate us. Hoederer! This party, it's yours, you can't have forgotten the efforts you made to forge it, the sacrifices you've had to ask for, the discipline you've had to impose. I beg you: don't sacrifice it with your own hands.[74]

Here it was Hugo who had taken on the mantle of Trotskyism. The experience he described fitted very well with that of the PCF, which served for three years in coalition governments from 1944 to 1947 before being ejected; and which then suffered crippling defeats that cost it over half its membership in the following years. Hugo's critique was precisely that which came from the Trotskyist left; indeed, it bore a certain resemblance to the arguments to be put forward by Ernest Mandel in 1952,[75] as well as echoing the position Sartre had argued on the *Les Temps modernes* radio programme in 1947.

But all that Hoederer could respond was: 'What verbiage! If you don't want to take risks you shouldn't be in politics'.[76] Here it was Hoederer who was retreating into the abstract. As Lenin would have reminded him, risk and compromise are real but always concrete, to be determined by the balance of forces in a specific historical conjuncture. In terms of such an analysis Hugo was, for the moment, way ahead.

Sartre himself pointed to another possible source of *Les Mains sales*, namely the case of Jacques Doriot, a popular PCF leader in the 1930s who advocated a united front against fascism before it was the PCF line, and was expelled for his pains.[77] (He went on to become an ardent pro-fascist). This does not contradict the account outlined here. The play was clearly not based on any specific historical events and Sartre could have been thinking of both Trotsky and Doriot as he wrote it. In either case the distinction between a united front and a popular front is crucial; and Sartre's failure to make the distinction led to the confusions which abounded in the play.

Needless to say, the critics linked to the PCF did not think much of the play. Neither Hugo nor Hoederer embodied the image which the Party wanted to project of itself, and since both were supposed to be Communists, this meant that the play lacked any positive point of reference. As late as the 1980s a sympathiser with the PCF was complaining that the play suggested that in a Communist Party 'political differences are settled by assassination and that leaders have a right to lie to their members'.[78]

Perhaps he had not noticed that Trotsky was indeed assassinated; as for lies, one need look no further than the absurd accusations made at the Moscow Trials, where one of the defendants 'confessed' to meeting Trotsky's son Leon Sedov at the nonexistent Hotel Bristol in Copenhagen.[79]

At the time the most entertaining, if not the most balanced, assessment came from Marguerite Duras. The future practitioner of the *nouveau roman* insisted on a rigorously naturalistic reading of Sartre's text; she pointed neatly to the intrinsic implausibilities of the plot, without ever querying why Sartre had adopted the particular style he had chosen for the play. The general line was to suggest that the play was funny despite itself, and that Sartre's aim was to satisfy the voyeuristic appetites of his bourgeois audience by revealing the 'secret, obscene conjugal life', the 'unspeakable behaviour' that went on inside a Communist Party.

She was particularly amused by the episode when Hugo was in prison and had been sent 'first chocolate-chocolates, then poisoned chocolates'. Clearly this was not a common method of dealing with dissent among intellectual members of Parisian cells of the PCF in the postwar period.[80] But as we have seen, the chocolate episode in the play was based on what really happened to the imprisoned Mercader.

However, Georges Altman of *Franc-Tireur*, himself a Communist in the 1920s, and by 1948 a target of PCF attacks, was able to give a much more balanced assessment of Sartre's achievement:

> We don't hesitate to say that, whether consciously or not, the reactionary critics who are trying to pull *Les Mains sales* over to their side are just as gravely mistaken as certain Communist critics who want to make this drama into a 'right-wing' work.
>
> … Sartre, who until the time of the RDR, has not been a political militant, has the merit of having discovered, through his writer's intuition, the language and movement of action, and what is truly touching in it. No! His workers are not, as is claimed, caricatures; the debate between them and the young bourgeois is passionately true and is expressed in very fine dialogue.
>
> … Hugo understands nothing, and doesn't want to understand; Hoederer understands that he doesn't understand.
>
> … For us, who will never make a separation between freedom and the revolution, to speak as Sartre has done in *Les Mains sales* is a revolutionary act.[81]

Les Mains sales did not pretend to be a realistic account of political events; it deliberately contained elements of melodrama and passages in which plot was sacrificed to argument; verisimilitude was not its strong point. Yet the play was deeply rooted in Sartre's own political development at the time. The contradictions of the play were Sartre's own contradictions. That was its strength – and its weakness. Sartre was now about to take to the political stage himself, and act out his contradictions in real life through the experience of the RDR.

Notes

1. *Sit* IV, p. 211.
2. *Choses*, p. 88; M. Merleau-Ponty, *Humanisme et terreur*, Paris, 1947, p. 86.
3. *Sit* IV, p. 228.
4. M. Merleau-Ponty, 'Pour la vérité', *Sens et non-sens*, Paris, 1966, pp. 271–303, especially pp. 286–87; originally published in *TM*, January 1946, pp. 577–600, especially pp. 588–89.
5. M. Merleau-Ponty, 'La Politique paranoïaque', *Signes*, Paris, 1960, pp. 309–28; originally published as 'Communisme-Anticommunisme', *TM*, July 1948, pp. 175–88.
6. Merleau-Ponty, *Humanisme*, p. xxix.
7. *Ibid.*, p. xxi.
8. *Ibid.*, p. 97.
9. *Ibid.*, p. vii.
10. J.-P. Sartre, *L'Existentialisme est un humanisme*, Paris, 1966, p. 131.
11. J.-P. Sartre, *L'Être et le Néant*, Paris, 1943, p. 722.
12. J.-P. Sartre, *Cahiers pour une morale*, Paris, 1983.
13. Sartre, *Cahiers*, p. 20.
14. *Ibid.*, p. 360.
15. *Sit* III, p. 193.
16. Sartre, *Cahiers*, p. 191.
17. Sartre, *Cahiers*, pp. 167–76.
18. At this time Trotsky's works were hard to come by in France. Most had disappeared and gone out of print during the Occupation, and Maurice Nadeau and Alfred Rosmer had taken on the job of getting them back into print.
19. L. Trotsky, 'Their Morals and Ours', in I. Howe, ed., *The Basic Writings of Trotsky*, London, 1964, p. 395.
20. Sartre, *Cahiers*, pp. 167–68.
21. Trotsky, 'Their Morals', p. 387.
22. Sartre, *Cahiers*, pp. 168–69.
23. Trotsky, 'Their Morals', p. 395.
24. Sartre, *Cahiers*, p. 169.
25. *Ibid.*, p. 171.
26. *Ibid.*, pp. 171–72.
27. Trotsky, 'Their Morals', p. 388.
28. Sartre, *Cahiers*, p. 173.
29. *Ibid.*, p. 176.
30. See J.L. Walsh, 'Sartre and the Marxist Ethics of Revolution', *Sartre Studies International*, Vol. 6, No. 1 (2000), pp. 116–24.
31. *Franc-Tireur*, 27 February 1948.
32. *Combat*, 20 January 1949.
33. Merleau-Ponty discussed *Their Morals and Ours* in *Humanisme et Terreur*, pp. 144–45, while de Beauvoir developed the formulation: 'The end justifies the means only if it remains present, if it is completely revealed in the course of the current enterprise'. (de Beauvoir, *Pour une morale de l'ambiguïté*, Paris, 1947, p. 180).
34. Sartre, *Cahiers*, p. 338.
35. K. Marx and F. Engels, *Collected Works*, London and Moscow, 1975–2001, 20: 14.
36. M. Merleau-Ponty, *Les Aventures de la dialectique*, Paris, 1955, p. 209.
37. See L.A. Bell, 'Different Oppressions', *Sartre Studies International* Vol. 3, No. 2 (1997), pp. 1–20; I.H. Birchall, 'Socialism or Identity Politics' and L.A. Bell 'Identity Politics?', *Sartre Studies International* Vol. 4, No. 2 (1998), pp. 69–78 and 79–84 respectively.
38. *Figaro*, 30 July 1945.

39. *Présence africaine* was launched by Alioune Diop, an SFIO senator from Senegal in 1947; its first issue made clear that it owed no allegiance to any philosophical or political ideology. Its *comité de patronage* contained Sartre, Camus, Gide, Senghor and Césaire, as well as the editorial board of the *Revue internationale*; early contributors included both Sartre and Naville. Clearly the PCF saw this as a serious threat to its hegemony.

40. G. d'Arbousier, 'Une dangereuse mystification: la théorie de la négritude', *La Nouvelle critique*, June 1949, pp. 34–47, especially pp. 37, 41.

41. *L'Humanité*, 1 June 1956.

42. *Choses*, p. 524.

43. A. Wurmser, *Fidèlement vôtre*, Paris, 1979, pp. 416–17.

44. *Heures claires des femmes françaises*, May 1950.

45. *C&R*, p. 415.

46. *Sit X*, p. 119. A little later in the same interview Sartre accepted the specificity of women's struggles, and stated that women's oppression did not derive from the class struggle, though it interacted with it. *Sit X*, p. 121.

47. S. de Beauvoir, *Le Deuxième Sexe*, 2 vols., Paris, 1949.

48. *Les Lettres françaises*, 23 June 1949.

49. *Action*, 17–23 November 1949.

50. As claimed by de Beauvoir in *Choses*, pp. 208–9. I was only able to consult the journal in microfilmed form, and the picture is wholly indecipherable; the caption reads: 'She calls for a robust embrace which will transform her into a quivering object'.

51. *La Nouvelle critique*, April 1951, pp. 32–44.

52. *Choses*, p. 209. See also S. de Beauvoir, 'La femme révoltée', *Nouvel Observateur*, 14 February 1972, pp. 47–54.

53. *Combat*, 22 December 1949.

54. G. Brereton, ed., *Les Mains sales* (Methuen's Twentieth Century Texts), London, 1963, pp. 8–9.

55. Report in *Franc-Tireur*, 18 January 1949.

56. *Choses*, p. 166.

57. *C&R*, p. 177.

58. S. de Beauvoir, *Lettres à Sartre*, Paris, 1990, 2: 345, 348–49, 356–57.

59. See B. Wolfe, *The Great Prince Died*, London, 1959; B. Wolfe, *Memoirs of a Not Altogether Shy Pornographer*, New York, 1972.

60. Masson, the murderer in Wolfe's novel, while not actually resident in the Rostov (Trotsky) household, spent much time there, and was intimate with its inmates.

61. D. McCall, *The Theatre of Jean-Paul Sartre*, New York, 1969, pp. 55–56. McCall based her comparison on Isaac Don Levine's book *The Mind of an Assassin* (New York, 1959). Although this was published long after Sartre wrote his play, much of the information contained in it was probably available to Wolfe, so the comparison is valid.

62. Levine, *The Mind of an Assassin*, p. 107.

63. Sartre, *Les Mains sales*, act 5. sc. 5.

64. Levine, *The Mind of an Assassin*, pp. 63, 106.

65. *Ibid.*, pp. 201–2.

66. *Ibid.*, pp. xi–xii.

67. *TDS*, p. 259.

68. I. Galster, *Sartre, Vichy et les intellectuels*, Paris, 2001, p. 230.

69. The name was perhaps reminiscent of the small right-wing grouping called *Pentagone* with which *Socialisme et liberté* had tried to develop contacts in 1941. (*Force*, p. 495). The headquarters of the U.S. Department of Defense, built in 1942, was not as well known then as now.

70. L. Trotsky, *Fascism, Stalinism and the United Front*, London, 1989, p. 106.

71. Interview with René Guilly, *Combat*, 31 March 1948; *TDS*, p. 247.

72. *TDS*, pp. 249, 260.

73. V.I. Lenin, *Collected Works*, Moscow and London, 1960, 31: 37.

74.   Sartre, *Les Mains sales,* act 5. sc. 3.
75.   *Ibid.,* act 5. sc. 3.
76.   *Ibid.,* act 5. sc. 3.
77.   *TDS*, p. 259.
78.   M. Adereth, 'Sartre and Communism', *Journal of European Studies* XVII (1987), p. 30.
79.   T. Cliff, *Trotsky: The Darker the Night, the Brighter the Star,* London, 1993, p. 342.
80.   M. Duras, 'Sartre et l'humour involontaire', *Action,* 21–27 April 1948.
81.   *Franc-Tireur,* 5 June

Chapter 8

THE RDR

The year 1947 saw the outbreak of the Cold War, and the exclusion of the PCF from government. This opened up a new situation in which Sartre had to reorient himself. In so doing he involved himself in a movement, which, very briefly, seemed to have the potential for making a real political impact.

In 1948 the Cold War intensified, leading to the Communist takeover in Czechoslovakia and the Berlin blockade; the outbreak of a new European war seemed increasingly probable. In France it was a year of bitter industrial struggle. Sartre had little hope of cooperation with the PCF, which continued to denounce him, yet the need for political engagement seemed more urgent than ever. It was in this context that Sartre embarked on his second experience of political organisation, in the *Rassemblement démocratique révolutionnaire* (Revolutionary Democratic Assembly) (RDR).[1] In later accounts Sartre minimised both his own role and the viability of the RDR;[2] in the 1970s, discussing with his Maoist comrades, he dismissed it as a 'bloody great stupidity' (*grosse connerie*).[3] Yet not only was it Sartre's most serious attempt thus far to develop a socialism wholly independent of Stalinism; it also, for a brief period at least, made a significant impact on political life in France.

In the months after its eviction from government in May 1947 the PCF had succeeded in mobilising strike action against low living standards. But the PCF leadership's aim was to serve Russian foreign policy rather than French workers. A highly critical editorial in *Les Temps modernes* (signed simply 'T.M'., indicating that Sartre endorsed it though he probably did not write it) stated in December 1947:

> The events of recent months are not only a setback for the Communist Party, they are also a setback for the working class.

Notes for this chapter begin on page 105.

'It's the Communists who are guilty of stupidities, and it's the working class which has to pay', said a trade unionist, a striker in 1938, who was subsequently out of a job for eighteen months... More than ever we face the question: is a minimum socialist policy possible today, and if so, which? In the intermediary countries of Europe, is there room for anything other than skirmishes between the Great Armies?[4]

The RDR is regularly described as Sartre's organisation, but the original initiative came from ex-Trotskyist David Rousset of the *Revue internationale* and Georges Altman, editor of *Franc-Tireur*, which, after adopting a pro-Communist position in the immediate postwar period, was beginning to distance itself from the PCF. Altman and Rousset had been among the initiators of a statement published in November 1947, to which Sartre put his name, under the title of 'First Appeal to International Opinion'. This argued that war could and must be avoided; but that for this European unity on a socialist basis was required.[5]

Meanwhile within the SFIO Léon Boutbien and Jean Rous had addressed a statement to the membership, warning of the dangers presented by Gaullism on the right and the 'adventurist politics' of the PCF on the left. They argued that the SFIO should withdraw from government and reorient its activity towards extraparliamentary action; they concluded with a call for a broad movement which would include all who wanted to resist reaction and defend the standards of working people: 'The time has come to counterpose to the RPF [de Gaulle's organisation, the *Rassemblement du peuple français*], which is the state totalitarian assembly in the service of big capital, the democratic and revolutionary assembly of the world of labour'.[6]

The two initiatives converged, and it was decided to appeal directly to the public. On 27 February 1948 *Franc-Tireur* carried the first public statement launching the RDR. This differentiated the new organisation from both Stalinism and social democracy:

Between the rottenness of capitalist democracy, the weaknesses and defects of a certain social democracy and the limitation of Communism to its Stalinist form, we believe an assembly of free men for revolutionary democracy is capable of giving new life to the principles of freedom and human dignity by binding them to the struggle for social revolution.

The first signatories included Rousset, Altman, Rous and Boutbien, Sartre, Paul Fraisse of *Esprit*, Roger Stéphane of *Combat*, Daniel Bénédite (who in 1940 had organised the escape from occupied France of such intellectuals as André Breton and Victor Serge), Badiou, the *maire* of Toulouse and Laminé-Guèye, the *maire* of Dakar.[7]

The RDR was to be a '*rassemblement*' (assembly) and not a party. This implied, of course, that members of the PCF, SFIO and other organisations could join without abandoning their own parties. It also suggested a less rigid and disciplined organisation. Throughout his life Sartre was suspicious of the idea of a party, and in his speech at the salle Wagram on 19 March 1948 he juxtaposed the concept of *'rassemblement'* to that of party:

> *That's why we are a Rassemblement;* a party cannot draw out the underlying appeal, which is contained in the demands of the masses – often unknown even to those who are making the demands – any more than a state bureaucracy can do so. The party apparatus, the bureaucratic apparatus, can only issue slogans. This revolutionary and democratic demand, which is contained in your everyday needs, can only be drawn out by yourselves, all of you acting together.[8]

The first few weeks seemed to vindicate the hopes of the new organisation's founders. On 12 March a public meeting was held at the *Sociétés savantes; Franc-Tireur* reported: 'The "audience"? Workers, mainly workers. Students too, shoulder to shoulder with the old militants'.[9] A week later *Le Monde* reported a similarly packed meeting at the *salle Wagram*.[10]

On this basis the leaders of the RDR naturally expected rapid growth, with hopes of up to 200,000 within three months.[11] Within a week of the founding statement the organisation was apologising for not being able to reply to the deluge of letters it was receiving: 'Among those joining, we can mention numerous members of the Ligue des Droits de l'Homme, primary and secondary teachers, Young Socialists and Christians... groups of workers from various factories in the Paris area... as well as several delegates from study circles at the *Ecole Normale Supérieure'*.[12]

Amid the elation that marked the first few weeks one supporter even composed a song for the organisation, celebrating the hopes of rapid growth through the recruitment of the likes of Thorez, de Gaulle, Truman, Salazar, Franco, Stalin, Pius XII and Ho Chi Minh.[13]

However, as soon as the RDR looked like achieving a level of significant influence, it came up against the opposition of the left parties. The founding statement had made clear that the RDR had no sympathy for Stalinism, yet at the initial press conference Rousset stressed that it welcomed unity with rank-and-file Communist workers: 'Never shall we consider Communist workers as "separatists", as de Gaulle's absurd criminal lie puts it. Even if we differ, sometimes fundamentally, about aims and methods, from the PCF, we are with the workers and middle classes struggling for their lives'.[14]

Obviously the PCF could not tolerate any such thing. The RDR meant that the threat which Sartre had seemed to pose to their student and intellectual audience was beginning to take shape. Moreover, Moscow was hostile. Dominique Desanti, who after her time in *Socialisme et liberté* joined the PCF in 1943, related that when the Wroclaw peace conference of 1948 was being planned, Zhdanov himself was strongly hostile to an invitation to Sartre because of his role in the RDR.[15]

Thus there was never any hope that rank-and-file members of the PCF would be allowed to participate in the RDR. On the contrary, the RDR was greeted with the same kind of abuse and slander of which Sartre himself had already been victim. Pierre Hervé described an RDR meeting at the salle Pleyel on 13 December 1948 as an 'anti-Soviet meeting organised... by a clique of intellectuals whose meretricious generalisations... fail to conceal a conscious acceptance of the capitalist order'.[16]

The only chance for the RDR to make any impact on the PCF would have been for it to recruit sufficient members outside the PCF for it to be ignored no longer. Hence the vital importance of the SFIO, where the situation was very different. Here was none of the monolithic unity that characterised the PCF; on the contrary, the party was divided into hostile tendencies. Its continuing acceptance of governmental responsibilities, and its consequent adoption of anti-Communism as a main pillar of its ideology, served only to heighten the tensions. In February 1948 the *Comité Directeur* (Executive) of the SFIO unsuccessfully called on the Socialist ministers to resign from government.[17] Jean Rous and Léon Boutbien had been among those who first initiated the call for the RDR, in the hope that it would provide a means of shifting the balance of power in the party to the advantage of the left. They thus had a rather different political agenda from that of the non-party supporters of the RDR, regarding it more as a means of regenerating the SFIO than as the basis for a new political movement. At the SFIO congress in July 1948 a motion to allow SFIO members to join the RDR was heavily defeated – 3,675 votes to 733 – and the previous ban upheld.[18] Now the RDR could not recruit from either of the main working-class parties.

There were also problems with the RDR's relations with the smaller organisations of the French left. While these generally counted their members in hundreds, they were activist organisations, and could have provided the RDR with key militants. But things were not to be so simple.

The *Jeunesses socialistes* had been dissolved by the SFIO in 1947 because of alleged Trotskyist influence. After the exclusion the group around André Essel continued to produce the paper *Drapeau rouge*, and fused with a group from the adult party, including Yves Dechezelles, known as *Action socialiste et révolutionnaire* (ASR). When the RDR was launched, *Drapeau rouge* greeted it with a sympathetic though not uncritical statement. But friction persisted among ASR members. Early in 1949 the organisation fragmented. One faction went to the RDR, another to the PSU,[19] while a third grouping went to the Trotskyist *Parti communiste internationaliste* (PCI).[20] Rather than uniting the left, the RDR had accelerated its fragmentation.

The main Trotskyist organisation in France, the PCI, was already divided before the advent of the RDR. Its congress, in November 1947, had rejected its previous orientation as opportunist and installed a new leadership (including Pierre Frank and Pierre Lambert) which stressed programmatic clarity.[21] At the time the PCI had 557 members, 38 percent of whom were workers.[22] It was a small organisation, but its militants were committed, politically serious activists. They could have made a useful contribution to the development of the RDR.

When the RDR was launched, the PCI leadership took a fiercely hostile attitude towards it; yet faced with the rapid growth of the RDR, they had nothing to say except to assert the programmatic superiority of their own organisation.[23] To a section of the membership such passive sectarianism seemed inadequate. A number of leading figures joined the RDR. On 27 March the PCI expelled thirteen members, including six from the central committee (among them Paul Parisot, Albert Demazière and Jean-René Chauvin). One historian hostile to the RDR estimates the PCI lost half its membership at this point.[24] Again the RDR had produced a split rather than unity. Those Trotskyists who joined the RDR contributed energy and political experience out of proportion to their numbers; two of the ex-PCI members, Parisot and Demazière, became full-time organisers at the RDR centre.[25] But because they had entered piecemeal, rather than as an organisation, they did not advance the political cohesion of the organisation.

Nonetheless a viable organisation had been born, which quickly developed an organisational structure. The leading body was a *Comité Directeur*, on which served Sartre, Altman and Rousset, and additionally P. Fraisse, Th. Bernard, Ch. Ronsac, D. Limon, J. Ferniot, B. Lefort, Rosenthal, Demazière and Aubin.[26]

In April the RDR publicised a series of public meetings to be held in provincial cities – Strasbourg, Toulouse, Montpellier and Lyons[27] – and by May a national organisation was established. The first issue of *La Gauche RDR*, the RDR's fortnightly paper, gave details of nine local groups in Paris, with dates of regular fortnightly meetings. The next issue listed twenty-seven *départements* where groups were being set up.[28] In May an appeal was launched to raise one million francs (equivalent to around £17,000 at 2002 prices).[29] Sartre personally donated some 300,000 francs.[30]

The RDR cast its net wide (Sartre missed the opening night of *Les Mains sales* because he was visiting a Masonic lodge which had shown interest in the RDR).[31] But the membership never exceeded four thousand at most. J.-R. Chauvin recalled that there were 'quite a few workers from the suburbs, but the majority of Paris members were students and intellectuals'.[32] Certainly the RDR was only a *groupuscule* in comparison with the mass organisations of the French left, but it did achieve a larger membership than any Trotskyist grouping between 1945 and 1968.

La Gauche RDR was edited by Jean Ferniot, a journalist on *Franc-Tireur*. Issues had two or four pages, and sold at 5 or 6 francs. It began as a fortnightly, but soon became monthly, and collapsed after issue No. 13 in March 1949. This was not the paper required by an organisation with the aspirations of the RDR. Initially it had appeared that *Franc-Tireur* would act as daily paper for the new organisation. But Altman was now paying the price of his flirtation with Stalinism in the immediate postwar period. A large number of his journalists were close to the PCF, and this, combined with repeated scurrilous attacks by the PCF, led to a serious internal dispute. *Franc-Tireur* survived, but Altman now had to justify his political independence, which meant that the paper could give only limited support to the RDR.[33]

Les Temps modernes was also lukewarm in its support of the RDR. Only two pieces appeared which referred explicitly to the RDR – a short interview with David Rousset, and the dialogue between Sartre, Rousset and Gérard Rosenthal (a lawyer, who had been active as a Trotskyist from 1928 to 1939) which later formed the first part of the book *Entretiens sur la politique*.[34] Thus even those centrally involved in the RDR, like Altman and Sartre, were not prepared to sacrifice the independence of the publications they controlled. Consequently the RDR lacked the journalistic support it needed to grow.

Yet for a time there was an active, enthusiastic membership. While only a minority of the RDR's members were industrial workers or even trade unionists, the organisation saw society in terms of class struggle, and unconditionally supported the working class. In the autumn of 1948 there was a major miners' strike in defence of wages and conditions.[35] RDR members gave practical support, notably providing accommodation for miners' children.[36]

Beyond such solidarity action, the RDR tried to develop a strategy for trade-union intervention. French trade unionism in 1948 was seriously weakened. The previous year the pro-American *Force Ouvrière* (FO) had split from the Communist-led CGT. Around half of the five million CGT members abandoned union membership altogether. Rousset argued that the task of the RDR was to campaign for trade-union unity; this must be rebuilt at the base, so the RDR should try to initiate factory committees involving nonunionised workers as well as representatives from the various unions.[37] On 4 May 1948 some 2,000 people at a meeting at the Mutualité heard Droeheiner (CGT), and Détienne (FO) speak in favour of trade union unity.[38]

In the RDR's May 1949 internal bulletin, Francis Fuvel (an ASR member from Lyons) proposed a trade union strategy for the RDR. He began by listing the traditional principles of French trade unionism: 'Class struggle, independence, democracy, internationalism, unity', and concluded that trade union activity must take the workplace as its starting point.[39] In Lyons RDR members had been working in the '*cartel* of trade union unity' set up by revolutionary syndicalists linked to the *Révolution prolétarienne*.[40]

In the autumn of 1948 the RDR produced a duplicated bulletin called *Le Cahier du propagandiste*. This aimed to provide concrete information on practical issues. The first issue was mainly devoted to a long article on the sliding scale of wages (wage increases automatically linked to inflation: the 'sliding scale' was a demand in the 'Transitional Programme' drafted by Trotsky for the Fourth International in 1938, and the importance given to it was probably an indication of Trotskyist influence within the RDR).[41] Thus there were activists in the RDR seriously concerned to develop an effective trade union strategy, even if time and resources did not permit much to be achieved in practice.

Another significant area of activity was anti-imperialism. On 18 November 1948 Sartre and other speakers addressed a largely Muslim audience on the question of Morocco. Sartre stressed the connections between the class struggle in France and colonial oppression: 'Those who are oppressing you are oppressing us for the same reasons'.[42] Early in 1949, the RDR launched a petition demanding a negotiated peace in Indo-China.[43]

The RDR also held public meetings throughout France to put forward its ideas. This involved a degree of risk, as on more than one occasion they were attacked by Gaullist thugs.[44] Obviously the far right believed the RDR deserved to be taken seriously.

Yet if the RDR displayed creditable activism and enthusiasm in pursuit of socialist aims, it was nonetheless based on considerable political confusion, which eventually produced its downfall. When smaller organisations criticised the RDR for its absence of programme, it was easy to dismiss this as the sectarianism of insignificant groups unwilling to involve themselves in a broader movement. But there was some truth in their criticisms. When Gilles Martinet wrote that the RDR had no doctrine but merely 'a set of doctrinal formulae which are both hasty and incongruous',[45] his language was unfraternal, but his criticism was valid.

The greatest strength of the RDR was its rejection of both Stalinism and social democracy, of both the pro-Moscow PCF and the pro-Washington SFIO. The greatest weakness was its inability to define the alternative. When Dominique Gauthiez defined the project of the RDR as being 'more revolutionary than the SFIO and more democratic than the PCF',[46] he left a profound ambiguity. The formulation could be understood as meaning that the PCF was indeed revolutionary and the SFIO indeed democratic, and hence what was needed was a synthesis of the two. Did the RDR occupy a political space *between* the PCF and the SFIO, or did it aim to transcend both and establish a position *beyond*? The question was left unanswered.

These issues were not clarified in the RDR's various statements. When Sartre, in 1974, said 'it was a reformist and not a revolutionary movement'[47] he was oversimplifying. The RDR did include many people who were, in some sense of the term, revolutionaries. But what the term meant was much harder to pin down. Only a small minority of RDR supporters conceived it in Leninist terms of smashing the bourgeois state. Sartre told an RDR meeting at the *salle Wagram*, amid enthusiastic applause:

> ... we shall be told that... the revolution is not for tomorrow. And I reply that, indeed, it is not for tomorrow, it's immediately if we wish. For in our view, the

revolution is not simply the last battle, or the final insurrection which enables a body or an already emancipated class to take power, revolution is a long programme, a long process of emancipation in democracy and freedom which we want to try and create beyond parties and beyond bureaucracies.[48]

This was not purely a theoretical question. It produced confusion on a number of practical points. When the RDR produced a draft policy on the Marshall Plan, it rejected 'a sterile attitude of negative hostility', urging working people to struggle against the militarisation of the plan, and to demand the rejection of clauses limiting trade with Eastern Europe.[49] Sartre had a similarly utopian perspective in demanding 'that the American contribution should be overseen and distributed by European socialist bodies, that it should be used for the building of a socialist Europe and that under no circumstances can there be any question of using it for remilitarisation'.[50] The whole purpose of Marshall Aid, as can be seen from subsequent U.S. policy, was to mobilise Western Europe against the Eastern bloc and to *prevent* the construction of a socialist Europe.

While the RDR sometimes appeared to be anticipating the movement for European unity that developed in the 1950s, the stress was primarily on the construction of a 'socialist Europe'. As Sartre put it in December 1948: 'To refuse to choose between the USSR and the U.S.A. does not mean yielding first to the one, then to the other, letting ourselves be tossed about between them. It means making a *positive* choice: that of Europe, socialism and ourselves'.[51]

Yet many of the RDR's supporters undoubtedly believed that Russia was in some sense socialist, albeit an undemocratic and authoritarian variant. Others thought it had nothing at all in common with socialism. For David Rousset it was 'a new historical social formation, where the state, owner of the economy, exploits the working masses'.[52] (The view that Russia was neither capitalist nor socialist had long been argued on the anti-Stalinist left, and had been developed theoretically by Bruno Rizzi and Max Shachtman.) In the difficult political conjuncture of the late 1940s, such confusions were hazardous. All too soon they were to undermine the RDR.

At the end of 1948 the RDR still seemed in a reasonably healthy state. On 13 December a major rally was held at the *salle Pleyel*. Four thousand people attended, with another two thousand turned away. David Rousset spoke about the Russian labour camps, in a stinging attack on Stalinism in the name of workers' democracy: 'On the basis of what political explanation can we admit the existence of concentration camps in the USSR? It is not enough to change the relations of production, it must also be carried out in the practice of workers by hand and by brain'.[53]

In early 1949 the Cold War was still intensifying – NATO was formed in April – and it became ever more difficult to maintain a nonaligned position. Rousset, Altman and Bernard went to New York in a bid to raise money for the RDR and *Franc-Tireur*. They had been encouraged by Irving Brown (who had played a key role in organising the FO split) to contact the U.S. unions. There was no objection within the RDR to seeking money from the international labour movement.[54] Yet, as Rousset described, when they met the U.S. unions the RDR representatives were a little naive about the source of the money:

> In France, there exists a fundamental tradition which seeks to maintain a very clear separation between the trade-union movement and the state... We discovered that such a separation was absolutely not understood by our American comrades.

> When we had explained the situation to them, they told us : 'We'll telephone the State Department. Mr X, a specialist in French matters, will talk to you'.[55]

Rousset and Altman were certainly not personally corrupted; in fact, if Rousset is to be believed, they did not make a good impression on the Americans.[56] But from now on there was a move away from the position of equal hostility to Washington and Moscow.[57]

The RDR's next venture was more ambitious than its earlier large public meetings. On Saturday, 30 April 1949, it took the initiative in organising an 'International Day of Resistance to Dictatorship and War'. Following a meeting of over 2,000 in the Sorbonne, some ten thousand people assembled at the *Vélodrome d'Hiver*. The net was cast wide – perhaps excessively so. The platform included Marceau Pivert (who in 1948 had moved the resolution against the RDR in the SFIO), and international figures such as Bob Edwards from Britain, the Italian Ignazio Silone and the Belgian trade unionist André Renard.[58]

Behind the scenes there were signs of disarray among the RDR leadership. Sartre, Merleau-Ponty and Richard Wright – 'realising we had been had', as Sartre put it later[59] – stayed away, fearing that some of the participants would exploit the occasion to advance a pro-American position. They sent a message which was repeatedly interrupted by applause, making clear their stance of opposition to both East and West: 'We are inclined to join with those who seek peace by peaceful means. As a result we condemn equally and for the same reasons the more or less disguised annexation of central Europe by the USSR and by the Atlantic Pact'.[60] Sartre's fears were justified. At the Sorbonne meeting the American ex-Marxist Sidney Hook openly expressed support for the newly formed NATO.[61] In the evening session there was pandemonium when an American scientist defended U.S. nuclear policy.[62]

Now it was downhill all the way. A two-day national conference on 28–29 June 1949 attempted to resolve the problems. The internal bulletin produced prior to the conference contained several articles analysing the difficulties of the organisation. The most interesting of these was what came to be known as the 'Chauvin–Sartre resolution'. This had been written by Jean-René Chauvin, one of the ex-PCI members who had joined the RDR. But Sartre was not a passive signatory; Chauvin recalled several discussions with Sartre: 'he was just discovering politics. He was discovering political action, militant action'.[63] Three other rank-and-file members of the RDR also signed the document – Henri Sack, a former member of the German Communist Party, Henri Massein, a former Trotskyist (one of the leaders of the PCI's 'entry' work in the SFIO Youth in the Lille area), and Georges Gousseau, a trade union militant.[64] It was the most serious attempt at honest accounting for what had gone wrong with the high hopes raised by the RDR just over a year earlier.[65]

The document began by recalling the ideals of nonalignment embodied in the foundation of the RDR:

> At its foundation the RDR defined itself as an assembly of proletarians and free men to struggle against war and dictatorship by social revolution. In face of both the Russian totalitarian state and the American democracy of the dollar, it proclaimed its complete independence. Rejecting both the exclusive use of parliamentary methods which are ineffective and the use of Stalinist methods which are antidemocratic, it intended to appeal to the initiative of the masses and to give democracy a popular base.

It was argued that there had been a divorce between the *Comité Directeur*, which had pursued 'spectacular demonstrations', and a membership which had failed to grow. Consequently there had been no genuine internal democracy:

> This deep contradiction continued to widen the gap between a rank and file which remained inorganic and without slogans and a *Comité Directeur* which failed to take responsibility. The concrete democracy which was to be the essential feature of our organisation remained on paper. Not that the RDR took on the form of a dictatorial party; it was pure anarchy.

This had led to a number of particular failures: *La Gauche* had been too ambitious and unable to mobilise the membership; the mass meetings had not connected to the concerns of the membership and hence had been abstract and even compromising, as when speakers at the peace rally defended NATO; because of the failure to recruit, the leadership had engaged in dubious political alliances; *Franc-Tireur* had failed to give support, particularly with regard to the Indo-China petition.

The document went on to reassert the basic principles which must underlie the RDR's political practice: opposition to dictatorship and fascism; defence of trade union rights; support for democratic movements against oppression, notably in Spain and in the colonies; opposition to war, especially in Indo-China:

> The RDR… condemns the Atlantic Pact, just like the Eastern Pact,[66] because for the peoples of Europe both constitute a permanent danger of war. It asserts its absolute independence with regard to both blocs, even in the event of war… The RDR reaffirms that the best way to fight against war and dictatorship is to prepare for socialist revolution.

It recalled the traditions of the nineteenth-century working class and of Marxism: 'Like the revolutionaries of 48 and 71 we must repeat: "No God! No Caesar! No tribune!" – "The emancipation of the working class will be the task of the workers themselves!" '

Consequently, the document argued, the RDR must involve itself in the day-to-day struggles of the working class forced onto the defensive by employers' attacks. This involved a set of concrete demands, including:

- defence of purchasing power through the sliding scale of wages;
- unemployment pay linked to the cost of living;
- 40-hour week without loss of wages;
- amnesty for workers prosecuted as a result of strike action;
- workers' control through extension of the powers of *comités d'entreprise* (factory committees).

At the same time it was necessary to revive the internal life of the RDR. In particular the document insisted that there must be no compromise with anti-Communism:

> Not only does the RDR not reject any unity of action with the PCF, but on the contrary it attempts to bring about unity between Socialist and Communist workers, whenever it is a question of defending the immediate interests of workers. However, it refuses to confuse these interests with those of the Russian bureaucracy...

The conclusion was optimistic: 'If we have enough cohesion, independence and skill we are bound to win at every point and on all counts'.

The document pointed to a reappraisal of the RDR's whole practice: a clarification of the basic principle of nonalignment, a concentration on working-class struggles, a recognition of the limitations imposed by a small membership and the need to relate large public rallies to the concerns of the membership. But the RDR national conference failed to rise to the challenge.

Instead a final resolution was adopted without any vote. Differences and setbacks were brushed aside behind a façade of unanimity.[67] The final resolution ignored obvious organisational problems and the fact that recruitment had fallen far short of the targets set in 1948. It went on to reaffirm the principle of total independence from Washington and Moscow, opposing both 'American capitalism and its European dependencies' and 'Soviet statism with its extensions known as "People's Democracies" '.[68] Rousset and Altman were present at the conference, but did not challenge this formulation, though it diverged sharply from the opinions they had recently expressed in print. Presumably they did not take the organisation seriously enough to want to fight for their positions. Behind formal unanimity was the reality of disintegration.

As is usual in such situations, demoralisation bred increasing internal factionalism.[69] Sartre spent the summer visiting Central America, and played no further part in the RDR. In October *Samedi Soir* reported that he had left the organisation following a dispute with Rousset; shortly afterwards *Le Monde* confirmed the resignation.[70] Fragments of the organisation dragged on for a few months; but in effect the RDR did not reach its second birthday. Sartre clearly saw Rousset as the main villain; he subsequently refused any cooperation or political dialogue with him.[71]

Was this sad end inevitable? Many have argued that the pressures of the Cold War rendered any nonaligned organisation impossible. In his notes on the failure of the RDR, Sartre stressed the inadequacy of voluntarism: 'New and definitive apprenticeship in realism. You can't *create* a movement'.[72] Jean-René Chauvin, however, claimed that Sartre 'had a very heavy responsibility for the failure of the RDR' because of his resignation after the unsuccessful conference. While admitting that he was speculating, he believed that the RDR's early ambitions could not have been achieved; but that if Sartre had stayed to fight the RDR might have become something like the *Parti socialiste unifié* (PSU) of the 1960s.[73]

The historical evidence gives some support to this claim. The 'Chauvin–Sartre resolution' was certainly correct when it stated:

> The RDR *exists*, it has an audience. The spectacular politics of the CD [*Comité Directeur*], which should have been carried out in a more discerning fashion, have nonetheless borne some fruit. For some time to come we still have a place in public opinion which is greater than the actual size of our forces. We must be able to take advantage of this.[74]

The initial enthusiasm for the RDR, the mass attendances at its rallies, the readership of *Franc-Tireur*, and even the determination of the PCF and the SFIO to crush the RDR before it could take off: all these facts suggest that there was a potential base for an organisation independent of Washington and Moscow. It could have limited the PCF's hegemony over the left; it might have given more effective coordination to the opposition to the Algerian War.

What was absent was political clarity. The RDR was against Washington and Moscow, against the PCF and the SFIO; what was it for? Did it advocate Russian planning plus American elections, or some completely different model of socialism? Some of its members were unambiguously revolutionaries, others reformists, others floated uncertainly between the two. While such an alliance would be acceptable in a single-issue campaign, it could only lead to confusion in an organisation claiming to fight on all fronts.

After the collapse of the RDR a series of other small groupings emerged during the 1950s before the establishment of the *Parti socialiste unifié* in 1960, showing that Stalinism and social democracy never established total hegemony over the French left. The fact that some ex-RDR members reappeared in the PSU, together with some of the RDR's critics, like Gilles Martinet and Naville, shows that despite the difficulties of forging an independent left in the period of the Cold War and the Algerian War, the independent left remained resilient; at all times there were voices willing to speak out against the domination of the PCF and to criticise it from the left. Throughout the 1950s there were individuals and groupings who defended an alternative conception of the socialist project, and the fact of their existence was perhaps the most significant legacy of the RDR.

Finally, what was Sartre's own role? As has been argued above, the RDR was much more than Sartre's organisation, although it was often perceived as such. In 1948 Sartre was at the height of his literary fame. He helped to draw large numbers to the RDR's rallies and was thus a major factor in the 'spectacular politics' which the 'Chauvin-Sartre resolution' rightly criticised for creating a breach between leadership and rank and file. But Chauvin noted that Sartre made a determined effort to involve himself in the day-to-day activity of the RDR. He did not confine himself to platform appearances at the various 'spectacular demonstrations', but came quite frequently to the meetings of the local branch in the fifth *arrondissement*, where Chauvin was branch secretary.[75]

Chauvin considered that Sartre was not 'a political brain', and lacked the 'political culture' of a Camus or a Merleau-Ponty.[76] A reading of the *Entretiens sur la politique* (discussions between Sartre, Rousset and Rosenthal) confirms this, showing that it was Rousset and not Sartre who dominated; in quantitative terms over 60 percent of the text was by Rousset. Rousset was also the RDR's most impressive orator, drawing more applause than Sartre.[77] It seems that Sartre was deferring to Rousset just as he deferred to Merleau-Ponty in the editing of *Les Temps modernes*. The fact that Sartre clearly respected Rousset during the RDR period is not negated – and may even be confirmed – by the contemptuous terms in which he later dismissed him: 'Rousset, an ex-Trotskyist, had absolutely nothing revolutionary about him except a big mouth'.[78]

For nearly two years in the RDR Sartre rubbed shoulders with Trotskyists, ex-Trotskyists and a variety of dissident Marxists. Throughout the next thirty years some of the principles and practices of the RDR, its non-alignment and its anti-imperialism, must have returned to inspire him. Sartre may not have been 'a political brain' but on a number of crucial occasions he made the right choice when more sophisticated individuals made the wrong one.

Notes

1. · For a full history, see I. Birchall, 'Neither Washington nor Moscow?', *Journal of European Studies*, XXIX (1999), pp. 365–404.
2. See *Sit* IV, pp. 223–25; Sartre, interview with Henri Magnan, *Le Monde*, 1 June 1955; *Adieux*, pp. 459–60.

3. *Raison*, p. 28.
4. 'En un combat douteux', *TM*, December 1947, pp. 962, 964.
5. *C&R*, pp. 194–97.
6. 'A l'entreprise néo-boulangiste il faut opposer le rassemblement démocratique et révolutionnaire', *La Pensée socialiste* No. 18, pp. 1–3.
7. *Franc-Tireur*, 27 February 1948; *C&R*, pp. 197–99.
8. J.-P. Sartre, 'Le Rassemblement démocratique révolutionnaire et le problème de la liberté', *La Pensée socialiste* No. 19, 1948, p. 5; a shortened version appeared as 'La Faim au ventre, la liberté au coeur', *La Gauche RDR* No. 1, 15–30 May 1948. See also J.-P. Sartre, D. Rousset and G. Rosenthal, *Entretiens sur la politique*, Paris, 1949, pp. 120–21 (discussion recorded 24 November 1948).
9. 'La première assemblée générale du RDR', *Franc-Tireur*, 13 March 1948.
10. 'Au Rendez-vous "démocratique et révolutionnaire"', *Le Monde*, 21–22 March 1948.
11. C. Ronsac, *Trois noms pour une vie*, Paris, 1988, p. 234; *Franc-Tireur*, 13 March 1948; 'Le RDR tient son premier meeting', *Combat*, 20 March 1948.
12. 'Le RDR', *Combat*, 4 March 1948.
13. Ronsac, *Trois noms*, p. 235.
14. *Franc-Tireur*, 11 March 1948.
15. D. Desanti, *Les Staliniens (1944–1956)*, Paris, 1975, p. 107.
16. P. Hervé, 'La Clique de ceux qui ont "rejeté en bloc la révolution"', *L'Humanité*, 15 December 1948.
17. *Combat*, 6 February 1948.
18. *Le Populaire*, 2 July 1948.
19. The *Parti socialiste unitaire* (not to be confused with the PSU of the 1960s) was a group with positions very close to the PCF; it contained individuals from an anti-Stalinist tradition such as Pierre Naville and Gilles Martinet.
20. See *La Vérité* No. 225, January 1949.
21. See Y. Craipeau, *La Libération confisquée*, Paris, 1978, pp. 161–94.
22. Jean-René Chauvin, interview with author, Paris, 20 March 1997.
23. P. Frank, 'Se définir pour s'unir', *La Vérité*, 19 March 1948; M. Mestre, 'A la recherche d'un "réformisme conséquent"', *La Vérité*, 12 March 1948.
24. J.-J. Marie, *Trotsky, le trotskysme et la IVe internationale*, Paris, 1980, p. 111.
25. Ronsac, *Trois noms*, p. 235.
26. *Le Cahier du propagandiste* No. 1, September 1948, p. 17 (J.-R. Chauvin archive).
27. *Franc-Tireur*, 2 April 1948.
28. *La Gauche RDR* No. 1, 15–30 May 1948, No. 2, 1–15 June.
29. *La Gauche RDR* No. 1.
30. Ronsac, *Trois noms*, p. 236.
31. *Choses*, p. 167.
32. Ronsac, *Trois noms*, p. 236; Chauvin interview.
33. C. Bellanger et al., *Histoire générale de la presse française*, Paris, 1975, IV 421–2; *La Gauche RDR* No. 7, October 1948; J. Ferniot, *Je recommencerais bien*, Paris, 1991, p. 198.
34. D. Rousset, 'Nos positions politiques', *TM*, July 1948, pp. 189–91; 'Entretiens sur la politique', *TM*, September 1948, pp. 385–428.
35. Sartre, Rousset and Rosenthal, *Entretiens*, pp. 143–44.
36. *La Gauche RDR* No. 7, October, 1948.
37. Sartre, Rousset and Rosenthal, *Entretiens*, p. 29.
38. *Franc-Tireur*, 5 May 1948.
39. F. Fuvel, 'Le RDR et le mouvement syndical', *RDR Bulletin intérieur* No. 2, May 1949, pp. 14–16 (J.-R. Chauvin archive).
40. *La Gauche RDR* No. 12, 11 February 1949.
41. *La Cahier du propagandiste* No. 1, pp. 1–12.
42   N. Lamouchi, *Jean-Paul Sartre et le tiers monde*, Paris, 1996, pp. 56–57. See *La Gauche RDR* No. 8, November 1948.

43. Lamouchi, *Jean-Paul Sartre*, p. 53; M.-A. Burnier, *Les Existentialistes et la politique*, Paris, 1966, pp. 71–72.
44. *Le Monde*, 13–14 June 1948; Ronsac, *Trois noms*, p. 236; *La Gauche RDR* No. 13, 11 March 1949.
45. 'Parti ou rassemblement?', *La Bataille socialiste*, 19 March 1984.
46. J. Rous and D. Gauthiez, *Un Homme de l'ombre*, Paris, 1983, p. 102.
47. *Adieux*, p. 460.
48. J.-P. Sartre, 'Le Rassemblement démocratique révolutionnaire et le problème de la liberté', *La Pensée socialiste* No. 19, 1948, p. 5; see also *Franc-Tireur*, 20 March 1948.
49. *La Gauche RDR* No. 3, 16–30 June 1948.
50. Sartre, Rousset and Rosenthal, *Entretiens*, pp. 109–10.
51. J.-P. Sartre, 'Il nous faut la paix pour refaire le monde', *Franc-Tireur*, 10 December 1948, reproduced in *C&R*, pp. 690–93. See also Sartre's interview in *New York Herald Tribune* (Paris edition), 2 June 1948, summarised in *C&R*, p. 201.
52. Sartre, Rousset and Rosenthal, *Entretiens*, p. 66.
53. *Franc-Tireur*, 14 December 1948.
54. Chauvin interview.
55. D. Rousset, *Une Vie dans le siècle*, Paris, 1991, p. 109.
56. Rousset, *Une Vie*, p. 110.
57. See articles by Altman in *Franc-Tireur*, 25 March 1949, and by Rousset in *Le Monde*, 29 April 1949.
58. *Le Monde*, 3 May 1949; *Franc-Tireur*, 2 and 3 May 1949. Edwards had been a member of the Independent Labour Party (ILP) in the 1930s, and Captain of the ILP contingent to Spain, linked to the POUM; from 1947 he was secretary of the Chemical Workers Union. Silone, the anti-fascist novelist, was an ex-Communist; in 1947 he supported Saragat's pro-American split from the Italian Socialist Party. Renard had been a Resistance activist in Belgium, and was a leader of the left in the Belgian union federation the FGTB.
59. *Raison*, p. 29.
60. *Franc-Tireur*, 3 May 1949.
61. S. Hook, *Out of Step*, New York, 1987, pp. 397–401.
62. *Combat*, 2 May 1949.
63. Chauvin interview.
64. A. Cohen-Solal, *Sartre*, Paris, 1985, pp. 522–23.
65. 'La Crise du RDR', *RDR Bulletin intérieur* No. 2, May 1949, pp. 8–10. The full text is reproduced in *L'Année sartrienne* No. 15 (2001), pp. 140–47; English translation in *Sartre Studies International* Vol. 6, No. 2 (2000), pp. 113–20.
66. The term is used figuratively; the Warsaw Pact was not formed until 1955.
67. Chauvin interview.
68. 'Pour un socialisme non étatique', *Franc-Tireur*, 30 June 1949.
69. Ronsac, *Trois Noms*, p. 253.
70. 'Pris d'une nausée politique, Sartre quitte le RDR', *Samedi Soir*, 13 October 1949; *Le Monde*, 27 October, 1949.
71. *C&R*, pp. 238, 292.
72. *Choses*, p. 194.
73. Chauvin interview.
74. *RDR Bulletin intérieur* No. 2, May 1949, p. 9.
75. Chauvin interview.
76. Chauvin interview.
77. 'Au Rendez-vous démocratique et révolutionnaire', *Le Monde*, 21–22 March 1948.
78. *Adieux*, p. 460.

Chapter 9

WHICH CAMP?

While Sartre was still apparently disoriented and disillusioned with the collapse of the RDR, Rousset had already moved on to the next stage of his political itinerary. On 12 November 1949 *Le Figaro littéraire* appeared with its entire front page devoted to an appeal:

> HELP THOSE DEPORTED in Soviet camps.

> AN APPEAL BY DAVID ROUSSET to the survivors of deportation to the Nazi camps.[1]

Rousset presented recently published information on the Russian labour camps and made numerous comparisons with the Nazi camps, of which he had already written extensively on the basis of personal experience. But he did not confine himself to humanitarian outrage at the atrocious conditions in the Russian camps. He also took the opportunity to develop his view of the nature of Russian society:

> The Nazi camps appear as a historical accident. They express and develop the violent contortions of Germany between the wars. Their sadism is the apocalyptic perversion of the will to life on the part of middle classes who had been humiliated and threatened with social death... In Russia... the class which organises the camps is neither humiliated nor threatened with death. It is, on the contrary, in full possession of considerable power and firmly resolved to control its future. So much so that the camps no longer appear as a pathological excrescence, but as the expression of normal relations, as the natural development of a new society.

This passage is crucial to any understanding of the intense passions which the debate about the Russian labour camps provoked, and, indeed, continues to provoke. At the time of the RDR Rousset had already put for-

---

ward the view that Russia represented a new social formation. Now he was using the campaign on the Russian camps to advance that view. He could scarcely expect unconditional support from those like Sartre and Bourdet who deplored the camps but did not share his political perspective. In the pages of *Franc-Tireur* Rousset insisted that precisely because Stalin claimed to be a socialist, repression in the USSR threatened to discredit the very idea of socialism.[2]

From the PCF, unsurprisingly, Rousset got vilification. The ineffable Kanapa found the moment right to compare the Buchenwald survivor Rousset to Goebbels and label him as 'a Hitlero-Trotskyist'.[3] The independent left was rather more ambiguous in its response. While Rousset had added a few details, the main picture of the USSR under Stalin as a brutally repressive society had been available since the 1930s, in the writings of Trotsky, Serge and many others, to anyone prepared to believe the evidence. Yet he had singled out the USSR as the sole target of his campaign and had launched his campaign in an openly right-wing paper. This use of the right-wing press was not forced on him; *Franc-Tireur* gave him enthusiastic support, with more coverage that it had ever given to the RDR,[4] and he could undoubtedly have run the campaign through *Franc-Tireur* without involving the right-wing *Figaro*.

Claude Bourdet, editor of *Combat* (himself a concentration camp survivor), refused support unless the investigation were expanded to all countries 'where men are deprived of freedom for political or social offences'; he referred in particular to 'the jails of Franco and Tsaldaris'.[5] The Trotskyist PCI issued a statement pointing out that Rousset was no longer a Trotskyist and accusing him of serving 'American imperialism' and the 'Cold War' rather than 'world socialism'.[6]

It is in this context that the response of Sartre and the *Temps modernes* must be set. In January 1950 *Les Temps modernes* published an editorial under the title 'Les Jours de notre vie' (The Days of our Life –a direct reference to the title of Rousset's book *Les Jours de notre mort*). A careful reading of this undermines all the claims of Sartre's opponents that he was 'soft on Stalinism'. Indeed, what is striking about it is just how much of Rousset's case had been accepted. The editorial stated quite bluntly 'there is no socialism when one citizen out of twenty is in a camp' and went on to develop this point:

> Two years ago one of us wrote in this journal that Soviet society is ambiguous and that in it can be found signs of progress and symptoms of retrogression. If there are ten million in concentration camps – while, at the other end of the Soviet hierarchy, wages and living standards are fifteen to twenty times higher than those of free workers – that quantity changes into quality, the whole system is transformed and changes meaning, and, despite the nationalisation of the means of production, and although the private exploitation of man by man and unemployment are impossible in the USSR, we wonder what reason we could still have for using the term socialism in connection with it.

Nonetheless the article went on to explain why *Les Temps modernes* would not align itself with Rousset's appeal:

> Whatever may be the nature of the present Soviet society, the USSR finds itself in general terms situated, within the balance of forces, on the side of the forces struggling against the forms of exploitation known to us. The degeneration of Russian Communism does not mean that the class struggle is a myth, that 'free enterprise' is possible or desirable, or in general that Marxist criticism is obsolete. From which we conclude that we should not show any indulgence towards Communism, but that in no circumstances can we form an alliance with its enemies. The only healthy criticism is therefore that which, inside and outside of the USSR, targets exploitation and oppression, and any politics which defines itself against Russia and confines its criticisms to it, is an absolution given to the capitalist world.[7]

Effectively there seem to be three reasons given, explicitly or implicitly, for offering some support to the USSR:

- that despite the internal regime it supported the forces of 'progress' on a world scale (a claim that might have difficulty standing up to an examination of Russia's role in China 1927, Germany 1933, Spain 1936–37 and the postwar carve-up in 1944–45);
- that Russia still somehow represented the 'idea' of communism, even if its actual practice negated it;
- that Lenin had argued that true revolutionaries 'denounce exploitation and oppression in their own country'.[8]

It was a half-hearted defence and one which would not have brought much pleasure to any Stalinist.

As well as 'Les Jours de notre vie' the issue of *Les Temps modernes* contained comments by Roger Stéphane and documents from the United Nations debate on forced labour. Stéphane pointed out that while in *Franc-Tireur* Rousset, replying to Bourdet, had expressed concern about Vietnam, Madagascar and North Africa, he had not shared these concerns with readers of the right-wing *Figaro*.[9] Certainly for Sartre and *Les Temps modernes*, Russian labour camps were not a matter of embarrassment or something to be shoved under the carpet, but an important issue requiring discussion.[10]

The *Temps modernes* editorial had been written by Merleau-Ponty, but Sartre later insisted that he approved every single word.[11] Sartre still retained from the RDR period a basic acceptance of a nonaligned stance, yet at the same time he also retained a belief that Russia was somehow different, not so much by what it did as by what it claimed to be.[12] It was a feeble argument and one that could lead to some strange conclusions – after all, Hitler called himself a 'socialist' and his party a 'workers' party'. It certainly had nothing in common with Marxism, for which 'it is not the

consciousness of men that determines their existence, but their social existence that determines their consciousness'.[13]

It is clear that Sartre's position was open to some criticism, and that it
lacked clarity. But it is also clear that he openly and unambiguously condemned the Russian labour camps and that nothing he said was likely to
bring comfort or assistance to the defenders of Stalinism.[14]

It is also important to understand that the 1950 editorial was not a bolt
from the blue. Rousset had not revealed anything qualitatively new about
Russia, and Sartre had been familiar with the arguments for some considerable time; there had been substantial discussion in *Les Temps modernes*
and elsewhere.

In 1948 Albert Camus had responded to the PCF fellow-traveller
Emmanuel d'Astier de La Vigerie. In his reply Camus referred to 'the concentration camps and the use of political deportees as a source of labour'.
He claimed that the camps were part of the state apparatus in Russia, just
as they had been in Nazi Germany, and he rejected the idea that they could
still be justified by the provisional requirements of an insurrectionary situation. He concluded that socialists should always reject concentration
camps as a means of government.[15]

Tony Judt has used this text in order to contrast Camus's allegedly
superior stance to Sartre's.[16] However, Judt failed to point out that *La
Gauche*, the journal which published Camus's article, was the organ of the
RDR, on whose *Comité Directeur* Sartre served. Moreover, as Altman's
prefatory note to the article pointed out, *La Gauche* had been the only journal to agree to publish Camus's article. Clearly Camus's position was
regarded as being within the ambit of the RDR, since he was shortly afterwards to speak on an RDR platform. It was thus partially thanks to Sartre
that Camus was able to present his argument.

More information on the Russian camps was made available by
Kravchenko, a Russian official who had defected to the West and in 1946
published a book called *I Chose Freedom*; this appeared in France[17] the following year and eventually sold half a million copies. On 30 March 1947
de Beauvoir wrote to Sartre from the U.S.A. where she had read
Kravchenko's book, describing it as 'gripping' and urging him to publish
extracts in *Les Temps modernes*.[18] In fact this did not happen, probably
because of the court case in 1949 when Kravchenko successfully sued the
PCF-controlled journal *Les Lettres françaises* for alleging that the book was
a forgery; this turned into a pitched battle between the PCF and its right-
wing enemies. But it is clear that *Les Temps modernes* was not opposed in
principle to publishing such material.

In June and July 1949 (five months before Rousset's appeal, when Sartre
and Rousset were still in the RDR) *Les Temps modernes* published two sets
of extracts from the notebooks of Victor Serge.[19] Serge had been a prolific
and sharp critic of Stalinism since his release from internal exile in Russia
in 1936 until his death in 1947; he knew about Stalinist repression from bit-

ter personal experience. Serge remained a marginal figure because neither the Stalinists (for obvious reasons) nor the right wing (because he still defended the traditions of October 1917) – nor even the Trotskyists (because Trotsky had quarrelled with him) – were enthusiastic to publish him. Only on the independent left did Serge get a hearing.[20]

Serge's text (a letter of 1946), the publication of which predated both Rousset's appeal and Merleau-Ponty's response, directly addressed the question of the camps and the social nature of the USSR; in fact, it tended to overstate the role of the camps in the USSR's economy:

> In this respect, I argue, in theoretical articles which I am sending to Paris that the existence of a penal labour force of some twenty million adults is the essential feature we have to take into account in seeking to define this *anti-socialist* regime. My argument is as follows. The privileged section of the population, enjoying conditions of life comparable to those of the average inhabitant of a civilised country, are 15% (in 1936; today, significantly less, as a result of the war), that is, 7–8% of adults. (This estimate was that of Leon Trotsky, myself and several others on the basis of serious cross-checking.) The penal labour force are 15 to 20 million, that is, about 15% of adults, twice the number of the privileged population. The fluctuations of these percentages are secondary; they define a social structure. The penal labour force constitutes a lumpen subproletariat, which literally has 'nothing to lose but its chains'; its condition is below that of slavery or serfdom. This is the new sociological fact. The owner of slaves or serfs had an interest in the preservation of his property. In Russia in particular, traditional patriarchal behaviour made serfdom less harsh. Law and custom always set limits to slavery and often fix conditions of possible emancipation. The huge horde in the Stalinist labour camps are, on the other hand, outside the law, beyond the pale of society, and enjoy the benefits of no traditions or known laws. They are pariah-slaves and, of course, this social category should be given a new name'.[21]

Sartre and Merleau-Ponty did not agree with Serge's analysis. Indeed, *Les Temps modernes* preceded the first extract from Serge's writings with a note (presumably by Merleau-Ponty) stating their reservations. Serge was accused of concentrating all his criticisms on the USSR and hence opening the door to alliances with the right against Stalinism. But the note ended in friendly fashion: 'It is in these terms that we should have liked to discuss with Victor Serge, if we had known his position. At least we can be sure that with him the discussion would have been useful and honest'. And it concluded by describing him as 'sensitive, intelligent, an extraordinary witness'.[22] (The next issue contained a very favourable review of Serge's novel *The Case of Comrade Tulayev* by Colette Audry.)[23]

But the most serious and developed analyses of the nature of Stalinist society to appear in *Les Temps modernes* came from the pen of Claude Lefort. Lefort had entered the *Temps modernes* team as a protégé of Merleau-Ponty; he has claimed that Merleau-Ponty was much more sympathetic to his positions than was Sartre. However, there is no corroborative evidence that there were any significant differences between Sartre and

Merleau-Ponty in the 1940s,[24] though Merleau-Ponty was undoubtedly more sophisticated. Lefort had been a member of the Trotskyist PCI since 1943, but had become increasingly critical of 'orthodox' Trotskyism. In 1949 he and Cornelius Castoriadis (who used the pseudonyms Paul Cardan and Pierre Chaulieu) decided that, after the disarray in the PCI caused by the exodus to the RDR and the PCI's adoption of a pro-Yugoslav position, there was no future for them there, and they launched the grouping that became known as *Socialisme ou Barbarie* from the name of the journal they published. Although *Socialisme ou Barbarie* was a small group – it never had more than eighty-seven members – it was to have a considerable influence. It was an organisation in constant evolution, moving ever further away from the Trotskyism, and eventually the Marxism, of its origins.[25] One of the main points of differentiation between *Socialisme ou Barbarie* and the PCI was its refusal to accept Trotsky's definition of Russia as being a 'degenerated workers' state'. Lefort had begun to develop this analysis in articles in *Les Temps modernes* before the split, much to the annoyance of his comrades in the PCI.[26]

One of Lefort's earliest contributions to *Les Temps modernes* was an article on revolutionary strategy in Indo-China.[27] Here he presented an exposition of Trotsky's theory of 'permanent revolution', using it to attack the mechanical version of Marxism which saw history as passing through a series of predetermined stages. He then used this framework to deliver a sharp attack on Ho Chi Minh and the Indo-Chinese Communists for abandoning the revolutionary opportunities available in the postwar period, especially as seen in the context of the international balance of forces.

He received an equally vigorous reply from the philosopher Tran Duc Thao,[28] who defended the policies of the Viet Minh.[29] It is striking that *Les Temps modernes*, which had a circulation well beyond the circles of the far left, was one of the few places where such a confrontation between Stalinism and Trotskyism could take place, with both sides presenting reasoned arguments rather than slanders.

In February 1948, just before his departure from the PCI, Lefort wrote for *Les Temps modernes* (at Merleau-Ponty's request)[30] a piece on the implications of Kravchenko's revelations for an understanding of Russian society.[31] He began by arguing that the originality of Kravchenko's work was to show powerfully 'the incoherence which reigns in the Stalinist economic system'.[32] This account undermined the claims that the 'planned economy' was the basis of Russian economic superiority; it maintained that the planning mechanisms did not work and led to great inefficiencies. Lefort justified his argument with references to the work of Charles Bettelheim, a Trotskyist from 1940 to 1943 and member of the *Revue internationale* circle, who was now moving to a position more sympathetic to Stalinism.

Lefort's conclusion was that Russia could in no sense be seen as any form of socialism or as transitional to it: 'There is no private property in the USSR; but there is nonetheless the same division as within capitalism between the forces of production and the forms of appropriation'.[33] Lefort deduced from this that Russia was an exploitative society, but that it differed in essence from both capitalism and socialism.[34] (Lefort and Castoriadis were at this point only at the very beginning of their elaboration of a theory of the nature of Russian society.) And, like Serge and Rousset, Lefort argued that the labour camps played an essential role in the economic life of the USSR:

> Forced labour is part of a deliberate mode of exploitation. For if to begin with the bureaucracy found itself using people it had thrown in prison for political reasons, the benefits it subsequently derived from these massive imprisonments led it to consider them – consciously – as a source of advantages and to multiply their numbers.[35]

The article also contained passages which could be seen as a critique of the positions held by Sartre – and by Merleau-Ponty. In his introduction Lefort noted the 'fundamental misunderstanding' which consisted in believing that to 'attack the USSR means defending the interests of world capitalism'. Those caught in the trap of that argument necessarily ended up justifying Stalinist policies by 'fallacious arguments or by a complicit silence'.[36] In his conclusion he returned to the question of the alleged commitment to 'communism' of the Russian leaders. He argued that those who claimed that this marked a substantive difference between Stalinism and capitalism failed to see that

> Marxist ideology is the best instrument of their domination... If ideology has such an important place in the life of bureaucratic society, it is not because socialism still lives despite the degeneration, but because alienation has reached a degree of perfection which is much higher than in a classic capitalist regime. The more man is alienated, the more he resorts to mystification.[37]

Such an attack did not pass unnoticed by the editors of *Les Temps modernes*. Lefort's article was followed by an editorial note (undoubtedly written by Merleau-Ponty) which explained that although the article had been commissioned, the review was in disagreement, less with its analysis than with its tone. The note went on to note that Lefort's accounts of planning, exploitation, terror and ideology were useful, but concluded:

> For him, the USSR is *the accused*. For us, with its greatness and its horrors, it is a project which has broken down. We must state whether we are Communists or not, and we say no. But the tone of the indictment seems to us to be out of place in a world which is nowhere innocent, and does not appear to be governed by an immanent reason.[38]

Lefort developed his position further in a second article devoted to showing that Trotsky's analysis of Stalinism was inadequate, because he continued to see the bureaucracy as a parasitic caste and not as a system of exploitation.[39] Thus far it might seem that his position was similar to that developed by Rousset. But there were two important differences. While

Rousset stressed the contrasts between West and East, coming more and more to support defence of the West, Lefort was concerned to show the similarities in the nature of exploitation on both sides of the Iron Curtain. And while for Rousset Russian labourers were seen primarily as victims of a repressive regime, Lefort stressed the role of workers in overthrowing the system of exploitation: 'We see Stalinism as a system of exploitation, which it is necessary to understand, just as it is necessary to understand modern capitalism, with a view to contributing to the working-class movement, which alone is capable of overthrowing them'.[40] It was this stress on working-class self-emancipation which prevented *Socialisme ou Barbarie* from drifting to the right, as so many other anti-Stalinists were to do. This was to become very clear in 1956.

It is evident, then, that in late 1949 the question of the Russian camps was not a new one for Sartre. The arguments had been developed at some length in the *La Gauche* and *Les Temps modernes*. While Sartre can be legitimately criticised for not having taken a personal stance on the question, critics such as Tony Judt should take note of the fact that the arguments had been well developed in *Les Temps modernes*.

It is also clear that in the period from 1947 to 1950, Sartre's position was essentially one of nonalignment, a rejection of both Western capitalism and Stalinism, tempered only by a rather vague sense that the Russian state's public commitment to the goal of 'communism' somehow made it progressive.

At around this time Sartre also showed some sympathy for Tito's Yugoslavia, which seemed as though it might be in some ways a preferable alternative to Stalinist Russia. He wrote a preface to Louis Dalmas's book on Yugoslav Communism. (Dalmas had been a Trotskyist activist during the Second World War and until 1947.)[41] In this Sartre stressed the 'ambiguity' of the Yugoslav experience. Unlike some on the left he rejected the idea that Belgrade was the new 'workers' Mecca'. But the fact of the emergence of a rival to Stalin would, he hoped, 'act from within on the consciousnesses of our Communist militants and make them rediscover their subjectivity'. The very existence of an alternative to Stalinism, whatever its intrinsic merits, meant that the USSR's claim to be the embodiment of a necessary historical process was challenged, and thus undermined the claims of a Marxism which professed itself independent of human freedom:

> Tito, if we are to believe Engels and Stalin, is supposed to be the objective product of the Yugoslav situation. But no, we shall be told, he rules by terror. So you can rule by terror against history? In that case, who can prove to me that the Politburo is not enforcing its existence in opposition to the Soviet population?[42]

Yet is also clear that Sartre's nonalignment tended to be a moral stance of equal repulsion from two modes of oppression, rather than based on any serious Marxist analysis. If he had paid more attention to the details of Lefort's argument, he might have avoided some subsequent problems.

The debate about the camps continued into 1950. One particularly lucid criticism of the *Temps modernes* position came from Jean-Daniel Martinet, son of Trotsky's friend Marcel Martinet, who wrote to *Les Temps modernes* pointing out that the facts about the Russian camps had been available since the 1930s and that the camps had to be seen as part of the 'state capitalist' organisation of the Russian economy. *Les Temps modernes* did not initially publish the letter, which appeared in *La Révolution prolétarienne*.[43] However, in June 1950 *Les Temps modernes* published the letter in full, with an extensive editorial reply, showing that Sartre and Merleau-Ponty felt sensitive to criticism from an apparently obscure journal of the far left.[44] The reply, probably written by Merleau-Ponty, conceded Martinet's main points, that the camps were an 'essential component' of the Russian system of production, and that this called into question 'the socialist character' of the USSR. It went on, rather uncomfortably, to argue that perhaps Martinet had been right, but 'too early'; that history was not predetermined, and that if the United States had pursued a different policy, the Peoples' Democracies might have developed more independently. It concluded with the rather feeble hope that if the Cold War lasted another twenty years, *Les Temps modernes* would at least have preserved the 'instruments of political discussion'. The whole argument was defensive and unconvincing. Merleau-Ponty was on the point of abandoning his stance of critical defence of the Eastern bloc, realising that his attempt to steer an intermediate course between Stalinism and the far left was unviable. Sartre would be left to pick up the pieces on his own.

Notes

1. Full text reproduced in Rousset, *Une Vie dans le siècle*, Paris, 1991, pp. 197–209.
2. *Franc-Tireur*, 14 November 1949.
3. 'Editorial' (signed Kanapa), *La Nouvelle critique*, December 1949, pp. 1–6.
4. *Franc-Tireur*, 11, 16, 17, 18, November 1949, etc.
5. *Combat*, 16 November 1949; Constantine Tsaldaris was the Greek Populist prime minister (1946–47) at the start of the civil war. See also Rousset in *Franc-Tireur*, 15 November 1949. Rousset's commission did turn its attention to exposing torture in Algeria, but only much later, in 1957. See for example L. Martin-Chauffier, 'Sept centres d'hébergement, neuf centres de triage visités en Algérie', *Figaro*, 13 August 1957.
6. Rousset, *Une vie*, p. 126.
7. 'Les Jours de notre vie', *TM*, January 1950, pp. 1153–68; reprinted as 'L'URSS et les camps', in M. Merleau-Ponty, *Signes*, Paris, 1960, pp. 330–43.
8. *TM*, January 1950, p. 1167.
9. 'La question du travail forcé à l'ONU', *TM*, January 1950, pp. 1228–36, especially p. 1235.
10. However, Sartre's claim, in his 1952 polemic with Camus, *Sit* IV, p. 104, that the *Temps modernes* statement had appeared a few days after Rousset's appeal, and that it had been set up in print *before* Rousset's appeal was published, does not fit the facts. *Les Temps modernes* appeared some seven weeks after Rousset's appeal and the editorial was clearly

presented as an answer to it. The claim was endorsed by M.-A. Burnier, but without any evidence to back it up, in *Les Existentialistes*, p. 59; see also J. Carat, 'La Rupture Camus–Sartre', *Preuves*, October 1952, p. 55. In late 1949 an article by Stéphane on the camps had been postponed to avoid any appearance of association with Rousset's campaign. See D. Drake, *Intellectuals and Politics in Post-War France*, Basingstoke, 2002, p. 68.

11. *Sit* IV, p. 225.
12. Camus recalled Sartre arguing in 1946 that while the deportation of several million people in the USSR was more serious than the lynching of a single Negro in the U.S.A., the lynching resulted from a historical situation that had lasted much longer than the USSR (A. Camus, *Carnets*, Paris, 1964, p. 186). De Beauvoir used a similar argument in *Pour une morale de l'ambiguïté*, p. 211.
13. K. Marx and F. Engels, *Collected Works*, London and Moscow, 1975–2001, 29: 263.
14. Many of Sartre's critics seem to have been unduly influenced by a reading of Simone de Beauvoir's novel *Les Mandarins*. This was a work of fiction and although it dealt with a group of left intellectuals in the post-Liberation period, there was no strict correspondence to historical reality. While there are undoubtedly some resemblances between Sartre and the character of Dubreuilh, who argued strongly against the publication of documents on the Russian labour camps, the fictional debate presented was actually quite distinct from the course of historical events (S. de Beauvoir, *Les Mandarins*, Paris, 1954, pp. 357–96).
15. *La Gauche* No. 7, October 1948; reprinted in A. Camus, *Actuelles*, Paris, 1950, pp. 199–207.
16. Judt, *Past Imperfect*, Berkeley and Los Angeles, 1992, p. 115. In retrospect it is clear that Sartre and Camus were developing in different directions in the late 1940s. At the time, it is doubtful whether either of them would have expected the sharp confrontation that was to arise in 1952.
17. V.-A. Kravchenko, *J'ai choisi la liberté*, Paris, 1947.
18. De Beauvoir, *Lettres à Sartre*, Paris, 1990, 2: 337.
19. V. Serge, 'Pages de Journal', *TM*, June 1949, pp. 973–93, *TM*, July 1949, pp. 71–96. The former but not the latter were published in V. Serge, *Carnets*, Paris, 1952.
20. Serge's *Memoirs* were serialised in *Combat* from 4 November 1949 onwards. However *Esprit*, for which Serge had written on Spain in the 1930s, had a fraught relationship with Serge; in 1946 he wrote to the editor, Mounier, accusing *Esprit* of having become 'pro-totalitarian and pro-Communist'. See M. Winock, *Histoire politique de la revue "Esprit", 1930–1950*, Paris, 1975, pp. 293–94.
21. *TM*, July 1949, pp. 92–93. Serge had a very low view of Kravchenko, whom he described as 'a fugitive who has never in his life thought of anyone but himself. And his fundamental motive has been to have a better life in the U.S.A. after a short period of uncertainty'. *TM*, July 1949, p. 92.
22. *TM*, June 1949, pp. 973–74.
23. *TM*, July 1949, pp. 173–76.
24. C. Lefort, *Un Homme en trop*, Paris, 1986, pp. 13–19.
25. See P. Gottraux, *"Socialisme ou Barbarie"*, Lausanne, 1997.
26. See P.F. (Pierre Frank?), 'Les Mains sales', *La Vérité* No. 228, 1949; P. Chaulieu, 'Les Bouches inutiles', *Socialisme ou barbarie* No. 1 (March–April 1949), pp. 104–111.
27. C. Lefort, 'Les Pays coloniaux', *TM*, March 1947, pp. 1068–94.
28. Tran Duc Thao, 'Sur l'interprétation trotzkyste des événements d'Indochine', *TM*, June 1947, pp. 1697–1705.
29. Ironically, Tran Duc Thao, who returned to Vietnam in 1951, was sacked from his teaching post at Hanoi University in 1958; in his self-criticism, he admitted links with *Les Temps modernes*, which he described as a 'Trotskyist group'. (O. Todd, *Fils rebelle*, Paris, 1981, pp. 219–22).
30. Lefort, *Un Homme en trop*, p. 13.
31. C. Lefort, 'Kravchenko et le problème de l'URSS', *TM* February 1948, pp. 1490–1516; reproduced in C. Lefort, *Eléments d'une critique de la bureaucratie*, Paris, 1979, pp. 117–44.
32. Lefort, *Eléments*, p. 120.

33. *Ibid.*, p. 131.
34. *Ibid.*, pp. 136–38.
35. *Ibid.*, pp. 139–40.
36. *Ibid.*, pp. 117–18.
37. *Ibid.*, p. 143.
38. *TM*, February 1948, p. 1516.
39. 'La Contradiction de Trotsky et le problème révolutionnaire', *TM*, December 1948–January 1949, pp. 46–69; in Lefort, *Eléments*, pp. 33–57.
40. Lefort, *Eléments*, p. 57.
41. See F. Charpier, *Histoire de l'extrême-gauche trotskiste*, Paris, 2002. pp. 137–50; for Sartre's interest in Yugoslavia see also p. 181.
42. 'Faux savants ou faux lièvres', *Sit* VI, pp. 23–68, especially pp. 24, 67, 49.
43. *La Révolution prolétarienne*, May 1950, p. 131.
44. 'L'adversaire est complice', *Les Temps modernes* No. 57, July 1950, pp. 1–11.

PART III

Rapproachement with Stalinism

Chapter 10

REORIENTATION

Following the collapse of the RDR, Sartre seems to have been politically disoriented. Some of the survivors of the RDR formed the CAGI (*Comité d'action des gauches indépendantes*), which ran candidates in the 1951 elections. But for the moment Sartre had no stomach for another attempt to organise the independent left; he retreated back to his literary and philosophical preoccupations, and wrote little of direct political significance for the next two years.

He was, moreover, increasingly isolated. In the RDR he had been working with people like Rousset, Rosenthal, Altman and Chauvin, who had considerably more political experience than himself. Moreover, since the founding of the *Les Temps modernes* he had worked closely with Merleau-Ponty, whom he perceived as a political mentor, and to whose judgement he often deferred. But from the outbreak of the Korean War in June 1950, Merleau-Ponty began to distance himself from Sartre, becoming increasingly critical of Communism and indeed of Marxism.

The final break with Merleau-Ponty came only in 1953; one of the factors that provoked it was a dispute about Sartre's old adversary from 1945, Pierre Naville (though Sartre does not actually name him in his account). When Naville contributed an article to *Les Temps modernes* about 'The United States and the Contradictions of Capitalism', Merleau-Ponty added an introductory note about the contradictions of socialism which he claimed Naville had ignored. In Merleau-Ponty's absence Sartre removed this note; after a growing divergence, it was the last straw which produced the final quarrel between the two men.[1]

In fact, it seems that neither Sartre nor Merleau-Ponty had read the full article. In the second part, which appeared five months later, Naville did indeed discuss the contradictions of the 'socialist' bloc: 'The establishment of this multistate socialist market which is also global in its principle, gives

---

rise to contradictions of a new type – for contradictions are also part of socialist development, although in a new form, free of the specific antagonisms of the capitalist economy'. On this basis he explained the Stalin-Tito split and predicted friction between the USSR and China.[2]

Left to fend for himself, Sartre engaged in a reconsideration of his position. Though he wrote little explicitly political, the works of the period from summer 1950 to summer 1952 indirectly show him grappling with a new set of problems. Rather than being drawn by the lure of totalitarianism, as some critics would have it, he was engaged in the difficult task of balancing and evaluating alternatives. If he did eventually opt for a *rapprochement* with Stalinism, it was not done innocently, and certainly not without an awareness of the contradictions involved.

Many accounts of Sartre's philosophy treat his novels and plays simply as illustrations of his philosophical work. The relation between the different parts of Sartre's work was in fact far more complex. Sartre did not simply repeat in fictional form ideas previously elucidated discursively. On the contrary, ideas were sometimes developed imaginatively before being translated into discursive terms.

For example, *Le Diable et le Bon Dieu* (1951) was written a year before Sartre's *rapprochement* with the PCF; yet in some ways it prefigured themes developed in *Les Communistes et la paix* – means and ends, freedom and history, revolutionary leadership. Indeed, it is arguable that if Sartre had not written *Le Diable et le Bon Dieu* he would not have prepared himself for the political changes of the following year.

The play portrayed Goetz, a barbaric military leader in sixteenth-century Germany, who wagered that he could become perfectly good. But intentions did not suffice; he gave his land to the peasants and established a utopian community, but this merely provoked a premature peasant revolt which seemed to have no chance of success. Finally the peasants appealed to Goetz to put his military skills at their service; he agreed, but only on condition that he could impose iron discipline – abstract 'goodness' had given way to a concrete understanding of means and ends.

Le Diable et le Bon Dieu was Sartre's own favourite among his plays.[3] It is easy to understand why. On the level of political and moral debate it was rich and complex, and it contained some fine dramatic moments, such as the delicious scene with the leper who was disgusted by those who came to kiss him to ensure their own salvation rather than his.[4] (One is reminded of accident victims in hospital being visited by prominent politicians.) Yet paradoxically, if it was Sartre's best play it was also his most Stalinist. As Goetz progressed from villain to saint to revolutionary, it was possible to see Sartre working his way through the arguments that would lead him to make his *rapprochement* with Moscow.

Thus Nasty, the peasant leader, argued that seven years were required to prepare the peasants' war of liberation; he urged Goetz not to give away his land to the peasants, but rather to serve their cause by offering Nasty a

base in one of his villages where he could prepare for revolutionary struggle. This sixteenth-century version of 'socialism in one country' was
clearly intended to be more 'realistic' than Goetz's utopianism,[5] while the
idea of 'premature' insurrection recalled Stalinist attacks on the Spanish
POUM and anarchists.

And when Goetz discussed with Nasty the possibility of enforcing military discipline, we can feel Sartre rehearsing his best macho Stalinist manner: 'Nasty, we shall have to hang the poor. Hang them at random, as an
example: the innocent along with the guilty'.[6]

The play was first performed at the time of a wave of purges and exe-
cutions in Eastern Europe, and it is hard not to take these lines as an
oblique defence of such miscarriages of justice. But it was a curious
defence. It is one thing to argue that a postrevolutionary state may need to
exercise revolutionary terror in its own defence, and that in the midst of
danger and encircling menace mistakes will inevitably be made so that
innocent victims suffer. People like Trotsky or Victor Serge, who experi-
enced revolutionary terror on the ground, would have no quarrel with
such a formulation. But a blanket threat to hang guilty and innocent alike
is very different, and in fact self-defeating. A few minutes' thought might
have led Sartre to realise that if the authorities made such a threat, then
many would draw the conclusion that they might as well be hung for a
sheep as for no lamb, and take the risk of being guilty in exchange for
whatever benefit it offered.

As for the Stalinists, the defence could hardly please them. In their
mythology the victims of the Moscow Trials in the 1930s, and of the Eastern European trials, were clearly guilty. (Hence Paul Eluard's refusal to
oppose the execution of the Czech intellectual Zavis Kalandra after an
extorted confession on the grounds that 'I already have too much on my
hands with the innocent who proclaim their innocence to worry about the
guilty who proclaim their guilt'.)[7] To shout one's mouth off about hanging
the innocent, as Goetz did, was not at all what was required.

Of course, Sartre's aim was not particularly to please Stalinists through
his depiction. As he had put it in *Qu'est-ce que la littérature?*, 'the Stalinist
politician has no desire whatsoever to find his image in literature because
he knows that a portrait is already a calling into question'.[8] In fact the Stalinists did not much like the play. Elsa Triolet, for example, complained that
Sartre was allowing the modern working class to be represented by a pre-
capitalist peasantry:

> Nasty wanted to lead into battle men who were not ripe to fight consciously.
> Therefore he lied to them. Nasty was not one of those leaders who knows how
> to be just one step in front of those who are following them. He no more resem-
> bles today's guides of the people than this horde of ignorant wretches resembles
> today's proletariat.[9]

Triolet would doubtless have preferred a Socialist Realist drama in which gentle but firm leaders shepherded a mass of robust and chaste workers, while evil Trotskyist saboteurs were hauled off to the gallows. Nonetheless she had a point. The sixteenth-century setting scarcely offered a serious opportunity for a study of the dynamics of revolutionary leadership in the twentieth. It was a point picked up in 1954 by Claude Lefort in his polemic with Sartre. Discussing Sartre's attitude to the working class in *Les Communistes et la paix*, Lefort enquired: 'And in fact, are the workers that you show us anything more than the peasants of *Le Diable et le Bon Dieu*? What other problem do you give them to solve except taking the decision to fight? That is, to follow their leaders?'[10] With some justice Lefort was accusing Sartre of underestimating the working class's capacity for consciousness and self-organisation.

In later years Sartre made some self-criticisms of his positions in the 1950s. After 1968, in an interview with Pierre Verstraeten, having abandoned his advocacy of a vanguard party in favour of a Maoist variant of spontaneism, he reconsidered how the play should have ended:

> When Goetz, at the penultimate stage of his journey, wants to be an ordinary soldier and obey like everybody else, to be just anybody, and I make him become a general, that is still the reflex of a classic intellectual. Today I do not see why he has to be a general, nor why anybody would especially want him in the ranks of the revolutionaries; but when I wrote the play, that is how I wanted it, that is how I thought. It seemed to me that history was blocked, and the intellectual, having a larger vision – in other words being in more direct contact with the universal – seemed to me necessary to get it going again. But now I no longer think this is quite the case.[11]

Apparently it had been a long time since Sartre had read his own play. For the revolutionary peasants had little interest in Goetz as intellectual; his 'larger vision' did not come into it. After all, his rather silly ideas about utopian communities had landed them in their present plight. He was prized for one reason and one reason only – for his skill in military matters. He was 'the best military leader in Germany'.[12] In terms of a distinction Sartre himself was to make, he was a 'technician' rather than an 'intellectual'.[13] Nasty's sole concern was to ensure that his skills were used to the benefit of the peasants.

There is an important historical source for this theme. In postrevolutionary Russia the Red Army set out to recruit Tsarist officers in order that they should put their military skills at the disposal of the proletariat in the civil war. The person in charge of this process was Leon Trotsky, as Sartre may have remembered. Trotsky recounted this debate in *My Life*,[14] which Sartre read in the 1930s.

'A portrait is already a calling into question'. In *Le Diable et le Bon Dieu* Sartre gave a portrait of his own state of mind on the eve of his *rapprochement* with Stalinism. Yet the dramatic form brought into focus the contradictions which undermined his own position. And it was those contradictions which gave the play its richness and its strength.

Saint Genet (1952) was one of the most complex of all Sartre's works. It developed his ideas on morality, art and language, and showed Sartre going far beyond the narrow scope of his earlier study of *Baudelaire* (1947) in the use of biography to explore the dialectic of individual freedom and historical context.

Yet to readers of 1952 the most provocative aspect of *Saint Genet* must have been its treatment of homosexuality. Sartre was developing the work on the oppression of Jews and women done by himself and de Beauvoir in the previous few years. But here the task was considerably harder.

In the cases of racism and sexism, there was at least verbal agreement on the left that oppression existed, even if there were divergences as to how it should be resisted. When it came to the oppression of homosexuals, it was a very different story. Homophobia was as widespread on the left as on the right. France had no laws against homosexual acts in private (with an age of consent set – by Vichy, and confirmed by de Gaulle – at twenty-one) and might thus be assumed to be a more tolerant society than Britain at that time. But when Sartre canonised the homosexual thief and jailbird as a 'saint', it provoked a widespread homophobic response. Robert Kemp's review in *Les Nouvelles littéraires* stressed the critic's repugnance at the obscenity of the text.[15] A couple of years later the young Jean-Marie Le Pen declared that 'France is ruled by homosexuals: Sartre, Camus, Mauriac'.[16]

Such homophobia was as widespread in the PCF as anywhere else. The ever-sensitive Jean Kanapa, in his 1947 diatribe against Sartre, had accused him of being a disciple of Heidegger who supported a Nazi regime in which 'homosexuals were labelled "supermen" ' (an eccentric account of history, to say the least), and claimed that Sartre was corrupting youth by putting homosexual characters in his novels.[17]

This grotesque abuse could not be simply put down to some postadolescent sexual complex in the brain of the young Kanapa. In the same year, Andrei Zhdanov made a speech in which *Les Temps modernes* was vigorously denounced for its interest in Genet:

> The journal *Les Temps Modernes*, edited by the existentialist, Sartre, lauds as some new revelation a book by the writer Jean Genet, *The Diary of a Thief*, which opens with the words 'Treason, theft and homosexuality – these will be my key topics'... The plays of this Jean Genet are presented with much glitter on the Parisian stage, and Jean Genet himself is showered with invitations to visit America. Such is the 'last word' of bourgeois culture.[18]

Zhdanov showed his usual scrupulous regard for fact. Genet did not visit the U.S.A. till the 1960s; he was refused a U.S. visa in 1965 on the grounds of his criminal record, 'sexual deviation' and alleged PCF membership; when he visited the U.S.A. in 1968 he crossed the border illegally from Canada.[19]

Zhdanov spoke to end debate, not to open it, and there was no need for him to repeat his message. Even twenty years later, Genet told an interviewer, publication of his work was banned in the USSR.[20] The PCF, fortunately, had no power to actually ban his work, but they loyally followed Zhdanov's line. Reviewing *Haute surveillance*, Guy Leclerc in *L'Humanité* said that 'societies have the writers they deserve' and compared Genet to a 'tramp rummaging in a dustbin'.[21] Among the few French writers who refused to sign a petition in support of Genet in 1948 were Louis Aragon and Paul Eluard, probably the two best-known PCF poets.[22] According to press reports, in late 1952 Genet attempted to join the PCF – perhaps stung by Sartre's taunt that 'as a Communist, Genet would be worthy of the hatred of the bourgeoisie; but he is only wicked'[23] – but was rejected, perhaps because Aragon deplored the 'immorality' of his work, and because the policy of the PCF was to refuse membership to 'conspicuous' (*voyant*) homosexuals.[24]

Homophobia on the left was not confined to the PCF. In 1956 Daniel Guérin – who as well as being an anti-fascist and an anti-imperialist was a persistent campaigner for gay rights – published in *France-Observateur* an obituary of Alfred Kinsey, in which he commended Kinsey's defence of homosexuality as natural, while arguing that he had failed to see the link between 'patriarchal, bourgeois and capitalist society' and 'the repression of sexuality'.[25] This provoked a number of shocked letters in which homosexuals were described as 'perverts', 'sick' and unnatural.[26] Guérin described in a later interview how, in the 1930s, he had been unable to broach the subject of his homosexuality with his associates on the anti-Stalinist far left, *pivertistes* and revolutionary syndicalists – as a result he had been 'two men' with 'two lives'.[27] Even the surrealists, who proudly proclaimed their revolt against all convention, condemned homosexuality[28] – a point picked up by Sartre in his critique of surrealism in *Qu'est-ce que la littérature?*[29]

Sartre was not immune to the attitudes of his own time, and it is possible to find traces of prejudice, especially in some of his earlier writings. Yet there was also profound empathy. Most critics, bemused by the supposed universality of 'hell is other people', have failed to notice that in *Huis clos* Sartre clearly presented the working-class lesbian Inès as a positive figure in contrast to the satirical depiction of the snobbish Estelle.

And set against the context of the prevailing homophobia it is clear that *Saint Genet* had to be read as a powerful protest against the oppression of homosexuals. As far as I have been able to establish, no publication of the PCF or any within its political orbit reviewed *Saint Genet*, obviously an indication of the embarrassment that the subject caused within Stalinist circles.

Saint Genet was published in June 1952, at the very moment when Sartre was making his *rapprochement* with the PCF. Within the text were indications of Sartre's reasons for choosing revolution rather than revolt (in some ways he seemed to prefigure Genet's own turn to political activism in his support for the Black Panthers and the Palestinians in the 1960s and 1970s). Yet *Saint Genet* also clearly expressed the very deep reservations that Sartre continued to have about Stalinism and especially its mechanical approach to oppression.

In the conclusion to *Saint Genet* Sartre argued that his aim had been 'to show the limits of psychoanalytic interpretation and Marxist explanation and to show that only freedom can give an account of the totality of a person'. Homosexuality was not the product of bourgeois perversion or childhood trauma, but, as he repeatedly insisted, the product of human choice.[30] In thus insisting that oppression was to be understood in terms of human freedom, Sartre was making a contribution to the restoration of freedom to the heart of Marxism, a place it had had since Marx's 1844 manuscripts, but from which it had been evicted by Stalinism. When Sartre sought reconciliation with the PCF in 1952, he was carrying in his intellectual baggage *Saint Genet* – clear proof that he had not wholly capitulated to Stalinism.[31]

On the very eve of his *rapprochement* with the PCF came Sartre's notorious public quarrel with his old friend Albert Camus in the summer of 1952. This was a public indication that Sartre's position had shifted; however, it was not planned in advance, but arose after Camus had complained bitterly about Francis Jeanson's review of his *L'Homme révolté* in *Les Temps modernes*, a review for whose content he held Sartre responsible, although all the evidence is that this was not the case. The quarrel has been much discussed and much misunderstood;[32] it was not a simple dispute between left and right, or between Communism and anti-Communism.

For although Camus often professed a political stance of rather moderate social democracy, he had a deep and long-lasting attachment to revolutionary syndicalism, and in particular to the journal *La Révolution prolétarienne*, which grouped together some of the veterans of pre-1914 syndicalism who had been expelled from the PCF in the 1920s, notably Alfred Rosmer and Pierre Monatte.[33] In 1953, the year after the quarrel, Camus wrote a preface to Rosmer's memoirs of the early years of the Comintern, *Moscou sous Lénine*, in which he stated: 'In my view, it is neither Kravchenko, a beneficiary of the Stalinist regime, nor the French ministers, responsible for a policy which is covering Tunisia in blood, who can criticise Stalin's dictatorship, but only Rosmer and those like him'.[34] Camus's argument here – that anti-Communists of the right cannot legitimately criticise Russia and that Stalinism can only be judged by those who share the aspirations of the October Revolution – came perilously close to positions often argued by Sartre and Merleau-Ponty. Perhaps that is why this particular text has been systematically ignored by those who seek to use Camus as a stick to beat Sartre with.[35]

Jeanson and Sartre were both well aware of Camus's attachment to revolutionary syndicalism. Jeanson, in his review of *L'Homme révolté*, took up

Camus' argument about whether revolutionary syndicalism was 'ineffective'. Camus alleged it would have been effective if Stalinism had not 'destroyed most of its gains'. Jeanson retorted that this precisely showed its ineffectiveness in face of actual reality.[36]

And Sartre, in defending Jeanson, spelt out the argument, saying with some justice that revolutionary syndicalism was now a '*historical* fact' and that 'one can, after all, consider a movement to be ineffective while at the same time admiring the courage, spirit of enterprise, abnegation and even effectiveness of those who took part in it'.[37]

Sartre went on to ask a vital question. If he was, as Camus had implied, a crypto-Communist, 'why is it me that they hate and not you?'[38] For there was ample evidence to show that the PCF press attacked Sartre far more frequently than Camus. Garaudy's *Une Littérature de fossoyeurs* (1947) devoted a whole chapter to Sartre, but only a few lines to Camus. The answer was clearly that Camus was perceived as being to the right of the Party – by 1955 he was to be a supporter of Mendès-France – and thus was a possible element in a future Popular Front. Sartre, however, was seen as staking out ground to the Party's left. Moreover, the *Révolution prolétarienne* nucleus were a group of splendid veterans of impeccable honesty; but they had failed to win any support among younger generations and were no threat whatsoever to the PCF's hegemony. The RDR, on the other hand, had momentarily looked like posing a threat to part of the PCF's audience, and therefore Sartre needed to be watched much more carefully.

In places Sartre's response to Camus made some very valid points about effective political action and the hypocrisy of the right; yet elsewhere he was savage and unfair. Perhaps he was still trying to convince himself, rather than to persuade Camus. Certainly this was not a man who had become trapped in the Manichaean universe of Cold War Stalinism. He was still very much aware that there was a left critique of Stalinism as well as a right critique, and that the left critique required to be approached with the utmost respect and seriousness. In offering the hand of friendship to the PCF, Sartre was not suffering from naivety. In retrospect Sartre's choice may seem wrong and, indeed, foolish, but, for better or worse, it was taken with a lucid recognition of a bleak reality.

Notes

1. R. Hayman, *Writing Against*, London, 1986, p. 284; see Sartre's account in his obituary of Merleau-Ponty, *Sit* IV, p. 259, and J.-P. Sartre and M. Merleau-Ponty, 'Les Lettres d'une rupture', *Magazine littéraire*, No. 320, April 1994, pp. 67–86.
2. P. Naville, 'Etats-Unis et contradictions capitalistes', *TM*, December 1952, pp. 899–914; 'Etats-Unis et contradictions capitalistes II', *TM*, May 1953, pp. 1714–35, especially p. 1734.
3. *Adieux*, p. 242.

4. J.-P. Sartre, *Le Diable et le Bon Dieu*, act 5. sc. 2.
5. Sartre, *Le Diable*, act 4. sc. 5.
6. *Ibid.*, act 7. sc. 5.
7. Cited by M. Polizzotti, *Revolution of the Mind: The Life of André Breton*, London, 1995, p. 567.
8. *Sit* II, p. 284.
9. E. Triolet, 'Le Grand Jeu', *Les Lettres françaises*, 14 June 1951.
10. 'De la réponse à la question', *TM*, July 1954, p. 166.
11. 'I Am No Longer a Realist', *Gulliver*, 1972; reproduced in R. Aronson and A. van den Hoven, eds., *Sartre Alive*, Detroit, 1991, pp. 83–99 (text in English).
12. Sartre, *Le Diable*, act 7. sc. 5.
13. *Sit* VIII, pp. 397–400.
14. L. Trotsky, *My Life*, New York, 1960, pp. 437–42.
15. R. Kemp, 'Répugnances', *Les Nouvelles littéraires*, 14 August 1952, p. 3.
16. M. Winock, *La République se meurt, 1956–1958*, Paris, 1985, p. 23.
17. J.-P. Sartre, *L'Existentialisme est un humanisme*, Paris, 1966, p. 97.
18. A.A. Zhdanov, *On Literature, Music and Philosophy*, London, 1950, p. 109.
19. E. White, *Genet* London, 1993, pp. 549, 582.
20. A. Malgorn, *Jean Genet: Qui êtes-vous?* Lyon, 1988, p. 167.
21. *L'Humanité* 12 March 1949.
22. E. White, *Genet*, p. 353.
23. J.-P. Sartre, *Saint Genet*, Paris, 1952, p. 194.
24. *Paris-Presse l'intransigeant*, 30 December 1952; J.-B. Moraly, *Jean Genet – la vie écrite*, Paris, 1988, p. 230.
25. D. Gúerin, 'Le Message de délivrance de Kinsey', *France-Observateur*, 30 August 1956, p. 14.
26. *France-Observateur*, 13 September 1956, p. 20; 20 September 1956, p. 20.
27. 'Daniel Guérin: d'une dissidence sexuelle à la révolution', *Masques*, May 1979, pp. 39–42.
28. Polizzotti, *Revolution of the Mind*, pp. 88–89, 294.
29. *Sit* II, p. 324.
30. De Beauvoir had already argued that lesbianism was 'behaviour chosen in situation' in *Le Deuxième Sexe*, 2: 192.
31. See I. Birchall, 'The Politics of *Saint Genet*', in B. Read, ed., *Flowers and Revolution*, London, 1997, pp. 177–87.
32. See I.H. Birchall, 'Camus contre Sartre: quarante ans plus tard', in D. Walker, ed., *Albert Camus, les extrêmes et l'équilibre*, Amsterdam, 1994, pp. 129–50.
33. See I.H. Birchall, 'The labourism of Sisyphus: Albert Camus and revolutionary syndicalism', *Journal of European Studies* xx (1990), pp. 135–65.
34. A. Camus, 'Le Temps de l'espoir', *Actuelles* II, Paris, 1953, pp. 147–56, especially p. 152.
35. Camus's links with the *Révolution prolétarienne* and with Rosmer in particular have been disregarded by most critics and biographers. Herbert Lottman's 700-page biography, *Camus*, London, 1981, does not have an index entry for Rosmer. At last Olivier Todd's biography of Camus, *Albert Camus*, (Paris, 1996), pp. 455–62, has repaired the omission.
36. F. Jeanson, 'Albert Camus ou l'âme révoltée', *TM*, May 1952, p. 2083.
37. *Sit* IV, p. 95.
38. *Sit* IV, p. 104.

Chapter 11

DANGEROUS LIAISON

Sartre's four-year romance with the PCF between 1952 and 1956 was not the most creditable period of his life, and it was certainly the one that provided most ammunition to his anti-Communist critics. A great many of the criticisms that have been made of Sartre's political conduct during this period are fully justified. Yet his position was complex and contradictory; to appreciate it fully it is necessary to place it in context. Sartre's political evolution in the 1950s is often presented as though it were simply a dialogue between two protagonists – Sartre and the Stalinist PCF. That dialogue did take place, but it was accompanied by a second dialogue, between Sartre and the various tendencies of the anti-Stalinist left.

Sartre's *rapprochement* with the PCF in 1952 marked a sharp break with the nonaligned politics he was pursuing in the late 1940s, when he vigorously rejected both Stalinism and social democracy, both Washington and Moscow. Certainly there were elements in his earlier thought that can be seen as preparing the way – the belief that 'the main enemy is at home', the recognition of the crucial importance of the workers organised in the PCF and CGT, the sense that Russia was somehow different, if only in its nominal adhesion to 'Communism'. And it was also the case that the ignominious collapse of the RDR reinforced the argument that there was nothing to the left of the PCF.

Sartre's first step towards *rapprochement* with the PCF came in December 1951, when he agreed to cooperate with the PCF over the case of Henri Martin, a sailor imprisoned for campaigning against the war in Indo-China.

But the crucial text for understanding Sartre's priorities during the 1952–56 period is the series of articles published in *Les Temps modernes* under the title *Les Communistes et la paix*.[1] In his obituary of Merleau-Ponty Sartre gave an account of how he came to write the articles. The immedi-

---

ate causes were the demonstration against the arrival in Paris of the American General Ridgway and the subsequent arrest of the acting leader of the PCF, Jacques Duclos, for being in possession of two pigeons. (It is rather unlikely that in 1952 the PCF communicated with Moscow by means of carrier pigeon – and even less likely that it used dead carrier pigeons.) Sartre noted the response on which his subsequent political choices were based: 'An anti-Communist is a dog, I stand by that. I'll stand by that for ever'.[2]

Les Temps modernes was not, of course, a monolithic publication, and there were a variety of political views among its contributors. The first instalment of *Les Communistes et la paix* did not appear on its own, but was one of a set of five pieces dealing with the aftermath of the Ridgway demonstration. Claude Lanzmann contributed a ringing denunciation of police violence, comparing the *préfet de police* to Herod, and arguing that only 'beautiful souls'[3] could deny the demonstrators' right to defend themselves.[4] RS (presumably Roger Stéphane) contributed a piece on the police chief, Baylot, based mainly on quotations which revealed the *préfet*'s anti-Communist paranoia.[5] An article by Marcel Saumane was highly critical of the PCF strategy in relation to the demonstration of 28 May, and the unsuccessful strike call the following week, which he described as 'one of the most serious mistakes made by the French Communist leaders for some years'. He accused the PCF of 'irresponsible "adventurism"', saying that even if the action was ordered by Moscow, the French leadership should have warned that the popular mood would not support such militancy; the fact that they did not revealed that they were out of touch.[6]

Most interesting of all was a piece by a 'metalworker' writing under the name Roger L.[7] He described the mood among the factory workers he worked alongside, noting that they showed little interest in the 28 May demonstration. They were, he argued, weary of PCF slogans. Duclos, he observed, was much less popular than Maurice Thorez, absent in Russia, and he claimed that rank-and-file workers did not believe the PCF line as presented in *L'Humanité* that workers in the non-Communist unions *Force Ouvrière* and the Catholic CFTC were class enemies. He argued that workers would be more likely to strike if their own interests were at stake – 'For grub, OK, but for Duclos, never'. The PCF in his view should have abandoned parliamentarism and international campaigns in favour of defending workers' immediate interests. The PCF's strategy had led to defeat: 'Today we can see the result: a few blokes politicised, four million voters; it seems contradictory but it allows Pinay to stick Duclos in jail without any problem'.[8]

It was a perceptive and interesting contribution, which in many ways undermined Sartre's claim of an identity between party and class. In some ways the analysis of working-class weariness with PCF politics was similar to what could be found in the writings of the *Socialisme ou barbarie* group, although Roger L. was rather more 'economistic' or 'syndicalist' in his outlook than *Socialisme ou barbarie*.[9] Taken as part of this package of five articles, Sartre's own contribution looked rather less like a total capitulation to Stalinism than has sometimes been claimed.

In *Les Communistes et la paix* Sartre set out his analysis of the French left. After analysing the events of the Ridgway demonstration, he went on to make clear that he was stating his 'agreement with the Communists on specific and limited subjects, arguing on the basis of *my* principles and not *theirs*'.[10] He stated that he would 'undertake to prove that *only* a Popular Front can restore strength to the labour movement'.[11] (The demand for a renewal of the Popular Front was an important theme in PCF propaganda in this period.) He satirised the absurdities of American-style anti-Communism, which could only develop in a situation where Communists scarcely existed. 'If you meet PCF members every day or even every month, how can you believe they eat babies?'[12]

Many parts of Sartre's argument were weak, and have not stood the test of time. Thus he denounced the alleged '*malthusianisme*' of the French economy,[13] using the term to refer to far more than population growth.[14] This revealed him as taking a far too pessimistic view of the French economy's potential for modernisation, as was to be shown over the coming decade.

His sneer at those who distinguished between 'that great liberal, Lenin, and… Stalin the autocrat' begged all the questions,[15] while his critique of liberalism also missed the point. Evoking a female refinery worker, he argued that her concept of freedom would be very different from that of an intellectual: 'I think she would be quite happy to give up the freedom of expression which is put to such noble use in the *Salle Gaveau* if she were liberated from the boring rhythm of the machines, from the jobs externally imposed on her, from the cold and the miserable environment of the factory'.[16]

He thus failed to recognise that the only way that the woman in question could hope to liberate herself was by effective organisation in the workplace; if she were denied the freedom to communicate and organise with her fellow-workers, then that hope would never be realised. That, precisely, rather than any abstract liberalism, was what lay behind the left critique of Stalinism, which Sartre, wilfully or not, refused to understand.

The central theme of Sartre's argument in the polemic was the question of the relation between party and class: 'The "proletariat constituted into a distinct political party", what is it, in France today, other than the totality of workers organised by the PCF? If the working class wants to detach itself from the Party, it has only one means available: to disintegrate into dust'.[17] The glorification of the party was thus the corollary of a belief that the working class was, if left to itself, wholly impotent.

This focus on the party was the theme of which Sartre was most critical in subsequent judgements on *Les Communistes et la paix*,[18] but these largely resulted from his continuing failure to develop a theory of the revolutionary party; in effect he made a flip-flop from substituting the party for the class to rejecting any need for a party at all.

It takes two to tango, and Sartre's *rapprochement* with the PCF could not have occurred unless there had been movement on the PCF's side as well as on his. In 1952 there were divergences within the PCF leadership; this was shown not only in the spectacular purge of veteran leaders André Marty and Charles Tillon (the former was accused of being a police agent), but also in strategic divergences about the relation between the PCF and the rest of the left. But in fact the government offensive (police raids, confiscation of newspapers) following the Ridgway demonstration actually led to an increase in support for the Party; Philippe Robrieux has noted that a number of non-Party intellectuals – including Vercors, Julien Benda, J.-M. Domenach, Paul Ricoeur, Jean Wahl – rallied round the Party when it was under state attack. It was in the context of a decision to be more open towards such non-Party support that the PCF responded to Sartre's advances.[19]

Sartre's article was welcomed by Pierre Daix in *Les Lettres françaises*.[20] Daix stressed the importance of unity in the struggle for peace: 'The problem is not that Sartre or other people don't like Communists, nor what the Communists happen to think of Sartre... but very simply to be aware that, if war breaks out, it will be too late to observe that all French people are condemned to the same annihilation'.

A more extensive response came from Jean Kanapa.[21] It would be interesting to know why Kanapa was selected for the job, when he had such a profound antagonism to Sartre. Possibly the PCF leadership thought that, if they could be seen to have instructed Kanapa to write such an article, it would be clear evidence that they were serious about dialogue.

His reply, directed to PCF members as much as to Sartre, was very guarded. He reminded Sartre, at some length, of the issues that separated them. He noted with regret that Sartre still believed in the existence of the Russian labour camps, even if he understood the way the campaign against them was being used. He criticised Sartre for his idealist philosophy and his 'taste for the morbid aspects of existence'. He found the articles accompanying Sartre's piece in *Les Temps modernes* 'very disagreeable'. And he affected to be highly offended by Sartre's suggestion that there might be differences of opinion within the PCF leadership. But he made clear that if Sartre wanted dialogue and cooperation the PCF would respond.

The union was consummated. For four years Sartre became – almost – the model fellow-traveller. In December 1952 he addressed the Communist-organised Peace Conference in Vienna. He spoke on pro-Communist platforms, in France and abroad, especially those concerned with the peace movement. He made numerous public statements and protests in accordance with the current Communist line. In 1954 he made his first visit to the USSR, and later that same year became a vice-president of the France–USSR Association.

During this period he wrote – or had ghost-written – various articles and gave a number of interviews. There were many ill-advised judgements in these. In 1954, on returning from the USSR, he published five articles in *Libération* in which he took a naively uncritical view of Russian society and made some appallingly dishonest claims about the freedom of criticism permitted there.[22] In a speech in February 1955 attacking German rearmament he referred to 'arming the Germans, our historic enemies, against Russia, our allies in 1914 and 1940'.[23] The year 1940 was presumably a mere slip; Sartre could scarcely have forgotten the Hitler–Stalin Pact. But since the whole Communist tradition emerged out of opposition to the First World War, the revival of the nationalism of 1914 was nothing less than grotesque. It seems clear that Sartre maintained mental reservations during this period – Jean Cau, his secretary, insisted that he kept his 'ironic lucidity intact'.[24] But his political judgement can be assessed only on the basis of published texts, and Sartre – in whose philosophy the notion of 'responsibility' plays a central role – must be held fully responsible.

But Sartre also insisted that freedom was always exercised in situation. The full complexity of Sartre's commitment in the 1952–56 period can be understood only by placing it in context. Thus many commentators, either by focusing too narrowly on the literary milieu or by looking only at a section of the political spectrum, give a fundamentally false picture of the balance of political forces in the early 1950s. Sartre has often been accused of going along with what was fashionable, or accepting current orthodoxy. Yet in French society as a whole the right was dominant throughout the 1950s. Governments were led by politicians of the centre or the right, from Pinay to de Gaulle; the only interruptions were the governments of Mendès-France (who excluded the SFIO as well as the PCF from his cabinet) and Guy Mollet (who intensified the war in Algeria). Although the PCF had a substantial popular vote, no prime minister between 1947 and 1958 owed his parliamentary majority to the PCF; Mendès-France made it clear he would not take office unless he had a majority without the PCF – thus Communist voters were effectively disenfranchised. Communism barely had any foothold in the French police or army, and to be a Communist militant in a factory was scarcely a comfortable life. In making his *rapprochement* with the PCF Sartre was very much swimming against the stream.

Moreover, the totality of Sartre's political practice in this period cannot be understood without reference to *Les Temps modernes*, a journal for which Sartre took responsibility, all the more so after his final break with Merleau-Ponty in 1953. Throughout Sartre's *rapprochement* with Stalinism *Les Temps modernes* remained an independent journal of the left. Sartre made it quite clear that the review would not be subordinated to a pro-PCF line; indeed, throughout the period *Les Temps modernes* continued to carry material that was critical of Stalinism and highly embarrassing to the PCF. In this task Sartre was aided by a number of allies from the anti-Stalinist left.

Thus in May 1952 Maurice Nadeau, veteran of the FIARI, who still felt a deep hatred of Russian 'socialist realism', wrote a sharply ironic critique of André Stil's novel *Au Château d'eau*, which had just won the Stalin Prize. In the summer of 1953 *Les Temps modernes* carried three major articles by Marcel Péju on the show trial in Czechoslovakia at which the former secretary-general of the Czech Communist Party, Slansky, was sentenced to death.[25] Péju began with a comparison which must have been highly offensive to any PCF reader. He said that the Czech events were as surprising as if Hitler, in 1942, had put Goebbels on trial, and Goebbels, before being executed, had admitted working for the Communist Party since childhood. Yet, he said, while such a split among Nazis would have given the left nothing but joy, to see similar events among Communists made us feel 'complicit and compromised'.

Péju did not pull his punches. His detailed account of the trial showed that the whole thing was very clearly rigged; that the evidence was implausible and that the charges were in no way proved; moreover he observed that the theme of anti-Zionism was developed to such an extent that the trial was overtly anti-Semitic. Tony Judt has noted Péju's article and asked how, if Sartre was 'reading the work of his own contributors', he could 'maintain his silence'.[26] But even before the articles appeared, in March 1953, Sartre published a reply to François Mauriac, who had criticised him for not condemning anti-Semitism in the USSR;[27] in this he had announced: 'In May *Les Temps modernes* will publish an article on the Slansky affair for which, as editor, I take full responsibility'. Sartre also took personal responsibility for Péju's articles in an interview in *Combat* later in 1953.[28] One might ask if Judt was reading the work of those he was criticising.

In his reply to Mauriac Sartre insisted that he opposed anti-Semitism anywhere in the world, and that while his aim was 'the rebirth of an independent left in close association with the Communist Party', independence would have no value if one could not speak the truth. But the article carefully evaded making any concrete judgement on what Sartre had subtly renamed 'Soviet anti-Zionism'. Sartre promised that he would deal with this in the forthcoming third part of *Les Communistes et la paix* – a promise which he strikingly failed to keep.[29]

In 1953 Dionys Mascolo (a PCF member from 1946 to 1949) published his book *Le Communisme*. This was not primarily a polemic against the PCF but rather a theoretical account of the idea of communism; it contained a sharp but fraternal critique of Sartre's essay 'Matérialisme et révolution'. It was, however, firmly anti-Stalinist, and at one point described Zhdanov as 'the modern Attila of theory'.[30] This was reviewed in *Les Temps modernes* by Sartre's old comrade, Colette Audry.[31] Audry was far from uncritical of the book, in particular disagreeing with Mascolo's criticisms of Sartre. But the review was generally favourable, and her treatment of PCF intellectuals as mindless transmitters of the official line was quite harsh. She concluded by citing Lenin as a point of contrast to modern Communist style and practice.

Three months later *L'Humanité* published an article by Kanapa, written in his usual frenetic style, in which he denounced a range of attacks on the PCF stemming from the book by the 'renegade Mascolo'. He cited the pro-American review *Preuves* (accused by the PCF, quite correctly, of being CIA-funded), and, in the same list of offenders, Colette Audry's piece in *Les Temps modernes*.[32]

This was not a piece of individual enterprise on Kanapa's part. Pierre Daix has recounted how he was summoned by François Billoux (a member of the PCF's Political Bureau during the 1950s and 1960s), who told him that Sartre was playing a 'double game' by publishing Audry's article (Audry's history was doubtless well known to the PCF leadership) and must be exposed. Daix was given an outline of the article which the Party Secretariat wanted to have written. Daix turned down the job, which was then given to Kanapa.[33]

Faced with a choice between the Stalinist Kanapa and Colette Audry, an anti-Stalinist of twenty years' standing, Sartre did not hesitate; he immediately penned a polemic which showed a powerful combination of wit and passion. 'One swallow doesn't make a summer and it takes more than one Kanapa to discredit a party'. He pointed out that on NATO, Indo-China and other issues Audry was on the same side as the PCF, and that for Kanapa to attack her was to undermine the whole strategy of uniting 'honest intellectuals'. (As ever the PCF was seeking friends to its right, not to its left.) He added that if Kanapa's accusations were justified, then the PCF was being inconsistent in cooperating with him: 'if I am a cop, your are cretins'. But he concluded, to show that he was not breaking off relations, 'the only cretin is Kanapa'.[34]

The unfortunate Daix was compelled to get his hands dirty after all by negotiating a settlement, which involved Kanapa writing a rather grudging reply in which he claimed that Sartre had misunderstood him. Daix later claimed that the PCF had been pressured into a withdrawal by Moscow, which gave 'great importance' to relations with Sartre.[35]

In 1955 *Les Temps modernes* produced a special 480-page issue entitled 'La Gauche' (the Left).[36] The journal opened its pages to a broad range of contributors; as well as *Temps modernes* regulars such as de Beauvoir, Lanzmann (who attacked *gauchistes* such as Trotskyists who had refused to support the Resistance for fear of aiding Anglo-American imperialism)[37] and Pouillon, there were representatives of the '*nouvelle gauche*' (Bourdet and Gilles Martinet), of the PCF (Victor Leduc and J.-T. Desanti) and independent left academics (Maurice Duverger, René Dumont).

The anti-Stalinist left was well represented. Colette Audry wrote that at the time of the Popular Front, Léon Blum 'held in his hand the fate of two proletariats' (the French and the Spanish) but failed the test.[38] The Trotskyist Jacques Danos was equally hard on the prewar Popular Front with a piece called: 'The Popular Front: how the left was led to defeat'.[39]

However, while the PCF may have been offended by particular contributors, the overall line was doubtless acceptable. The unsigned editorial introduction and conclusion focused on the advocacy of a new Popular
Front, a governmental alliance of the PCF and the SFIO, arguing that 'only
a Popular Front government based on the PCF and the SFIO' could help to
establish a neutral zone in Europe and that 'only such a government could
renew the economic structures of the country, and only such a government could liberate the overseas peoples from an anachronistic colonialism'.[40] Marceau Pivert was thus not wholly unfair when he commented
that 'this collection of opinions excludes anti-Stalinist tendencies, those
which do not consider Stalinism to be in any way a component of the
authentic left'.[41]

Nonetheless Sartre's resolute defence of the political independence of
Les Temps modernes in this period showed clearly that in his *rapprochement*
with the PCF he did not put all his eggs into one basket. He continued to
distrust the PCF and maintained his contacts with those who would join
with him in opposing it if necessary.

As in other periods we can look to Sartre's literary work for some clues
to the underlying contradictions in his political stance. His play *Nekrassov*,
first performed in 1955, told the story of how a criminal, Georges de
Valera, succeeded in passing himself off to Paris journalists as a
Kravchenko-style Russian defector. Their appetite for anything that could
be used in the anti-Communist crusade was such that they believed his
most grotesque inventions, thus providing scope for a vigorous satire of
the French press in particular and Cold War anti-Communism in general.

Nekrassov was in many ways a unique episode in Sartre's career. Sartre's
other plays, however radical, were normally presented to an overwhelm-
ingly bourgeois audience. But since *Nekrassov* was written during his
period of alliance with the PCF he did succeed in achieving a partly proletarian audience, as the PCF encouraged workers from factories and the
Paris suburbs to attend the performances.[42] It was also his first and only
comedy, and revealed a talent for humorous writing that might otherwise
not have been suspected.

Sartre now got rave reviews from Communist critics – but from few others. A play whose main subject was the absurdities of the anti-Communist
press could hardly expect a lot of sympathy from journalists. Yet *Nekrassov*
did not lack ambivalence, and in some ways the play embodied the contradictions of *Les Communistes et la paix*.

One person who picked up on the play's ambiguities was Roger Quilliot, who pointed out in the SFIO's monthly journal that many of the criticisms Sartre made of the bourgeois press could find parallels in the
Communist world; he added, doubtless hoping to embarrass Sartre in the
eyes of his Communist friends: 'Sartre is too clearsighted not to have
thought of it'. As he put it: 'Whether Sartre wishes it or not, his play is
ambiguous, and in aiming at one form of McCarthyism, he hits all of them,

whether red or white'.[43] Quilliot had a point, and there was certainly a double edge when Sartre made his newspaper editor say: 'But come on, I'm a progovernment paper! There'll surely be a government when the Russians occupy Paris'.[44]

In *Les Communistes et la paix* Sartre singled out 'left anti-Communists' for special treatment, and he did the same in *Nekrassov*. The main target was the character of Demidoff, whom Sartre used to satirise, unkindly but not wholly unfairly, the perpetual fragmentation of the far left. When de Valera confronted Demidoff, he presented him with a brief *curriculum vitae*:

> You came to France in 1950: at that time you were a Lenino-Bolshevik and you felt very isolated. For a while you came close to the Trotskyists and you became a Trotskyisto-Bolshevik. When their group broke up, you turned to Tito and you were known as a Titisto-Bolshevik. When Yugoslavia was reconciled with the USSR, you put your hopes in Mao Tse-tung, and you proclaimed yourself a Tungisto-Bolshevik. Since China didn't break with the Soviets, you abandoned that course and you now call yourself a Bolshevik-Bolshevik.[45]

A few moments later Sartre, who knew there were no jokes like the old jokes, revealed that Demidoff's organisation had only one member. Yet behind the satire Sartre was doubtless reflecting on the destructive factionalism he had encountered in the RDR. It was the failure of the far left to preserve a united organisation that had driven Sartre, rather reluctantly, into the arms of the PCF.

But on one charge, at least, Sartre can definitely be declared innocent. It was *Nekrassov* which gave birth to the longstanding and apparently ineradicable myth that Sartre said he would not criticise Russia 'in order not to make Billancourt despair'. In the play Véronique, a Communist journalist, talking to de Valera, argued that the effect of his alleged revelations about Russia would be to cause demoralisation and despair among the small minority who believed him in the Renault factory at Billancourt. When she left he, perversely, began to sing 'Let's make Billancourt despair'.[46]

From this to making Sartre responsible for the statement that we must not make Billancourt despair is quite a long way. To make a dramatist responsible for all the statements of his characters would leave Shakespeare and Molière responsible for some perverse opinions. Moreover, it was a statement that could not be made publicly without undermining itself; if one explains why one is suppressing the truth one ceases to suppress it. It is as though a doctor said to her patient: 'I won't tell you that you're terminally ill because it would depress you'.

In an interview in *Le Monde* just one week before the first night of *Nekrassov*, Sartre made clear that his position was the exact opposite; asked if he would publish material critical of the USSR, he replied:

If I were convinced of the truth of new facts, even though the revelation of them might perchance embarrass the PCF, I should reveal them: either it would just cause a bit of a stir, and we should continue to agree on other points in common; or else things would work out differently, and if so too bad.[47]

Sartre's argument, as presented elsewhere – for example in his polemic with Camus[48] – was that the motive of anti-Communists in publicising criticisms of Russia, even if they were true, was to weaken the PCF, which was the main organisation of the working class in France. The logic of this was not to suppress criticisms, but to argue that the left should make its criticisms in its own press and through its own organisations.

Why, then, has the position been so persistently attributed to Sartre? Obviously it served the interests of his political opponents to suggest that he was a servile and openly dishonest supporter of the USSR. Yet, although the alleged 'quotation' was repeatedly used, in good or bad faith, by Sartre's right-wing critics, it appears it did not originate with them.

In June 1955, André Wurmser, reviewing the play in *L'Humanité*,[49] told right-wing journalists that they were 'collaborating in what Sartre calls "making the poor despair"'. Subsequently, on 29 November 1955, the PCF held a large public meeting with a mainly student audience in Paris in order to reply to Merleau-Ponty's recently published book *Les Aventures de la dialectique*. Among the speakers was the inevitable Kanapa, who told the audience: '*We do not want*, to quote the very appropriate expression of J.-P. Sartre, *them to make Billancourt despair*'.[50] It would indeed be ironic if the 'cretin' Kanapa had been the person to provide ammunition for the anti-Communists by attributing the statement to Sartre. It remains unresolved whether he did so from stupidity or from malice.

Notes

1. *TM*, July 1952, pp. 1–50; October–November 1952, pp. 695–763; April 1954, pp. 1731–1819; reprinted in J.-P. Sartre, *Sit* VI, Paris, 1964, pp. 80–384.
2. *Sit* IV, pp. 248–49.
3. The term derived from Hegel's *Phenomenology of Mind*, though it was often used as a simple insult by PCF writers.
4. *TM*, July 1952, pp. 51–54.
5. *TM*, July 1952, pp. 65–69.
6. *TM*, July 1952, pp. 55–60.
7. One of the PCF's leading militants in Renault was called Roger Linet. Linet was not wholly uncritical of the PCF line at this period. However, given the level of discipline in the PCF, it seems highly unlikely that he would have written in *Les Temps modernes* under such a transparent pseudonym. See R. Linet, *Renault 1947–58*, Paris, 1997, pp. 223–51.
8. *TM*, July 1952, pp. 61–64.
9. Compare, for example, D. Mothé's *Journal d'un ouvrier*, Paris, 1959, which showed the role of the PCF at Renault Billancourt in relation to the Algerian War, the Hungarian

Revolution and the accession of de Gaulle in 1958, as viewed by a shop-floor worker who was a member of *Socialisme ou Barbarie*.

10. *Sit* VI, p. 168.
11. *Sit* VI, p. 254.
12. *Sit* VI, p. 161.
13. *Sit* VI, pp. 269ff.
14. The Malthusian attitude to the economy was defined by Philip Williams as: 'a conviction that the market was fixed and one trader's gain meant another's loss, a preference for high profit on a low turnover, and a willingness to mitigate competition sufficiently to keep the weaker firms afloat'. P.M. Williams, *Crisis and Compromise*, London, 1964, p. 3.
15. *Sit* VI, p. 82.
16. *Sit* VI, p. 115.
17. *Sit* VI, p. 195.
18. See, e.g., interview with *Il Manifesto*, September 1969, cited *C&R*, pp. 480–81.
19. P. Robrieux, *Histoire intérieure du parti communiste*, Paris, 1980–84, 2: 308.
20. *Les Lettres françaises*, 28 August 1952, pp. 1–5.
21. J. Kanapa, 'J.-P. Sartre, *Les Communistes et la paix*', *La Nouvelle critique* 39, September–October 1952, pp. 23–42.
22. *Libération*, 15, 16, 17–18, 19, 20 July 1954.
23. J.-P. Sartre, 'La Leçon de Stalingrad', *France–URSS* No. 115, April 1955, pp. 4–5.
24. J. Cau, *Croquis de mémoire*, Paris, 1985, p. 245.
25. M. Nadeau, 'André Stil, prix Staline', *TM*, May 1952, pp. 2091–99; M. Péju, 'Hier et aujourd'hui – le sens du procès Slansky', *TM*, May 1953, pp. 1775–90; June 1953, pp. 2009–23; July 1953, pp. 139–64.
26. T. Judt, *Past Imperfect*, Berkeley and Los Angeles, 1992, p. 184.
27. *Figaro*, 17 March 1953.
28. *Combat*, 31 October–1 November; C&R p. 266.
29. J.-P. Sartre, 'Réponse à M. Mauriac', *L'Observateur*, 19 March 1953, p. 7; see *Sit* VI pp. 253–384.
30. D. Mascolo, *Le Communisme*, Paris, 1953, especially pp. 375–406, 402.
31. *TM*, November 1953, pp. 926–33.
32. J. Kanapa, 'Un "nouveau" révisionnisme à l'usage des intellectuels', *L'Humanité*, 22 February 1954; reproduced *Sit* VII, pp. 94–98.
33. P. Daix, *J'ai cru au matin*, Paris, 1976, pp. 342–44.
34. *Sit* VII, pp. 98–103.
35. Daix, *J'ai cru*, pp. 344–46; for Kanapa's reply see *L'Humanité*, 24 March, 1954.
36. *TM*, May 1955.
37. *TM*, May 1955, p. 1635.
38. *TM*, May 1955, p. 1796.
39. *TM*, May 1955, pp. 1803–26. Danos and Marcel Gibelin, who also contributed to the issue, were the authors of *Juin 36* (Paris, 1952), the classic Trotskyist account of the Popular Front; English translation as *June '36*, London, 1986.
40. *TM*, May 1955, pp. 1538, 2006, 2015.
41. *Revue socialiste*, October 1955, p. 334.
42. *Adieux*, p. 244.
43. R. Quilliot, 'De Nekrassov à Merleau-Ponty', *Revue socialiste*, December 1955, pp. 551–55.
44. J.-P. Sartre, *Nekrassov*, act 4. sc. 3.
45. *Ibid.*, act 6. sc. 13.
46. *Ibid.*, act 5. sc. 8.
47. Henri Magnan, 'Sartre nous dit… ', *Le Monde*, 1 June 1955.
48. *Sit* IV, pp. 104–5.
49. *L'Humanité*, 24 June 1955.
50. R. Garaudy et al., *Mésaventures de la dialectique*, Paris, 1956, p. 146.

Chapter 12

Debate with the Far Left

For Sartre, as we have seen, 'an anti-Communist is a dog'. But he did go so far as to recognise that there was more than one breed of the species. In fact, in *Les Communistes et la paix* he carefully distinguished between 'left' and 'right' varieties, while arguing for their essential symmetry:

> The 'left' anti-Communist doesn't want to hear any mention of working-class weariness: he shows us a proletariat of steel plunged to the hilt into the corpse of the bourgeoisie. The 'right' anti-Communist shows us the bourgeoisie in the form of a young giantess holding in her arms a dying proletariat. In either case, it means passing over in silence anything that looks like reciprocal conditioning, in short, denying the class struggle.[1]

He attributed to the 'left' anti-Communists a belief in spontaneity which he scorned as being nothing but wishful thinking:

> Has anyone ever seen a proletariat without combativity? And didn't Marx say that it would be revolutionary or it would not be? So it *is*, it *must be*, or else the anti-Communist Marxists would lose hope and their reason for existing. Therefore there *must* exist within it an impulse, deceived, misled, perverted by the wicked. Can no trace of it be found? That's because it is not directly accessible to our senses.[2]

Trotskyism in particular was dismissed because it based 'the abstract rationalism of an oppositionist on a pragmatic irrationalism'.[3]

Sartre's analysis assumed that no serious political force could exist to the left of the PCF, and that those individuals or groupings which claimed to stand to its left were either insignificant or malicious. The reality was considerably more complex. There was a political space to the left of the PCF and Sartre became involved in debate with various elements of it,

---

both in *Les Communistes et la paix* and in other polemics arising out it. These are a matter of public record and cannot be written out of history.

One of Sartre's targets in *Les Communistes et la paix* was Georges Altman, with whom he had worked in the RDR, and whom he now saw as a typical representative of the 'left anti-Communists'. In the three years since the collapse of the RDR, Altman and his paper *Franc-Tireur* had taken an increasingly pro-American and anti-Communist position. Sartre understood quite clearly the responsibilities of the PCF in the matter: 'M Altman... is not a traitor, not even a wicked man. But the Communists treated him with the technique used by Charles Boyer in *Gaslight*: you make the patient believe by repeated devices that he is mad and evil. After three months of this treatment, M. Altman is already more than half convinced'.[4]

Nonetheless, Sartre felt with some justice that Altman had gone over to the enemy. Altman set out his response to the Ridgway demonstration in a signed editorial[5] which was quoted in *Les Communistes et la paix*. He began by arguing that the repression faced by Communists in France was far less severe than that faced by oppositionists in the Eastern bloc, and blamed the situation on the absence of a left alternative to the PCF: 'if .. a bold social democracy were able to take away from the Stalinists the monopoly of defending the workers, we shouldn't be in this situation'. He described the PCF's anti-Americanism as a form of racism, and added 'Now it isn't even a question of Communism any more, but of "Russianism" (*russisme*)'. His conclusion was a clear refusal to take up the issue of defending Communists:

> And then today we are asked to freely consent to let ourselves be strangled. Very sorry! From now on we shall only have the heart to protest in favour of the Communists when they are willing to stop deporting, imprisoning, killing and causing the disappearance of all those who do not think as they do.

Altman's attack on the absence of civil liberties in Stalinist regimes was wholly justified. Yet the real issue was obscured. Altman made no distinction between the ruling parties of the Eastern bloc and the PCF, very much excluded from power by France's right-wing government. If it was true that the PCF was mechanically loyal to Russian instructions, it was also true that the PCF and the CGT had mass support from the French working class. If Sartre overstated the case by claiming that the working class would not exist without the PCF, Altman erred in the opposite direction by denying the PCF's working-class base altogether.

Not surprisingly, Sartre's positions in *Les Communistes et la paix* provoked considerable discussion among all sections of the French left. Many of those coming from a revolutionary anti-Stalinist tradition considered that Sartre was guilty of betrayal by his association with the PCF.

For example, a left current still existed in the SFIO, a successor to the *gauche révolutionnaire* of the 1930s in which Colette Audry had been active. In January 1953 the former leader of the *gauche révolutionnaire*, Marceau

Pivert, contributed a stinging attack on Sartre and *Les Communistes et la paix* to the *Revue socialiste*; the official journal of the SFIO.[6] Pivert argued a position on Russia similar to Rousset's, namely that Russia was a new form of society that was neither capitalist nor socialist. He claimed that 'there is no longer a capitalist class in Russia or the satellite countries'. The corollary was that the working class did not exist either; Russian workers had been transformed into 'gagged slaves'. The logic was that workers were better off in capitalist France than under Stalinist dictatorship. A further corollary was that the PCF desired to become a new ruling elite in the Russian style, and that Sartre had become an agent of this aspirant dictatorship: 'So now we have J.-P. Sartre transformed into a recruiting sergeant for the PCF, that is, a machine for crushing individuals and the working class in order that the elite caste of totalitarian bureaucrats may triumph'.

Pivert argued for 'a third way, a third camp', which would be that of democratic socialism. He went on to maintain that the masses were right to refuse to follow the PCF's call for a peace demonstration because the Stalinists refused to adopt the slogan of Liebknecht: 'The main enemy is at home'. Paradoxically Pivert failed to see that this was precisely the logic that lay behind Sartre's position – namely that the first enemy to be confronted must be that in France.

The *Revue socialiste* also carried a second piece attacking Sartre, this time by the veteran Spanish revolutionary Julián Gorkin,[7] ex-Communist, ex-Trotskyist and former leader of the Spanish POUM. The main thrust of his article was devoted to denouncing Stalinism, while never making clear whether this implied taking the pro-U.S. side. In fact the article did not go very far politically, for Gorkin adopted the easier option of attacking Sartre's personality. He recalled his own acquaintance with Sartre, remembering that Sartre had made himself at home in a worker's flat, but had made André Gide walk up four flights of stairs: 'Pride and disrespect towards one of the literary glories of France; smug humility in dealing with a proletarian'.

Sartre took no apparent notice of these attacks from the ranks of the SFIO. The various manifestations of the Trotskyist left proved rather more demanding. In this period he was obliged to confront both orthodox Trotskyism and the post-Trotskyism of the *Socialisme ou barbarie* grouping.

Orthodox Trotskyism was represented by the French section of the Fourth International (International Secretariat). In *Les Communistes et la paix* Sartre devoted some fourteen pages to a detailed critique of an article by E. Germain in *La Vérité des travailleurs*.[8] Germain was the pseudonym of the well-known economist and Fourth International leader Ernest Mandel.

Germain had begun by referring to the Marty–Tillon affair, in which two veteran leaders of the PCF had been purged. One of the issues raised had been the question of the PCF's strategy at the time of the Liberation, and whether in fact it had been possible to make a bid for power at that time. Germain pointed to the effects of the PCF's policies, showing that the

Party's membership had fallen from one million to half a million, and that of the PCF-led CGT from six million to two-and-a-half million. He contrasted the balance of class forces at the end of the war with that existing in 1952: 'Then fascists, cops and collaborators were arrested; now trade-union activists are sacked and Communist militants are arrested'. The clear implication was that if the PCF could risk an aggressive action like the Ridgway demonstration in 1952, it could have dared much more in 1944.

Germain examined what a revolutionary strategy in that period would have been. It was not simply a question of making a bid for state power, but rather of developing class consciousness and organisation, working towards what the Bolsheviks described as 'dual power':

> We don't say that power should have been seized on 28 August 1944. That would indeed have been adventurism. But we say that throughout the period 1944–1945 there were *hundreds of opportunities* to create and develop the seeds of a new form of power, which in any case the masses had themselves formed (liberation committees, factory committees, patriotic militias). The duty of a true Communist leadership, following the example of Lenin, would have been to develop to their maximum extent these positions which had been won, and to exploit these possibilities as much as possible. What would have happened later would have resulted from the evolution of the relations of forces that nobody can ever foresee precisely.

Sartre responded that since on Germain's own analysis the PCF had a pro-Moscow leadership opposed to any attempt to take power in France, the conditions simply did not exist: 'What then becomes of the "possibility" of 1944? The die was cast. And if a few enthusiasts believed that they were going to lead the working class to victory, it was because they had seen the details of the situation without considering it as a whole'.[9]

Mandel wrote a reply which was submitted to *Les Temps modernes* but not published.[10] He rejected Sartre's appeal to reality: 'It's the very argument used by Hegel to sanctify the absolutist state, an argument which Marx mocks mercilessly'. And he observed that in Bolivia and Ceylon the Trotskyists had the majority of the working class; on Sartre's own logic he should support Trotskyism in those countries.[11]

He went on to undermine Sartre's argument about the relation of party and class, showing that Sartre's formulation was oversimplified and mechanical:

> Does the proletariat becomes a class – a class for itself, since it is a class in itself by the fact of its place in the process of production – by constituting itself into a political party? Of course. But what Marx has in mind here is not an act of joining, repeated thousands of times over, in relation to a specific day-by-day policy of a particular party. What Marx has in mind is the historical conquest – repeated periodically at great turning points in history – of class consciousness, by breaking with the organisations, the ways of thought and action of the opposing class.[12]

Mandel neatly turned Sartre's own earlier positions back against him, showing a knowledge of his work and quoting Sartre's own words: 'To try and save others without their involvement means destroying all value in the salvation that is imposed on them',[13] and 'I think I recall that class struggle and emancipation of the proletariat were conceived by Marx as always having to go hand in hand'.[14]

Unlike Pivert, Mandel did not see the PCF as existing outside the working class; he saw it as rooted in the actual realities of French working-class life. But at the same time he saw how the tendencies to reformism and bureaucracy resulted from its position in society: 'the reformist bureaucracy originates from the links between the labour movement and bourgeois society'.[15] He concluded by stressing that what was crucial was not any particular form of organisation, but the advancement of working-class consciousness and self-confidence, for it was only on these that the self-emancipation of the working class could be based: 'Trotskyism is the art of adapting means to the end, the art of arriving at victory over capitalism by the only means which ensure a rapid and genuine transition towards socialism: the blossoming of the working class's awareness of its own strength and of its self-confidence'.[16]

With its clarity and focus on working-class consciousness, Mandel's article was one of the most acute critiques of *Les Communistes et la paix*. If Sartre disregarded it and made no answer at the time, it may nonetheless have crept into his consciousness. For after the experience of 1968 Sartre radically changed his estimation of the possibilities in 1944:

> Since 1945, the Western Communist Parties, in particular the French CP, have been trained by Stalinism not to take power. The world had been divided up at Yalta, the division was good, and the Soviets intended to respect the contract… All the men who, in the PCF, tried to push forward the gains which the Communists had made by their admirable attitude during the war, who tried to win reforms that were in some sense revolutionary, who urged workers to be more combative, were recalled to order by the Party, reduced to silence or expelled. Because it was not the Party's objective to make the revolution.[17]

It is possible to hear more than an echo of Mandel's words in these lines. They were also a return to the position Sartre himself had argued in his 1947 radio broadcast, showing that Sartre's pro-Stalinism of the 1950s was only a temporary aberration.

Perhaps the most interesting of the groupings of the anti-Stalinist revolutionary left was *Socialisme ou barbarie*, which had emerged from a split in the Trotskyist movement in the late 1940s. *Socialisme ou barbarie* rejected the Bolshevik notion of a vanguard party; it did not attempt to recruit or to build an alternative leadership for the working class. The strength of *Socialisme ou barbarie* was the fact that it looked beyond the official organisations that claimed to represent the working class to the actual experience of the working class on the shop floor. The journal carried many descriptions of day-to-day working life, notably those by Daniel Mothé, a milling-machine operator at the Renault Billancourt vehicle factory. In the mid-1950s *Socialisme ou barbarie* represented the most innovative current of the French revolutionary left.

Needless to say, *Les Communistes et la paix* did not please *Socialisme ou barbarie*; it promptly provoked Castoriadis, writing as Pierre Chaulieu, to a vigorous and vehement (though often witty) diatribe against Sartre.[18] Unlike Pivert, who saw the PCF as wholly outside the working-class movement, Chaulieu stressed its contradictory nature; it had a genuine working-class base, but its pro-Russian policies obstructed its claim to working-class backing. As a result its capacity to mobilise was declining, though workers still supported it in union and parliamentary elections because the SFIO offered no alternative, and because they recognised that the collapse of the Communist-led CGT trade-union federation would lead to an employers' offensive.

In this recognition of the need to defend existing organisations there are some points of contact with Sartre's position; but Chaulieu poured scorn on any attempt to seek united action with the PCF. Invoking the case of Trotsky, Chaulieu mocked: 'Someone who had led two revolutions, one of them successful, and created the first proletarian army, spent his last years trying to create an independent proletarian organisation ready to form a united front with the Communist Party, until the day that the Stalinists murdered him'.[19]

Chaulieu made the same accusation of worship of the accomplished fact as Mandel, but expressed it in more venomous personal terms. He claimed that for Sartre it was not ideas but results that mattered – in Sartre's own words, 'the true idea is the effective idea'. For Sartre, he alleged, effectiveness amounted to getting five million votes in the elections or filling the *Vélodrome d'Hiver* (a large stadium in Paris frequently used by the PCF for mass rallies). This was the basis on which Sartre had approached the PCF.[20]

Chaulieu jeered at Sartre's concern for efficacy as set out in his dispute with Camus: 'Touchingly, he pointed out to him that they were both bourgeois, but that at least he, Sartre, "would take care to pay the price"... That day, the infant mortality rate in the working-class suburbs of Paris fell'.[21] Chaulieu totally rejected Sartre's identification of party and class:

> Is it necessary to add that just because every party expresses at a given moment of its existence a necessary stage for this development of the proletariat, it by no means follows that one should always support the strongest 'workers'' party in the country where one is? Only someone with the temperament of a sycophant or a parliamentarian could draw such a conclusion.[22]

Chaulieu did not entirely deny Sartre's good intentions, but saw him as having no concept of working-class self-emancipation. Back in 1900 Sartre would have been a paternalist factory owner; today, with nothing but his royalties, he was a Stalinist.[23] Chaulieu was very sceptical about Sartre's response to the Ridgway demonstration, saying that he would have been indifferent to the failure of a strike for economic demands, but a strike for political ends – ends of which Chaulieu obviously disapproved – inspired long articles in *Les Temps modernes*.

Chaulieu also took up the question of the nature of Russian society. He observed that Sartre saw Russia as a 'workers' state', thereby neglecting the basic fact of exploitation. He noted that Sartre invoked the argument that Russian workers did not oppose their exploitation; but he commented that the same observation had been used to claim that Russian workers had been turned into slaves and no longer had the capacity to emancipate themselves.

Sartre did not respond to Chaulieu. But he had been unable to avoid a sharp confrontation with the other leading member of *Socialisme ou barbarie*, Claude Lefort, who was a member of the *Temps modernes* team. As time went on the tensions between Lefort's views and Sartre's became unbearable. Despite Merleau-Ponty's efforts to mediate, which succeeded in removing a few particularly intemperate passages from the exchange,[24] the debate was a bitter one, with some sharp blows and vicious insults. Many of Lefort's points were indisputably valid, and Sartre's aggressive style can best be explained by the fact that he was covering up his own vulnerability and vacillation. Ronald Aronson is probably correct in speculating that 'Sartre's alignment with the Communists could only be accomplished by considerable internal violence'.[25]

Lefort's article[26] was written as a critique of the first two sections of *Les Communistes et la paix*. He began by challenging Sartre's claim that 'the PCF is the only pole around which those who are opposed to war can gather'.[27] He countered this with the argument that working-class organisation was formed in struggle, and that the basic forms of organisation derived from the direct economic needs of workers in the production process:

> If we observe the way in which workers, from the beginning, conduct their struggle, oppose bourgeois legality in practice, create autonomous organs of struggle, factory committees or soviets, in other words act according to new social norms, then it is clear that their demands, whatever their explicit scope, are revolutionary. A factory committee has no function or meaning in a system of exploitation and it is therefore the negation of it even if its objective is only an increase in wages or a new contract.[28]

Lefort argued that it was precisely the nature of capitalist production which made the working class the potential revolutionary class that it was. Since methods of production were in a state of constant revolutionary change, the proletariat was required to continually rethink its perception of the world and its forms of organisation. So for Lefort the position of the proletariat in production had to be the starting point of any analysis.

He went on to elaborate a theory of the roots of Stalinism, which he saw as the product of a tendency to bureaucracy that had a long history in the labour movement, but which had now given rise to a separate social layer.[29] Sartre had attacked the notion of working-class spontaneity; Lefort responded that in this attack, Sartre's target was in fact the concept of autonomous history or experience, since he maintained that the class was nothing without the party and could have no manifestation independently of it.[30]

Lefort rejected any notion that the emancipation of the working class could be achieved by a group external to the working class and substituting itself for it. While not taking a wholly negative view of Bolshevism, he argued that Bolshevism was a product of specific Russian conditions rather than a model for universal imitation. And he insisted that before 1917 Lenin had always stressed the self-activity of the class rather than the role of the party leadership; it was only with the isolation of the Russian Revolution and the decline of mass participation that Lenin had moved towards the position that the party must substitute itself for the class.

Yet after an effective onslaught on many of Sartre's positions, Lefort's conclusions were surprisingly modest. He proposed no organisational alternative, no political strategy for the present period. All that intellectuals such as himself could do was to analyse the situation and trust in the spontaneous activity of the class:

> As soon as we realise that praxis is struggle and the process of becoming of the class, Stalinism can be restored to its place in proletarian experience and the most important question becomes clarifying this experience and helping it to develop, not seeking to replace the current party by another party which, being imposed from outside, would necessarily have the same features.[31]

Sartre was dismissed as an empiricist for wishing to involve himself in political action in the immediate present; Lefort predicted that he would soon abandon even the claim to revolutionary politics, and would come to argue that the revolution was a myth, and that pacifism was the only virtue in the present period.[32]

Sartre was stung to reply in the same issue of *Les Temps modernes*.[33] The combination of the validity of much of Lefort's case, and the malice of Lefort's concluding prediction, doubtless helped to account for the unusually vindictive tone of Sartre's reply. There were some witty but malevolent gibes – 'if I were a "young employer", I should be a Lefortist'; 'The *Figaro*, which like you aims, probably for different reasons, to separate the class from its apparatus...'.[34] Sartre strongly denied identifying the party with the class: 'Where did I write that the party was identical to the class? It would be like calling the piece of string which binds the asparagus a bunch'.[35] He sneered at *Socialisme ou barbarie*, which contained only a few exceptionally theoretically minded workers, and was remote from what Sartre saw as the reality of working-class life, since the majority of workers voted Communist.[36]

The main thrust of Sartre's reply was to deny Lefort's claim that the proletariat's role in production was sufficient to make it revolutionary. On the contrary, he stressed the need for revolutionary organisation and the deliberate cultivation of revolutionary consciousness. He denied Lefort's argument about the revolutionising effect of the labour process, claiming that the effect of deskilling was to brutalise workers rather than to radicalise them. He argued that this could only be counteracted by the effect of Communist organisation in the class; to ask for a working class without Communists was to presume that the proletariat could organise spontaneously and that parties and unions had no value.

The Communists, he claimed, represented an active minority within the class, who had an impact on the majority who remained outside parties and unions. He thus sought to establish a dialectical interaction between class and leadership: 'I see that leaders are nothing without the masses, but the class has no cohesion and power except to the extent that it trusts its leaders'.[37]

Moreover, he argued, by rooting the PCF in a tendency towards bureaucracy within French society, Lefort missed the importance of the Russian influence on French Communism. In a passage which must have been profoundly upsetting to Kanapa and his other PCF friends, Sartre invoked Trotsky and Rosa Luxemburg on his side of the argument, claiming that 'the task is not to show the party dictating to the masses what their opinion should be. The party is distinguished from the masses only inasmuch as it unites them'.[38]

He pointed out that left oppositionists like Trotsky and Serge had always recognised historical alternatives, and had claimed that the degeneration of the Russian Revolution was not inevitable, but that Lefort had abandoned this recognition of historical choice – what Sartre called 'Trotskyist possibilism'[39] – by claiming that the rule of a working-class minority must inevitably turn into an exploiting bureaucracy. Sartre claimed that Lefort's position had been better when he was an orthodox Trotskyist, and believed that there was at least a fifty-fifty chance of success.[40]

Sartre concluded by turning the tables on Lefort; it was not Sartre who worshipped the accomplished fact, but rather Lefort who accepted existing reality passively. Sartre concluded by accusing Lefort of 'quietism' and labelling him a 'solipsist'.[41]

Lefort's reply to all this did not appear for over a year, although it was dated 'June 1953'. Either this was a misprint for 1954, or there was some dispute which delayed publication; Lefort by now was in Brazil.[42] He responded irritably to the tone of Sartre's polemic, and contrasted his own political record favourably with Sartre's, recalling the latter's misfortunes with the RDR and his flirtation with Titoism. He made some other telling points, for example noting that Sartre's account of the 1936 Popular Front was borrowed from a work by two Trotskyists,[43] who, he claimed, confirmed Lefort's view of the importance of spontaneity, and of the role of the PCF.[44] He observed that in Sartre's discussion of the PCF and the USSR 'you simply validate two unknowns each by the other'; the revolutionary credentials of the PCF were proved by its dependence on Russia, those of Russia by its support for the PCF. And he scornfully rejected Sartre's dismissal of 'abstract freedom', arguing that workers' ability to make demands, to defend their conditions through trade unions, had been the precondition for social progress.[45]

He was scathing about the role of the PCF in the factories, saying that if Sartre were to ask actual proletarians about the Party,

> they would tell you that the PCF's policy is disastrous for the proletariat, that they saw its true face in 1947, when it was sharing power with the bourgeoisie and the CGT was walking hand in hand with the employers, when Stalinist squads came to Renault to attack strikers with clubs; that the PCF only defends workers' demands to the extent that they are useful to it in putting the employers in difficulties, but that they are not concerned about achieving them; that the staggered or rotating strike, allegedly a means of harassment, is demoralising, that those involved feel isolated each time and are in fact defeated one after the other.[46]

He reminded Sartre that the PCF was not the sole organisation of the working class, but that the class had created many different organisations.

The crux of Lefort's reply was the social and historical role of the working class. He accused Sartre of seeing only the negative effects of technological change, thus presenting a brutalised working class, incapable of emancipating itself. And he argued against Sartre's views of the effects of deskilling that

> labour is not so mechanised that it does not leave each worker a margin of initiative whose effects concern all those participating in the same task. Here is an automatic lathe which trims down metal cones, and here is another which points them. Between the workers operating them there is an elementary solidarity, so that one respects the angle he must establish sufficiently for the other to be able to carry out his pointing. And this solidarity is even more perceptible on a production line where the mistakes of one worker ruin the work of his neighbour or of all the others.[47]

He threw back again at Sartre the accusation of worship of the accomplished fact. If, as Sartre argued, the PCF must be supported in France because it was the only political party representative of the workers, then the same logic would require support for the Labour Party in Britain or the American union bosses.[48]

While not idealising Leninism, Lefort pointed out that blind anti-Communists and pro-Stalinists converged in equating Leninism and Stalinism. The PCF, however, he claimed, was neither revolutionary nor reformist, but was preparing the way for a new type of power, in order simultaneously to eliminate the bourgeoisie and to install a new form of exploitation.[49]

So ended the debate, with neither side offering a convincing way forward. But despite all the illusions and misjudgements, Sartre's political priorities in the 1950s remained rooted in his alignment with the exploited and oppressed. From this he derived two basic principles, principles that helped him to remain on the road when so many others skidded off it.

The first was the principle that Sartre and Merleau-Ponty argued in their editorial on the Russian labour camps,[50] and which Sartre reiterated in his polemic with Camus, the principle of Lenin and Liebknecht that the main enemy is at home. This principle implied that revolutionaries could not rise above national boundaries in order to establish an impartial league table of the degree of repression in various societies. They existed within a particular nation state, and the place where they could most effectively fight was on their own territory. Moral indignation about repression abroad could all too easily be a soft option compared with facing the employers and police of one's own society.

Secondly, Sartre insisted that alignment with the working class could not be envisaged other than in terms of the organisations which, for better or worse, continued to hold the loyalty of the majority of conscious and active workers. The PCF could not be written off, ignored or by-passed. Although, as *Socialisme ou barbarie* correctly reported, many workers were sceptical of the PCF's political intentions, they recognised that they would be even worse off if they had no organisation at all. If a right-wing government had succeeded in banning the PCF – not a wholly implausible scenario: the West German Communist Party was banned in 1956 – it would have been a major setback for the working class and no one calling themselves socialist could doubt which side to take.

In his polemic with Sartre, Lefort recommended the book *The American Worker* by Paul Romano, which had been translated in *Socialisme ou barbarie*.[51] The book contained a vivid description of the reality of factory life and was sharply critical of the role of trade unions. Nonetheless Romano recorded: 'In spite of the workers' dislike of the bureaucracy, they would positively defend their union against an attempt to bust it. As one worker put it; "Any union is better than no union" '.[52]

Sartre, despite everything, understood this basic principle. True, he often lapsed into a fetishisation of party organisation which led him to defend the indefensible. But he was always aware that a rejection of all organisation would lead to complete scepticism. Contrary to Lefort's prediction, Sartre remained a revolutionary while many of the adherents of *Socialisme ou barbarie* eventually drifted into the morass of postmodernism. Whatever his misjudgements, Sartre never abandoned the possibility of political action. And when, in 1956, the ice broke and the range of possibilities suddenly broadened, Sartre was able to revise his position.

Notes

1. *Sit* VI, p. 254.
2. *Sit* VI, p. 214.
3. *Sit* VI, p. 232.
4. *Sit* VI, p. 82.
5. G. Altman, 'Le temps du délire', *Franc-Tireur*, 29 May 1952.
6. M. Pivert, 'J.-P. Sartre, la classe ouvrière et le stalinisme', *Revue socialiste* 63, January 1953, pp. 76–84.
7. *Revue socialiste* 66, April 1953, pp. 424–35.
8. E. Germain, 'On pouvait prendre le pouvoir en 1944–45', *La Vérité des travailleurs*, October 1952, pp. 2–3.
9. *Sit* VI, p. 222.
10. 'Lettre à Jean-Paul Sartre', *Quatrième Internationale*, January 1953; reproduced in E. Mandel, *La Longue marche de la révolution*, Paris, 1976, pp. 83–123. Mandel did write for *Les Temps modernes* after 1956 – articles on the Belgian general strike (April 1961), neocapitalism (August–September 1964), Soviet planning (June 1965), etc.
11. Mandel, 'Lettre à Jean-Paul Sartre', pp. 86–88.
12. *Ibid.*, p. 99.
13. *Ibid.*, p. 106, citing F. Jeanson, *Le problème moral et la pensée de Sartre*, Paris, 1947, pp. 354–55.
14. *Ibid.*, p. 106, citing Sartre, Rousset and Rosenthal, *Entretiens*, p. 23.
15. Mandel, 'Lettre à Jean-Paul Sartre', p. 110.
16. *Ibid.*, p. 122.
17. *Sit* VIII, pp. 212–13; see also J. Gerassi, *Jean-Paul Sartre – Hated Conscience of his Century*, vol. I, Chicago, 1989, p. 183.
18. P. Chaulieu, 'Sartre, le stalinisme et les ouvriers', *Socialisme ou barbarie*, August–September 1953, pp. 63–88.
19. Chaulieu, 'Sartre, le stalinisme', p. 66. Trotsky was well aware of this contradiction; a contradiction which he perceived as being in the nature of Stalinist parties rather than in himself; shortly before his death he defended his position vigorously in discussions with the leaders of the American Socialist Workers Party. 'I know. They have even shot at us. But some tens of thousands of workers are with them… the question is the Stalinist workers. The working class is decisive'. See 'Discussions with Trotsky' (12–15 June, 1940), in *Writings of Leon Trotsky 1939–40*, New York, 1973, p. 262.
20. Chaulieu, 'Sartre, le stalinisme', p. 65.
21. *Ibid.*, p. 65.
22. *Ibid.*, p. 88.
23. *Ibid.*, p. 83.
24. *Sit* IV, p. 257.
25. R. Aronson, *Jean-Paul Sartre: Philosophy in the World*, London, 1980, p. 222.
26. C. Lefort, 'Le marxisme et Sartre', *TM*, April 1953, pp. 1541–70.
27. Lefort, 'Le marxisme', p. 1541.
28. *Ibid.*, pp. 1546–47.
29. *Ibid.*, pp. 1556–58.
30. *Ibid.*, p. 1562.
31. *Ibid.*, p. 1568.
32. *Ibid.*, p. 1569.
33. J.-P. Sartre, 'Réponse à Lefort', *Les Temps modernes*, April 1953, pp. 1571–1629; reproduced in *Sit* VII, pp. 7–93.
34. *Sit* VII, pp. 13, 83.
35. *Sit* VII, p. 8.
36. *Sit* VII, pp. 20–21.
37. *Sit* VII, p. 60.

38. *Sit* VII, p. 60.
39. *Sit* VII, p. 82.
40. *Sit* VII, pp. 91–92.
41. *Sit* VII, p. 93.
42. C. Lefort, 'De la réponse à la question', *TM*, July 1954, pp. 157–84.
43. J. Danos and M. Gibelin, *Juin 36*, Paris, 1952. Danos and Gibelin were both contributors to the special edition of *Les Temps modernes* on 'La Gauche' in 1955. It may have been Lefort who first drew Sartre's attention to their work.
44. Lefort, 'De la réponse', p. 171.
45. *Ibid.*, p. 183.
46. *Ibid.*, p. 160.
47. *Ibid.*, pp. 173–74.
48. *Ibid.*, p. 179.
49. *Ibid.*, p. 182.
50. 'Les Jours de notre vie', *TM* 51, January 1950, pp. 1153–68.
51. *TM*, July 1954, p. 165.
52. P. Romano and R. Stone, *The American Worker*, Detroit, 1972, p. 25.

Chapter 13

LAYING THE GHOST

The year 1956 was to be a momentous one, in which the hegemony of Moscow over the international Communist movement was severely shaken, though not destroyed. The fixed certainties of the map of the left were undermined, and the prospects for an independent anti-Stalinist left improved markedly. Sartre's *rapprochement* with the PCF was coming to an end. As a result he was obliged to seek new allies and to redefine his relations with both the PCF and the anti-Stalinist left.

Already at the beginning of the year there were signs of growing friction. In January, Pierre Hervé, a leading PCF intellectual who had vilified Sartre at the time of the RDR, published a book called *La Révolution et les fétiches*,[1] in which he made implied criticisms of the PCF's dogmatism. He was promptly expelled from the Party.

In February Sartre devoted an article to the affair. Unaware of the storms ahead, Sartre chose his words carefully in order not to provoke his friends in the PCF. He observed that the PCF displayed 'extraordinary objective intelligence' and that it was rarely mistaken. But he went on to note that as far as PCF intellectuals were concerned, they had failed to develop Marxism as an intellectual tool, leaving the field to non-Marxists like Guillemin and Lévi-Strauss. He concluded: 'In France, Marxism has stopped'.[2]

Some of Sartre's friends on the anti-Stalinist left welcomed the new orientation. Daniel Guérin, former *pivertiste* and regular contributor to *Les Temps modernes*, wrote an article in *Combat* in which he noted that it would be easy to raise 'quibbles' (*chicanes*) about Sartre's past errors and his continuing illusions about Stalinism. But that would be petty and would neglect what was positive in Sartre's article, namely the 'thrashing' he had given to the Stalinist intellectuals and the perspectives he had opened for a Marxism liberated from Stalinism. With only the mildest hint of irony he

---

added that though others had said this before, 'the fact of being right before Sartre does not take away from Sartre the merit of being right today'.[3]

A more provocative rejoinder came from Pierre Naville, who responded to Sartre's argument in an article entitled 'Les mésaventures de Nekrassov'. Here he argued that Marxism must not be confused with Stalinism, and that it would be the progress of the class struggle that would lead to a renewal of Marxism:

> If Stalinism can be liquidated, it is because in the last resort the evolution of the USSR itself and of the whole world, the overthrow of the society which has been observed there for the last twenty years, justify the ideas of Marx such as they were interpreted by the likes of Lenin, Rosa Luxemburg and Trotsky rather than the distortions to which they were repeatedly subjected by the imitators of Stalin.[4]

Sartre replied promptly. He began by noting that Naville could not be compared with right-wing critics of the PCF because of his life and works and his record of struggle. He insisted that Naville and his colleague from *France-Observateur*, Gilles Martinet, were not anti-Communists at all, and criticised the PCF for the attacks made on them. Yet Sartre claimed that Naville's philosophical method meant he was unable to grasp dialectics:

> This mechanistic materialist makes use of the language and arguments of Marxism but he is incapable of discovering the dialectic in things or in ideas. He claims that science needs contradictions to live, but contradictions, wherever they may be, seem scandalous to him: is it not striking that he rushed to write his article because he thought he had discovered one in mine?[5]

The dispute could be traced back to the criticisms Naville had made of Sartre's *L'Existentialisme est un humanisme* in 1945. But because Sartre's criticisms of Stalinism focused on its philosophical method (reductionism, mechanical materialism), rather than on its political strategy (popular frontism, socialism in one country), he evaded rather than responded to Naville's points. Sartre still believed that anyone who attempted to position themselves to the left of the PCF automatically found themselves moving to the right, whatever their personal intentions. From this it was a short step to the cheap insult that anti-Communists were simply making a career out of permanent opposition. With a joke plagiarised from George Orwell's account of the professional anti-fascist in *Coming Up for Air*[6] ('A queer trade, anti-Fascism. This fellow, I suppose, makes his living by writing books against Hitler... what'll he do if Hitler ever disappears?'), he mocked:

> Finally, they must admit their constant concern to remain in the opposition. From Naville to Altman, they have all felt the same threat: 'Stalin was our reason for living; if the Russians denounce his errors, what will become of us?' Altman worked within the Apocalypse: what will be left of him if his terrifying effects are taken away from him? Film reviews in the *Canard enchaîné*? And Naville, who had been delivering judgements for thirty years: is he going to have to retire?

He ended with a quite unfair claim that Naville's methodology was complicit with Stalinism, and that Naville was stuck in the past:

> To him it seems unbearable that someone can preserve their independence and call himself the ally of the Communists. I understand his pain and I can forgive it: today such an attitude is easy; in his day, it was impossible… He should be careful: already, when he goes up to speak from the platform, his finger raised, his eye lifeless, his mouth open, you have the impression of seeing a monolith trotting along. If he goes on like this, this old champion of anti-Stalinism will soon be the last Stalinist in France.[7]

Naville responded, both with a short piece in *France-Observateur*,[8] and with a longer piece, issued in pamphlet form.[9] Naville was indignant at what he called Sartre's use of 'the vocabulary of police state Stalinism'. But he went on to make some significant substantive points. Firstly he criticised Sartre for following PCF sectarianism in writing off the SFIO, by lumping it and the Christian Democratic Mouvement Républicain Populaire together in the same reactionary sack. He insisted: 'Behind this label SFIO there are men, and among them many workers. There are even three and a half million voters, which is far from nothing'.[10]

Naville stood by Trotsky's definition of Russia as a workers' state, albeit bureaucratically distorted. He claimed it was Sartre who had failed to take the question of contradiction into account: 'And the contradictions do not disappear in the rudimentary socialist regime which exists in the USSR. We can even say that it is in such a regime that they should appear most clearly, since by definition it is there that they should be used and transcended in a rational and profitable fashion'.[11]

He threw back in Sartre's face the accusations of mechanical materialism by claiming that it was Sartre, the alleged champion of free will, who had collapsed into passivity by his worship of the accomplished fact, his acceptance of the criteria of power and size as outweighing everything else: 'Should we see there a Hegelian justification: all that is real is rational? The root of this pseudorevolutionary conservatism, which here I shall call quietism?'[12]

Another veteran anti-Stalinist who joined the debate was Maurice Nadeau. He sharply attacked Sartre's position on Pierre Hervé, writing: 'Here again we encounter Sartre's old animosity against the PCF's heretics, which, for example, has always made him compare Trotskyists to spies or police agents'.[13]

In his reply to Naville Sartre protested that Nadeau was using a 'Stalinist' method of criticising him, claiming he had always said the exact opposite.[14] And it is true that in 'Matérialisme et révolution' Sartre had argued against the view that Trotskyists were 'objectively' police informers.[15] But Sartre did take it as a premise that there was nothing to the left of the PCF; hence the logic of his position was that any move away from the PCF must be to the right. Nadeau did have a valid point, albeit one expressed somewhat intemperately.

But while these relatively trivial disputes were going on, the world was rapidly moving forward. In February the Twentieth Congress of the Communist Party of the Soviet Union consolidated Khrushchev in power and promised reform; but the most dramatic event was Khrushchev's so-called 'secret speech' – published in millions of copies around the world over the next few months – in which he denounced the crimes of Stalin. There was nothing new here to those who had read their Trotsky or their Serge, but coming from such a source it threw faithful Communists into disarray.

The PCF was one of the most loyally Stalinist parties in the world. At the Twentieth Congress, when foreign Communists gave their fraternal addresses, Maurice Thorez and Mao Tse-tung were the only ones to invoke the name of Stalin alongside Marx, Engels and Lenin – certainly not a slip of the tongue.[16] Until 1958 the PCF leaders were backing the Molotov faction against Khrushchev.[17] Indeed, it was only in 1973 that the PCF formally recognised that the Khrushchev speech was authentic; until then it had been dismissed as a Western forgery.

Sartre reacted slowly to these events. The May issue of *Les Temps modernes* promised that as a conclusion to *Les Communistes et la paix* an article by Sartre would appear shortly replying to Pierre Hervé and others.[18] Who the others were to be, and from what points of the political spectrum they would come, remains unknown, for the article never appeared, overtaken by events.

The same issue contained a short article by Eduard Kardelj, a member of the Yugoslav government, commenting on the Twentieth Congress of the CPSU. This was an anodyne piece, in which Stalin was never even named. But it was prefaced by an editorial note which, presumably, reflected the rather naive optimism of Sartre and his circle at this time that Communism was entering a phase of reform, and that the *rapprochement* would be continued indefinitely:

> The Twentieth Congress of the Communist Party of the USSR has marked the end of the Stalinist era and the return of Communism to its principles. It thus justifies the attitude of all those who, like us, while having no tolerance for the deviations of Stalinism, refused to break with the USSR and the Communist movement.[19]

But in the autumn workers began to write history for themselves, casting aside the empty schemas of intellectuals. Hungarian workers, who had had exaggerated expectations of Khrushchev's promises, staged an insurrection which was suppressed by Russian troops with the utmost brutality. Faced with the spectacle of 'proletarian' tanks being deployed against flesh-and-blood workers, Communists around the world had to choose between symbol and substance. Compared to many other countries the PCF had relatively few defections over Hungary – largely because of the enormous patronage it enjoyed in terms of jobs in factory committees and local authorities – but the events left many of its members shocked and questioning.

For Sartre, the Hungarian rising, like the Ridgway demonstration four years earlier, was a revelation; once again the chains were broken. In *France-Observateur* Sartre, in company with Leiris, Schwartz, Prévert, Audry and others, denounced the Russian intervention, saying that socialism 'is not brought at bayonet point'. But they denied the right of criticism to those who had backed American imperialism in Guatemala in 1954, or who supported the Franco-British invasion of Egypt taking place at that very moment.[20]

Sartre gave a much fuller statement in an interview with *L'Express*.[21] His condemnation of the Russian intervention was unequivocal. He called it a 'crime' and stated: 'I condemn entirely and unreservedly the Soviet aggression'. While making clear that he did not blame the Russian people for the acts of their leaders, he declared that he was breaking off relations with Soviet writers who failed to denounce the intervention. He was scathing about the Socialist Party, which had called on Communist workers to abandon the PCF and join the SFIO – exchanging, as he put it, those who 'approve the crushing of Budapest' for those who 'torture in Algeria'.

But Sartre had not yet entirely broken with his past and some striking contradictions remained in his statements. Thus he argued: 'Some people say: "it was necessary to save the 'bases of socialism' in Hungary". If the bases of socialism had existed in Hungary, socialism would have saved itself unaided. The Red Army intervened to save in Hungary the bases of socialism in the USSR'.

Sartre quite reasonably implied that if the working class had actually held power in Hungary, there would have been no need for the Red Army to prevent it abandoning that power. But on the basis of this logic, what grounds were there for calling the USSR 'socialist'?

Sartre's comments on the Khrushchev speech also showed that he had not yet thought through the logic of his position. This he considered to have been probably 'the gravest mistake', since 'the solemn public denunciation, the detailed exposé of all the crimes of a sacred figure who for so long represented the regime is an act of madness when such frankness is not made possible by a prior and substantial raising of the standard of living of the population'.

Sartre here betrayed a lack of confidence in the ability of working people to absorb and deal with the truth, thus revealing how corrupted he had been by his alliance with the PCF; apparently at this time he could envisage socialism only in terms of something carefully dispensed from above, not as the result of workers themselves coming to terms with the truth. Certainly Sartre was right to see the Khrushchev speech as being 'instead of a full and frank explanation, merely a string of anecdotes'. But he seemed to think complete silence would have been better, while the bureaucracy reformed itself behind closed doors.

As for the PCF, Sartre again found himself grappling with contradictions which certainly existed in reality, but also in his own history. He observed that the PCF was 'in contact with the masses', yet its apparatus 'owed total allegiance to the most intransigent tendency in the Soviet government'. As a result, he declared, he would never be able to resume relations with the present PCF leadership, whose positions resulted from 'thirty years of lies and sclerosis' (the figure was significant, for it dated the degeneration from the defeat of the Left Opposition in the 1920s). Sartre pledged himself to oppose any attempt from the right to ban the PCF, yet seemed confused as to how far his former strategy of influencing the PCF from without remained valid.

Sartre published a much more considered and extensive account of the Hungarian events in the special issue of *Les Temps modernes* which appeared in January 1957, and which had been prepared by François Fetjö, Ladislas Gara and Communist Gérard Spitzer (who was to be expelled from the PCF in February 1957 for his involvement). Sartre's essay, 'Le Fantôme de Staline', offered no comfort to the obdurate Stalinists of the PCF in its denunciation of the Russian intervention; but he also attempted an analysis of Stalinism that generated a set of problems which formed the centre of his theoretical preoccupations in his remaining twenty-three years.

'Le Fantôme de Staline'was just as unequivocal as the *L'Express* interview in its condemnation of the Russians and their French apologists. Sartre took pleasure in comparing the PCF to James Burnham, ex-Trotskyist turned anti-Communist. Burnham believed that contented, well-paid workers could be suddenly provoked into militancy by a handful of Communists; likewise the PCF's advocates apparently believed that otherwise contented workers in socialist Hungary could be incited to revolt by fascist propaganda.[22]

Sartre also made it clear that his disillusion with the East had not in any way endeared him to the West; on the contrary, he argued, anti-Communist conservatives in the West were the 'natural allies of Stalinism'; both wanted to preserve the Cold War and to save arms manufacturers from the 'spectre of peace'.[23]

But Sartre was still caught up with arguments that went back to the late 1940s. In *Les Communistes et la paix* he had polemicised against both 'left' and 'right' anti-Communists. In 'Le Fantôme de Staline' he recognised a presence on his left which had to be included in the debate: 'Even the Communists admit today that it was not merely a fascist putsch; only the Trotskyists maintain that the insurrection had an entirely progressive character. The truth is situated somewhere between these two claims which are equally unfounded and schematic'.[24]

Presumably Sartre was referring to Lefort and his friends in *Socialisme ou barbarie* – no longer strictly Trotskyists – who had been the most enthusiastic about the Hungarian workers' councils. In accusing the left supporters of the Hungarian insurgents of schematism, Sartre was technically correct – no revolution is pure, and undoubtedly there were fascists and nationalists trying to exploit the situation – but he thereby evaded the real question, namely, which was the most important of the class conflicts involved? Sartre was to come back to this point in *Questions de méthode*. He still quite explicitly rejected the position argued, in rather different ways, by Rousset and Lefort, that the societies of the Eastern bloc were exploitative, class societies: 'It is absurd to claim that this bureaucracy *exploits* the proletariat and that it is a *class*, or else words have lost their meaning'.[25]

Sartre's analysis owed more to existentialism than to Marxism. Free-market capitalists were in 'bad faith', while Russian bureaucrats were acting 'authentically': 'the Communist leaders have assumed the entire responsibility for the regime in its greatness and its defects. The liberal bourgeois pleads not guilty: he didn't make the world, and like everyone else he obeys the inexorable laws of the economy'.[26] It was an interesting observation about the difference in ideology between free-market societies and those with 'planned' economies. But it fell a long way short of an adequate distinction between two different socioeconomic systems.

Hence for Sartre the USSR must still be defended, despite all its horrors: 'Should we call this bloody monster which lacerates itself socialism? I reply frankly: yes. It was even the *only* socialism in its primitive phase, there was no other, except perhaps in Plato's heaven, and it was necessary to will that, or not to will any socialism at all'.[27]

Sartre claimed 'all men of the left' would recognise that the USSR must survive '*for the cause of Communism*'. Yet when nothing but 'a vague reference to a future socialism' was used to justify the killing of 'flesh and blood men, even though they are workers, even though they are Communists', Sartre found the situation unacceptable. Hence he returned to the arguments about ends and means he had developed on reading *Their Morals and Ours*:

> We agree with those who say: the end justifies the means; but we add the indispensable corrective: it is the means which define the end. The USSR is not imperialist, the USSR is peaceful, the USSR is socialist, that is correct. But when its leaders, in order to save socialism, launch the people's army against an allied country, when they make their soldiers, those abstract beings, shoot on workers who can no longer put up with their poverty, when, without taking into consideration the concrete demands of the situation, they decide on their course of action on the basis of the impact it will have *elsewhere*, on other countries, and ultimately on the world, they make socialism into a mirage and transform the USSR, despite themselves, despite itself, into a predatory nation.[28]

Unconditional defence of a mirage; a predatory but peaceful nation! Here Sartre's logic was stretched to breaking point. But Sartre was merely responding to a problem which confronted many of those who had broken with Stalinism in 1956. The Khrushchev speech had confirmed the crimes of Stalin to those who had not known – or had not wanted to know – about them before; from now on they could not be denied. Yet, as Sartre had pointed out in the *L'Express* interview, the Khrushchev speech was highly inadequate – 'a string of anecdotes'. It failed to relate Stalin to the overall power structure in the USSR – and for good reason, for Khrushchev himself owed his place and his career to that selfsame structure.

Classical Marxism had always argued that the legal and political super-structure of any given society was to be understood in terms of the relations of production which constituted the base of that society. But if it was held that the economic base in Russia, by virtue of the so-called planned economy, was socialist, while the political dictatorship of Stalin had breached even the most elementary socialist principles, then clearly the model was not working. There were two solutions. One was to abandon the idea that the economic base was socialist; the other to argue that the relation between base and superstructure was much more complex, much more 'mediated' than classical Marxism had allowed for.

Sartre opted for the latter view. The logic was essentially reformist; for if the bureaucracy was relatively autonomous then it was possible to envisage the eradication of abuses without calling into question the supposedly noncapitalist nature of the basic economic relations on which the society was founded. Sartre was to grapple with this problem in two volumes of the *Critique*, but never came to a satisfactory conclusion.

Many years later, in 1970, when Sartre had begun to free himself from his insistence that the USSR was in some sense 'socialist', he argued the point much more lucidly, seeing the complete vacuity of the Khrushchev speech:

> Not an idea, not an analysis, not even an attempt at an interpretation. A 'tale told by an idiot, full of sound and fury'. Let's be clear: Khrushchev's intelligence is not in question; but he was speaking in the name of the system: the machine was sound, but its chief operator was not; happily, this saboteur had relieved the world of his presence, and everything was going to run smoothly again. In short, the new staff were getting rid of a cumbersome corpse just as the old staff had got rid of living people. However, it was *true* that Stalin had ordered massacres, transformed the land of the revolution into a police state; he was *truly* convinced that the USSR would not reach communism without passing through the socialism of concentration camps. But as one of the witnesses very rightly points out, when the authorities find it useful to tell the truth, it's because they can't find any better lie. Immediately this truth, coming from official mouths, becomes a lie corroborated by the facts. Stalin was a wicked man? Fine. But how had Soviet society perched him on the throne and kept him there for a quarter of a century?[29]

It was not, however, simply the class nature of the Eastern bloc states that was at stake. Some of Sartre's opponents, like Pivert, had seen the USSR as a new form of class society in which workers had been transformed into slaves. For them there could be no dynamic of change, either from above or from below. Camus summed up this position in a speech on Hungary in March 1957: 'There is no possible evolution in a totalitarian society. Terror does not evolve, unless for the worse, the scaffold does not liberalise, the gallows are not tolerant. Nowhere in the world have we seen a party or a man holding absolute power fail to use it absolutely'.[30]

As against this rather mechanical analysis, Sartre recognised that within the complicated balance of forces in Stalinist societies, there was a dynamic of change. This still differentiated him from those like Lefort and *Socialisme ou barbarie*, who stressed the importance of workers' self-activity and the creation of workers' councils, and who saw a potential alternative to 'actually existing' socialism in working-class creativity.

Sartre's firm condemnation of the Russian intervention in Hungary marked a clear break with his politics of the previous four years. However, he did not satisfy his critics on the left, who continued to point to the limitations and contradictions of his analysis. In a letter written in February 1957 the Trinidadian Marxist C.L.R. James wrote: 'Sartre is a complete Trotskyite'.[31] The news would probably have been equally surprising to Sartre and to the French Trotskyists of the time, though it might have been more acceptable to PCF leader Maurice Thorez, who around the same time accused Sartre of falling into 'the old Trotskyist raving' because of his opposition to Russian intervention in Hungary.[32] Yet James (an ex-Trotskyist who believed Russia to be state capitalist and who held positions similar to those of *Socialisme ou barbarie*) had grasped something of the contradictions involved in Sartre's reactions. Sartre recognised that there was a bureaucracy in the Eastern bloc – much too well paid but hardworking – but did not conceive of it as a class with interests directly opposed to those of the workers. In this sense James was right; Sartre's position was closer to that of Trotsky himself, who had seen Stalin's Russia as a 'degenerated workers' state', than to the views of Lefort, Rousset or James.

But the sharpest critique came from Sartre's old adversary, Claude Lefort, in an article published a year later. This was a reply not only to Sartre, but to an article by Marcel Péju on Poland, the only instance where *Les Temps modernes* explicitly polemicised against *Socialisme ou barbarie*.[33] Lefort was scathing in his attack on Sartre. He argued that even when Sartre was criticising the Communist Party, he was effectively serving its ends:

> Sartre, once again, but in circumstances of exceptional significance, made himself the only advocate of the CP who could be listened to. Fajon, Stil and Duclos declaimed, and their lies were so crude that militants scarcely took any notice of them. Sartre, on the other hand, while raging against these lies, explained to his Communist readers, students and intellectuals, why they should remain in the Party.[34]

Despite his renunciation of the vanguard party, Lefort was here clearly driven by sectarian logic; he was obviously much more angry with Sartre than with the Stalinists. Indeed, his style here became a mirror image of the Stalinist method. In 1948 *L'Humanité* had proved that *Franc-Tireur* was a Gaullist paper by the fact that it attacked de Gaulle; here Sartre was shown to be a friend of Stalinism precisely because he attacked it.[35]

However, Lefort went on to make some legitimate criticisms of Sartre's position. He claimed that since Sartre failed to see Hungary as an exploitative society, he was unable to fully comprehend the spontaneous and creative nature of the proletarian upsurge. Sartre was thus dodging the essential problem, namely 'the demolition of a pseudosocialist regime by workers who take on socialist aims', and was making a static analysis, by taking the demands of a particular demonstration to show that the masses wanted no more than a Hungarian 'Gomulkism'. (Polish leader Gomulka had tried to initiate cautious reforms while avoiding a Hungarian-style confrontation.):

> To claim that at a given moment the masses are demanding nothing more and nothing less than what they are demanding is to engage in bad idealist psychology. To know exactly what the masses are demanding, they must be observed acting over time. But, precisely, Sartre refuses to do this, he doesn't want to consider the continuity of their action.

He also argued that Sartre was wrong to talk of the danger of a 'reactionary threat' in the sense of the restoration of private property, since the social forces capable of restoring private capitalism did not exist in Hungary. (Lefort was doubtless right at the time; he can scarcely be blamed for failing to predict the very different world that was to exist after 1989.)[36]

Sartre's new analysis implied a major change in his strategy towards the PCF. 'Le Fantôme de Staline' concluded:

> Our programme is clear: through a hundred contradictions, internal struggles, massacres, destalinisation is in progress; it is the only policy which, at the present time, serves the interests of socialism, peace and the closer cooperation of workers' parties. With our resources as intellectuals, read by intellectuals, we shall attempt to assist with the destalinisation of the French Party.[37]

It was a realistic strategy, and indeed all the evidence is that Sartre's work did have some substantial impact on the slow destalinisation of the PCF. But a serious contradiction remained. Sartre had made the question of Hungary central; yet this did not necessarily relate to the domestic activities of the PCF. After all, the prewar Popular Front had enjoyed its greatest successes at the time of the Moscow Trials. Like many Communists and fellow-travellers who broke with Stalinism in 1956, Sartre did so on the basis of a sincere and passionate opposition to the crushing of the Hungarian insurrection; but the break did not involve any critique of the popular front strategy which was central to the PCF's policy inside France.[38]

In 'Le Fantôme de Staline', Sartre had written, stressing that he had been repeating the same thing for the last ten years:

> Only a Popular Front can save our country: it alone can cure our colonial cankers, rescue the economy from Malthusianism, give it a new momentum, organise, under workers' control, a mass production to raise the French standard of living;

it alone can lay the bases of a social democracy, regain national sovereignty, break the Atlantic bloc and put French might at the service of world peace.[39]

For a popular front to institute workers' control would be a historical novelty; Sartre had clearly not studied the restraints and limitations on the 1936 Popular Front programme. Even more importantly, where was this popular front to come from? In 'Le Fantôme de Staline' Sartre devoted several pages to analysing the obstacles to a popular front. In the *L'Express* article he had been even more brutal – the PCF 'owed total allegiance to the most intransigent tendency in the Soviet government', the SFIO was the party of 'those who torture in Algeria' and the Radical Party 'has never really been on the left'.[40] But the SFIO and the Radicals had been central to the Popular Front of the 1930s; it is hard to imagine what possible meaning the term could have if they were to be excluded.

In 1956 Sartre had, with some considerable courage and lucidity, placed himself on the right side of the barricades. But the road ahead was still strewn with difficulties and obstacles, and there was no clear objective in sight.

Notes

1. P. Hervé, *La Révolution et les fétiches*, Paris, 1956.
2. 'Le réformisme et les fétiches', *Sit* VII, pp. 104–18.
3. D. Guérin, 'Sartre et la chute de l'idole', *Combat*, 5 April 1956. I am grateful to Dr David Berry for drawing my attention to this article.
4. *France-Observateur*, 8 March 1956; also published in *TM*, March–April 1956, pp. 1504–9; reproduced in P. Naville, *La Révolution et les intellectuels*, Paris, 1975, pp. 130–37.
5. 'Réponse à Pierre Naville', *TM*, March–April 1956; reproduced in *Sit* VII, pp. 119–43, especially p. 133.
6. G. Orwell, *Coming Up For Air*, Harmondsworth, 1962, p. 145.
7. *Sit* VII, p. 141–43.
8. 'Les nouvelles mésaventures de J.-P. Sartre', 19 April 1956.
9. Both are contained in Naville, *La Révolution et les intellectuels*.
10. Naville, *La Révolution*, p. 145.
11. *Ibid.*, p. 213.
12. *Ibid.*, p. 203.
13. M. Nadeau, 'Sartre et "l'affaire Hervé"', *Les Lettres nouvelles*, April 1956, pp. 591–97, especially p. 592.
14. *Sit* VII, p. 129.
15. *Sit* III, p. 170–71.
16. P. Robrieux, *Histoire intérieure du parti communiste*, Paris, 1980–84, 2: 431.
17. See 'The Khrushchev Speech, the PCF and the PCI' (interview with J. Pronteau and M. Kriegel-Valrimont), in R. Miliband and J. Saville, eds., *The Socialist Register 1976*, London, 1976, pp. 58–60.
18. *TM*, May 1956, p. 1728.
19. *TM*, May 1956, p. 1619.

20.   'Contre l'intervention soviétique', *France-Observateur*, 8 November 1956, p. 4.
21.   J.-P. Sartre, 'Après Budapest, Sartre parle', *L'Express*, 9 November 1956, pp. 13–16.
22.   *Sit* VII, p. 159.
23.   *Sit* VII, p. 265.
24.   *Sit* VII, p. 168.
25.   *Sit* VII, p. 225.
26.   *Sit* VII, p. 219.
27.   *Sit* VII, p. 236.
28.   *Sit* VII, pp. 276–77.
29.   *Sit* IX, p. 252.
30.   'Kadar a eu son jour de peur', *Franc-Tireur*, 18 March 1957.
31.   A. Grimshaw, ed., *The C.L.R. James Reader*, Oxford, 1992, pp. 267–68.
32.   *L'Humanité*, 18 February 1957.
33.   M. Péju, 'Retour de Pologne', *TM*, July–August 1957; see P. Gottraux, *"Socialisme ou barbarie"*, Lausanne, 1997, p. 266.
34.   C. Lefort, 'La Méthode des intellectuels progressistes', *Socialisme ou barbarie* No. 23, January–February 1958; reproduced in C. Lefort, *Eléments d'une critique de la bureaucratie*, Paris, 1979, pp. 251–52.
35.   See E. Fajon, 'Un Journal de M de Gaulle', *L'Humanité*, 12 October 1948. In Lefort's favour it may be noted that a longstanding PCF loyalist, André Wurmser, wrote in his memoirs, *Fidèlement vôtre*, (Paris, 1979), p. 439, that: 'The most intelligent exposition of the causes of the Budapest upheaval was that by Jean-Paul Sartre, and I have never understood why he concluded that he would no longer shake hands with French Communists'.
36.   Lefort, 'La Méthode', in *Eléments*, pp. 251–52, 256, 260–61, 264.
37.   *Sit* VII, p. 307.
38.   The case in Britain of Edward Thompson, who wrote a powerful indictment of the Hungarian events, but continued for the next thirty years to argue for a popular front line in the peace movement, provides an interesting parallel.
39.   *Sit* VII, p. 290.
40.   Sartre, 'Après Budapest', *L'Express*, 9 November 1956, pp. 15, 16.

PART IV

Towards a New Left

Chapter 14

FROM PRACTICE TO THEORY

During his period of *rapprochement* with the PCF Sartre's political writings had been of a polemical nature; precisely because of the profound contra-dictions in his position he had not attempted to give a theoretical exposi-tion of his views. But the crisis of 1956 forced him to return to theory. Indeed, it was the questions posed by 1956 that provided the impetus for the theoretical labours of the next two decades – the *Critique de la raison dialectique* with its unpublished second volume, and the massive but also incomplete biographical study of Flaubert, *L'Idiot de la famille* (1971–72).

The starting point, and in many ways the most impressive piece of work, was a short essay on Marxism and existentialism. This was written in 1957 for a Polish journal.[1] An adapted version appeared in *Les Temps modernes*[2] and was published as the introductory section of the *Critique de la raison dialectique* in 1960 under the title *Question de méthode*. In this essay Sartre alternated, often in a tortuous and obscure manner, between methodological questions of a high level of abstraction and the immediate political questions posed by the crisis of Stalinism. While he claimed in the preface that he was addressing the question: 'Have we today the means of establishing a structural and historical anthropology?', much of *Question de méthode* returned obsessively to problems raised in his polemics of the 1940s and 1950s. Two themes in particular dominated the essay:

- the place of the individual in the Marxist view of history and the development of a nonreductionist Marxism which would allow a rel-ative autonomy to the individual human being;
- the current state of Marxist scholarship and the question as to how Marxism could be renewed as a critical method.

Early in the essay he took up the question of the Marxist response to the Russian intervention in Hungary. On the one hand, Sartre noted, as he already had done in 'Le Fantôme de Staline', that the Stalinists saw the intervention as the necessary suppression of a counterrevolutionary rising; on the other hand 'former Trotskyists' (i.e., *Socialisme ou barbarie*) saw it as Soviet intervention against workers' councils. For Sartre both these accounts were oversimplifications, and hence he declared the need for a method that would enable him to transcend the dichotomy.[3]

The fact that after 1956 Sartre's politics were torn between Stalinism and anti-Stalinism was thus played out in his theoretical endeavours. Paradoxically, the existentialist philosopher of choice had begun to construct a philosophy on the basis of a reluctance to make a clear choice for or against Stalinism.

This led to the more general methodological question of the role of the individual in history. To what extent were individuals to be seen merely as representatives of a social class and bound by historical determinations, and to what extent were they free to act within a given situation? The problem was summed up in a couple of sentences which were to become famous: 'Valéry is a petty bourgeois intellectual, there is no doubt about that. But not every petty bourgeois intellectual is Valéry'.[4]

Sartre's formulation was a neat and effective one, which undermined a great deal of the reductionist nonsense that had emanated from the PCF's intellectuals in the Stalinist years. But it was not as original as is sometimes supposed. Rather than being a novel summarisation of the marriage of Marxism and existentialism, it was very much an echo of something Leon Trotsky had written in the 1930s: 'Not every exasperated petty bourgeois could have become Hitler, but an article of Hitler is lodged in every exasperated petty bourgeois'.[5]

Whether Sartre remembered Trotsky's remark, consciously or subconsciously, or whether the two thinkers had converged on similar formulations from very different starting points, is a secondary question. The point is that here Sartre was returning to the authentic Marxist tradition, which in the dialectics of social evolution had always stressed the scope for human action within the constraining limits of material circumstances. This was made clear by Marx's statement that 'Men make their own history, but they do not make it just as they please; they do not make it under circumstances chosen by themselves, but under circumstances directly encountered, given and transmitted from the past',[6] or Engels' assertion – endorsed by Sartre in *Question de méthode* – that 'Men make their history themselves, only they do so in a given environment which conditions it'.[7] This in turn leads back to the analysis of Stalin in the second volume of the *Critique*: Stalin 'makes himself the man for the situation by the answer he gives to the demands of the moment'.[8] Stalin is thus neither inevitability nor monstrous inexplicable aberration.

The Valéry quote was the basis for Sartre's biographical explorations, especially his monumental study of Flaubert. Moreover, Sartre's stress on the individual enabled him to avoid the complacent orthodoxy of a left that took collectives for granted as something given once and for all. Thus Sartre deeply distrusted the bourgeois notion of 'progress', adopted by the Stalinists and made into a basis for clichés ('all progressive forces', etc., etc.) Again, notably during the Algerian War, Sartre's view of the individual helped to cut through the Stalinist use of mass forces as an alibi for inactivity. Time and again the PCF concealed its own passivity behind the excuse of not 'isolating' itself from the 'masses'. Sartre's practice, especially at the time of the Manifesto of the 121, was predicated on the belief that an individual initiative, while it could and should not be substituted for the masses, could help to set a dynamic of mass action in motion. This perspective was to be validated by the events of 1968, when actions, first by the Paris students, then by workers at Nantes, detonated a general strike.

The other central theme of the *Critique* was the status of Marxism. In trying to establish the basis for a defence of the Marxist methodology, Sartre once again found himself caught up in the debate between Stalinism and the anti-Stalinist left. Thus one of the earliest arguments he developed in the *Critique* was the claim that: 'An alleged "transcendence" of Marxism would at worst be simply a return to premarxism, at best merely the rediscovery of a thought already contained within the philosophy that has been believed to be transcended'.[9]

But this was the very argument which Naville had deployed against Sartre some fifteen years earlier: 'Today, taking up again, in whatever form, a position prior to Marxism, is what I call returning to Radicalism'.[10]

Sartre's defence of this position was disconcertingly brief. By simple assertion, with no elaboration or proof, he identified three 'moments' of philosophy since the seventeenth century – those of Descartes and Locke, of Kant and Hegel, and of Marx.[11] It is perhaps best to take this, not as a historical analysis, but merely as a personal statement by Sartre that he had abandoned the attempt set out in 'Matérialisme et révolution' to develop existentialism as an alternative revolutionary theory to Marxism, and that he henceforth intended to work within the framework of Marxism. Existentialism was now demoted to being merely an 'ideology', a 'parasitic system' attempting to integrate itself within Marxism.[12]

However, Sartre claimed, 'Marxism has stopped', repeating the same phrase he had used in his response to Pierre Hervé the year before. This he linked directly to the encirclement of the USSR and the consequent withdrawal into socialism in one country.[13] He thus reiterated the claim he had made in 'Le Réformisme et les fétiches', that the only serious development of Marxism had been made outside the Communist Party.[14] The significance of this is that Sartre was now openly declaring himself not only as a Marxist, but as one determined to work independently of the Communist Party.

Sartre spent little time in *Question de méthode* dealing with the orthodox thinkers of the PCF such as Garaudy and Kanapa. The only thinkers from within the Stalinist tradition to whom he devoted any significant consideration were Lukács and Henri Lefebvre.

As Sartre was probably aware, Lefebvre was coming to the end of his involvement with the PCF, in which he had been perhaps the most distinguished philosopher, though never a wholly reliable one, till the aftermath of 1956. By temperament he had more in common with the far left. In the 1960s he was to develop links with the Situationists, themselves influenced by *Socialisme ou barbarie*.[15] Sartre praised highly his work on sociological methodology, saying of it: 'It remains regrettable that Lefebvre has not found imitators among other Marxist intellectuals'.[16] Sartre found in Lefebvre something very similar to what he himself was to describe as the 'progressive-regressive method' in the *Critique de la raison dialectique*.

But Sartre was much more interested in the independent Marxists who had pursued their work outside the Stalinist framework. Although he could be sharply critical of their work, there was always a recognition that their mistakes were honest errors rather than the product of political expediency.

One thinker commended in *Question de méthode* was Lucien Goldmann, author of *Le Dieu caché* (1955), which explained the development of Jansenism – and hence Pascal's *Pensées* and Racine's tragedies – by reference to the historical development of the *noblesse de robe*.[17] Goldmann had come out of an anti-Stalinist tradition in Romania, and persistently attempted to defend a tradition of Hegelian Marxism and in particular the early work of Lukács against the Stalinist distortion of the Marxist method.[18]

But the Marxist thinker to whom Sartre gave greatest critical attention in *Question de méthode* was Daniel Guérin, a frequent contributor to *Les Temps modernes*, who in 1957 found himself the target of Sartre's polemical zeal. The issue at stake was the interpretation of the French Revolution.[19]

Guérin's *La Lutte de classes sous la première république*[20] (published in 1946) claimed that while the French Revolution was, in Marxist terms, a bourgeois revolution, it also contained the embryo of a proletarian revolution. The Paris wage-earners, the *bras nus* (bare arms), began to act independently of the Jacobins, whom Guérin saw as linked firmly to the big bourgeoisie. In this sense the Jacobins played a conservative role in relation to the threat from below. (Here Guérin was using concepts borrowed from Trotsky's theory of 'permanent revolution'.) While Guérin was quite clear that the *bras nus* could not have taken and held power, he saw their organisations as forerunners of the direct democracy of the Paris Commune and the Russian soviets.

Guérin's account was not politically innocent. It was a challenge to the whole republican tradition of revolutionary historiography for which, in Clemenceau's words, the Revolution was a bloc. The dominant academic historians of the Revolution, Mathiez and Georges Lefebvre, had taken the Jacobins as their heroes. The Jacobin tradition was central to the political mythologies of the Popular Front and the Resistance, and Guérin was thus polemicising against the notion of a Resistance uniting all classes against the foreign invader.

Not surprisingly, Guérin had had a rough ride from Stalinist historians. His interpretation was a challenge to the whole popular front tradition, and also to the use of the analogy of the Terror to justify Stalinist repression. It was necessary for the PCF not so much to refute Guérin as to discredit him. In fact the work of Soboul, Rudé and others was to show the seminal qualities of Guérin's researches, but such was the hegemony of Stalinism over left historiography that Guérin's work was banished from academic respectability.[21]

We do not know when Sartre first read Guérin's work, but in the years before the *Critique* it was drawn to his attention in two of the polemics that marked his period of *rapprochement* with the PCF. In 1953 Claude Lefort cited Guérin to show how proletarian consciousness was formed spontaneously as early as 1792.[22] Two years later, Merleau-Ponty in *Les Aventures de le dialectique* devoted some fifteen pages to a consideration of Guérin's 'very fine book'. But while recognising the book's merits, he claimed that Guérin's material challenged Marxist categories despite the author's intentions, and that Guérin replaced the history that actually occurred with what might have happened: 'If the proletarian revolution is not ripe, then Robespierre is relatively progressive, and the ultraleftism of the *bras nus* is relatively counterrevolutionary'.[23]

In preparing the *Critique* Sartre was to read extensively on the French Revolution, studying the work of Jaurès, Lefebvre and Soboul as well as of Guérin.[24] In the *Critique* the French Revolution would become a major source of examples and models; but Guérin's main thesis of embryonic proletarian revolution would be discussed only very briefly and tangentially.

The main attack on Guérin came in *Question de méthode*. In a footnote Sartre insisted that 'with all its errors... it remains one of the very few *enriching* contributions by a contemporary Marxist to historical studies'.[25] But he challenged Guérin's claim that the declaration of war on Austria by the Girondin government in 1792 was 'an episode in the commercial rivalry between France and England'.[26] In an early chapter of his book Guérin had placed the 1792 war in the context of the Franco-British wars of the eighteenth century, examined French attempts to exclude British textile imports in the late 1780s, argued that the war against Austria was fundamentally directed against Britain, and concluded – in the passage which probably shocked Sartre most profoundly – that economics was more significant than ideology: 'On the French side, the claim of bringing freedom to neighbouring countries seems to have been only a pretext concealing very material interests'.[27]

Sartre attacked Guérin for reductionism, starting by summarising his attempt to link the Girondins to 'a bourgeoisie of merchants and shipowners', and accused Guérin of trying to make historical events fit into 'prefabricated moulds'. While he conceded that 'the Girondins, in their actual politics express the class which produced them and the interests of the social layers which support them', he claimed that Guérin avoided the question of political praxis, and that political reality was irreducible.[28] Guérin was accused of an a priori method which omitted the mediation of concrete human beings, and was also found guilty of 'economism' for underestimating the importance of political, as opposed to economic, factors in assessing Robespierre's attitude to the war. Sartre concluded his attack on Guérin – and Lukács, whom, since the 1949 debate he had believed guilty of a similar reductionism – by linking their methodology to bureaucracy: 'thus the perpetual movement *towards identification* reflects the unifying practice of the bureaucrats'.[29]

Sartre's primary concern here was not with the facts of revolutionary history, but with methodology. He enquired: 'Why do we react against Guérin's brilliant but false proofs? Because concrete Marxism must study real men in depth and not dissolve them in a bath of sulphuric acid'.[30] This led, naturally enough, into the argument about Valéry and the petty bourgeoisie.

That Sartre's concern was methodological rather than historical was made clear from the outset, when he discussed the problem of *situation*: 'There is no doubt that Marxism enables us to *situate* a speech by Robespierre, the policy of the Mountain towards the *sans-culottes*, economic regulation and the laws of the "maximum" voted by the Convention just as much as Valéry's poems or Hugo's *La Légende des siècles*'.[31] Such leaps from poetry to politics and back were symptomatic of Sartre's healthy contempt for the boundaries of academic disciplines; however, they left some tricky loose ends. Certainly the work of a poet cannot be read off from class alignment, and few Marxists have supposed it could be. A denial of the class base of government policies is altogether different, and would involve jettisoning the Marxist theory of the state.

When *Questions de méthode* appeared in *Les Temps modernes* in 1957, Guérin responded indignantly.[32] He was legitimately angered by the fact that Sartre appeared to be lumping his work together with the sclerotic Marxism that he denounced in *Questions de méthode*. Guérin claimed that his work served precisely to undermine the type of 'Robespierrist and Stalinist dogmatism of the bourgeois revolution' that he would have expected Sartre to object to. He further noted that Sartre chose to make his attack on 'a relatively secondary passage', insisting that even if he were wrong on the question of the war, his main argument would stand. Guérin charged Sartre with rejecting the complex reality of history in favour of an oversimplified concept of the petty bourgeoisie. He conceded that Marxism sometimes underestimated the role of the human will, but argued that Sartre had moved too far in the opposite direction, and in his attempt to rid Marxism of dogmatism had ended up by abandoning the capacity of Marxism to give class explanations of historical phenomena; he had thus reverted to the old idealist view that individuals make history. Guérin described Sartre's argument as an 'anti-Marxist diatribe'.

Guérin offered an intriguing explanation for Sartre's attack, namely that 'Sartre's true target is not me, but Lukács'. Guérin claimed that Sartre was so offended by Lukács' reductionist claim that his philosophy was merely one of petty-bourgeois revolt that he was using anything that came to hand to pay off old scores.

Sartre's response to Guérin's letter consisted of three short sentences: 'Guérin's reply not only demonstrates that he hasn't understood a word I was saying: it shows – and this is much more serious – that he doesn't understand the first thing about his own book. I therefore confine myself to assuring him that it is an *excellent* book. His best, by far'.[33] Sartre's customary wit covered up an inability to reply to Guérin's arguments.

But the key to the exchange did not lie in a mere confusion between Lukács and Guérin. It must be understood in terms of the intellectual and political evolution of the two men. Both had attempted in difficult circumstances to liberate Marxism from the constraints of Stalinism, but their starting points had been very different.

From the 1940s Sartre had seen reductionism as one of the main defects of Stalinism. His work after 1956, especially the *Critique*, was a prolonged polemic against reductionism, summed up in the image of the 'bath of sulphuric acid'. Sartre did not, however, oppose the main theme of the PCF's political strategy in France, the recreation of a popular front. As was made clear in 'Le Fantôme de Staline', this remained Sartre's political perspective at the time of his polemic with Guérin.

Guérin's political evolution had been very different. He had come to political maturity during the bitter social struggles of the 1930s, in particular the Popular Front government of 1936 which had opposed a wave of factory occupations which Guérin described as an 'abortive revolution',[34] and the Spanish Civil War, in which popular frontism had paved the way for Franco's victory. By writing *La Lutte de classes* Guérin challenged the historical roots of the popular front tradition; in his analysis of the 1792 war he showed that foreign policy had roots in class interests, and that there could be no struggle for national liberation which rose above class interests. This was the real issue at stake; hence the bitterness of the confrontation.

Sartre's concern with the role of the individual led him to see biography as a major area of intellectual concern. *Question de méthode* contained many references to Flaubert, showing that Sartre was already formulating the main themes of *L'Idiot de la famille*. (Already in 1956 he and Garaudy had agreed to make parallel studies of Flaubert from Marxist and existentialist standpoints.) A major influence here that is often neglected was the work of Isaac Deutscher. Deutscher, a Trotskyist activist in the 1930s, was best known for his major biographies of Stalin and Trotsky; indeed, for a whole generation the latter work reclaimed the figure of Trotsky from the lies and slanders of Stalinism. Moreover, by studying a key figure in the Russian Revolution, Deutscher was precisely confronting what Sartre saw as a central question – the interaction between individual and historical process.

In the 1950s *Les Temps modernes* published a number of pieces by Deutscher, including his critique of Orwell, in which he made a sharp attack on Orwell's understanding of Stalinism while at the same time avoiding the crude abuse to which Orwell was subjected by the Stalinists.[35]

In 1957 it published three major extracts from the first volume of Deutscher's biography of Trotsky.[36] (The whole volume was subsequently to appear in the Julliard series of books known as the *Temps modernes* collection, launched by Sartre and Merleau-Ponty in 1950.) These extracts constituted the whole of Chapter 9, 'Trotsky in the October Revolution'.[37] Here Deutscher showed Trotsky's essential role in the insurrection, something that for nearly thirty years had been written out of history by Stalinism. But he also showed the complex interaction between the individuals Lenin and Trotsky, the Bolshevik Party as a whole, and the proletarian masses. It was precisely such interaction that Sartre himself sought to study in his work on Flaubert, with the use of what he called the 'progressive-regressive' method, which showed the interaction of individual and social structure. In his reply to Naville in 1956 Sartre had specifically drawn attention to Deutscher, referring this time to his biography of Stalin:

> Leave aside the content: Naville doubtless condemns it; but we can find in it an interesting application of the Marxist methods to the knowledge of a single person; by the perpetual reversal of perspectives, Deutscher shows us simultaneously the objective movement of history through the historical individual and the mark made by the individual on the historical movement.[38]

This is a striking account of Sartre's own method. Yet two major studies of Sartre as biographer fail to even mention the name Deutscher.[39] This is indicative of just how much the influence of the anti-Stalinist left has been neglected in the study of Sartre's Marxism.

Sartre's long and tortuous dialogue with Marxism of both the Stalinist and anti-Stalinist varieties continued with the *Critique de la raison dialectique*. The first volume appeared in 1960; Sartre wrestled with a second volume, but never completed it to his satisfaction, and the manuscript was published after his death in 1985. The two volumes were impressive in their range and contained many interesting and provocative ideas; but there were also many unsatisfactory arguments and loose ends; clearly the work did not live up to the claims of some of its initial admirers.[40] What follows is not intended as a full account of the work, but merely an examination of some of the themes relevant to the present book.

The first volume of the *Critique* was not primarily concerned with a direct analysis of the Russian experience. But it can be understood as a response to the problems raised by the Khrushchev 'secret speech' and the process of destalinisation. The account of Stalin's crimes given by Khrushchev (and slowly and very reluctantly accepted by the PCF) was clearly inadequate, and left a major problem for anyone who still accepted the Marxist framework. How had such gross breaches of legality on the level of the 'superstructure' been possible if the 'economic base' continued to be socialist? Sartre had rejected the option, posed in most coherent form by *Socialisme ou barbarie*, of seeing the USSR as being nonsocialist. On such an analysis, the visible horrors of the Moscow Trials would flow naturally from the day-to-day exploitation of Russian workers in the process of production.

Sartre was therefore in a position comparable to those medieval astronomers who refused to accept that the earth moved round the sun. It was possible to maintain a geocentric model of the universe, but as each new observation was made, the system became more and more complex and required more and more contorted movements to be attributed to heavenly bodies.[41] Likewise, Sartre's attempt to give an account of the relation of base and superstructure which would fit the experience of Stalinism required a model in which the mediations between base and superstructure became ever more complex.

Ronald Aronson was thus quite right to argue that while most readings of the first volume of the *Critique* have grasped its 'formal and metatheoretical Marxist ambitions', nonetheless 'the imposed self-sufficiency of Volume One has forced them to miss the concrete political purpose which, for Sartre, lay at the heart of the project: to determine why the Bolshevik Revolution followed the course it did, and to explore the prospects of its thawing into a genuine socialism'.[42] (Aronson's metaphor left open the question as to whether frozen urine would ever 'thaw' into lemonade.)

In the never-completed second volume of the *Critique*, Sartre attempted to go to the heart of the matter with an analysis of the conflict between Stalin and Trotsky. In considering the circumstances of postrevolutionary Russia in the 1920s, Sartre claimed to have discovered 'the implicit coexistence of Stalinism and Trotskyism'.[43] Such a discovery was, to say the least, implausible. Thirty years of murder, persecution and lies could scarcely be brushed aside as a mere misunderstanding. Why had Stalin and his allies devoted such energy to vilifying and destroying Trotsky and his followers? Was it merely a clash of personalities? Or was Stalin simply, as Khrushchev had argued, 'a very distrustful man, morbidly suspicious'?[44] Sartre went on to develop this argument:

> Stalin himself, through a hundred treacheries, despite everything helped the Chinese, the Spanish, etc., to the extent of what he believed *possible* without unleashing armed intervention by the West; and Trotsky himself, in exile, gave the proletariats of the world the task of defending the USSR, in the event of its being attacked, because, despite everything, the bases of socialism existed there.[45]

This was rather like claiming that a policeman and a burglar shared a common commitment to the distribution of wealth. A reading of Harold Isaacs on China,[46] or, in the case of Spain, of his former teacher Katia Landau, would have shown Sartre that Stalin strangled the Chinese and Span-

ish revolutions rather than assisting them. Deutscher's biography of Trotsky also set out the issues clearly, especially in the case of China.[47]

Yet on this basis Sartre claimed that Stalin and Trotsky could have come
to an agreement on a 'minimum programme'. This would apparently have
consisted in recognising that support from revolutions abroad was not
going to come in the immediate future and so it was necessary to build
socialism in Russia, while at the same time recognising that this would
only be 'presocialism' and that Communism could only be achieved on a
world basis. But if such a minimum programme had been possible, why
had things turned out differently? Sartre fell back on secondary factors of
personality, such as the fact that Trotsky had spent much time in the West
before 1917, while Stalin had barely left Russia, or that Trotsky was an
intellectual by nature.[48]

Sartre accepted that there existed a bureaucracy in the USSR and that
the emancipation of the workers required the abolition of that bureaucracy. Yet he stood by the position developed in 'Le Fantôme de Staline'
that the bureaucracy was not a class. The consequence was that the
removal of the bureaucracy would not be in any sense comparable to a
proletarian revolution:

> That in no way means that the elimination of the bureaucracy must necessarily
> be achieved by calm progress: circumstances alone can determine the speed
> and violence of this elimination. All that can be said is that the totality of the
> process – a more or less complete agreement or a series of difficult adaptations
> or bloody disturbances – is located in the framework of a *reformist* praxis.[49]

Sartre's position here was strongly reminiscent of the classic Trotskyist
position that Russia was a 'degenerated workers' state' and that therefore
the forthcoming revolution would be 'political' rather than 'social'. Yet
after 1968 Sartre frequently took positions which denied any socialist content to the regime in the USSR. It may be that this led him to abandon the
second volume of the *Critique*.

For the logic of Sartre's position led into a quagmire. In the first volume
of the *Critique* he had dismissed the 'very idea' of the dictatorship of the
proletariat as 'absurd', arguing that 'historical experience has undeniably
shown that the first moment of socialist society could be – considered on
the still abstract level of power – nothing but the indissoluble aggregation
of bureaucracy, Terror and the cult of the personality'.[50] This was a strange
appeal to inevitability by the philosopher of freedom! But things were to
get worse in the second volume, where Sartre argued that 'in certain historical circumstances, [socialism] can be a synonym of *hell*'.[51] In his attempt
to reconcile the followers of Stalin and Trotsky, Sartre had now reached a
stage of self-destruction. To tell those who believed that the USSR was
more or less a workers' paradise that in fact it was 'hell' was likely to lead
to a complete termination of dialogue. On the other hand, to anyone trying to build an independent socialist movement, the formulation was sin-
gularly useless. After all, if told that socialism would mean bureaucracy,

terror and quite possibly hell, average workers would quite reasonably tend to think they would be better off sticking with capitalism. In trying to play the middle against both ends, Sartre was setting himself up for the fate of all those who walk in the middle of the road. Small wonder he found it impossible to complete the *Critique*.

But if the *Critique* was a failure in its attempt to deal with the Russian question, it raised a number of important issues as spin-off. The question of explaining Stalin's role meant asking how much room for manoeuvre he had had. Could a kinder, gentler Stalin have pursued the same general policy but in a slightly less hellish way? Thus Sartre argued in one of his examples that 'the difference in standard of living between the Western worker and the Soviet worker was, at the beginning, so substantial that the situation *proposed* the "iron curtain"; but it did *not require* them to lie ceaselessly about the conditions of European workers'.[52]

Such an attempt to distinguish between necessary and contingent components of Stalinism risked a lapse into the purely arbitrary. Yet at least it pointed to a more intelligently critical approach to the history of the Russian experience than those dictated by the worship of an infallible Stalin on the one hand and the demonisation of Cold War anti-Communism on the other. If Sartre failed to resolve his problems in theory, the rethinking involved in *Question de méthode* led to a renewed period of activism, especially with regard to the Algerian War. And Sartre's influence, in terms of both theory and practice, was to assist with the emergence of a genuine left outside and independent of the PCF.

Notes

1.　The same issue of the journal, *Twórczość*, also contained articles by Henri Lefebvre, Edgar Morin and Maurice Nadeau. See M. Kelly, 'Towards a Heuristic Method: Sartre and Lefebvre', *Sartre Studies International* Vol. 5, No. 1 (1999), pp. 9, 15.

2.　*TM*, September 1957, pp. 338–417; *TM*, October 1957, pp. 658–98. While the text that appeared in *Les Temps modernes* was entitled 'Questions de méthode' it was published in the *Critique de la raison dialectique* (Paris, 1960), under the title 'Question de méthode'.

3.　Sartre, *Critique*, p. 26.

4.　*Ibid.*, p. 44.

5.　L. Trotsky, *Fascism, Stalinism and the United Front*, London, 1989, p. 259. I am grateful to Mr Peter Glatter for first suggesting this comparison.

6.　K. Marx and F. Engels, *Collected Works*, London and Moscow, 1975–2001, 11: 103.

7.　Engels put the argument in these words in a letter to H. Starkenburg of 25 January 1894. See K. Marx and F. Engels, *Selected Correspondence* (Moscow, 1956), p. 549 (the volume of *Collected Works* containing Engels' 1894 correspondence has not yet appeared). Sartre claimed the Engels quotation came from a letter to Marx. Pietro Chiodi, in *Sartre and Marxism* (Hassocks, 1976), p. 41, attributed it to a letter to Borgius. Engels may have used the same or similar words on other occasions. Cf. Sartre, *Critique*, p. 60.

8.　J.-P. Sartre, *Critique de la raison dialectique* tome II, Paris, 1985, p. 208.

9.　Sartre, *Critique*, p. 17.

10. J.-P. Sartre, *L'Existentialisme est un humanisme*, Paris, 1960, p. 127. By 'Radicalism' Naville meant the republican, Jacobin politics of the middle-of-the-road Radical Party. (See Chapter 6 of this volume). In 1967 Naville himself cried victory at Sartre's conversion to Marxism: 'The best representatives of existentialist or phenomenological philosophy themselves, after having thought that they were making a clean sweep of the ground, have come to pitch their tent on the outskirts of Marxism, and it's a very significant achievement' (P. Naville, *Le Nouveau Léviathan*, Paris, 1967, p. vii).

11. Sartre, *Critique*, p. 17.

12. *Ibid.*, p. 18.

13. *Ibid.*, p. 25.

14. *Sit* VII, pp. 11–12, 132. In *Les Aventures de la dialectique*, (Paris, 1955), pp. 43–80, Merleau-Ponty had coined the term 'Western Marxism' (*marxisme occidental*) to describe Lukács's *History and Class Consciousness*. The term was applied by Perry Anderson to Marxist thinkers outside Russia since the 1920s. Anderson saw the central feature of 'Western Marxism' as a divorce between theory and practice, going so far as to assert: 'When the masses themselves speak, theoreticians – of the sort the west has produced for the last fifty years – will necessarily be silent' (P. Anderson, *Considerations on Western Marxism*, London, 1976, p. 106). It should be stressed that in this sense Sartre was never a 'Western Marxist'.

15. See M. Kelly, 'Towards a Heuristic Method: Sartre and Lefebvre', *Sartre Studies International*, Vol. 5, No. 1 (1999), pp. 1–15.

16. Sartre, *Critique*, p. 42.

17. Sartre, *Critique*, p. 75.

18. According to his biographer the young Goldmann was accused of Trotskyism by the Romanian CP in the early 1930s with 'some justification'; he admired Trotsky and called Stalin a murderer; however, there was no organised Trotskyist current in Romania at this time. See M. Cohen, *The Wager of Lucien Goldmann*, (Princeton NJ, 1994), p. 36.

19. See I. Birchall, 'Sartre's Encounter with Daniel Guérin', *Sartre Studies International* Vol. 2, No. 1 (1996), pp. 41–56.

20. D. Guérin, *La Lutte de classes sous la première république*, 2 vols, Paris, 1946; revised edition Paris, 1968.

21. See N. Carlin, 'Daniel Guérin and the Working Class in the French Revolution', *International Socialism* 47 (1990), pp. 197–223.

22. *TM*, April 1953, p. 1545.

23. *Les Aventures de la dialectique*, pp. 283-98, especially pp. 283, 285.

24. *Adieux*, pp. 236, 258, 260.

25. Sartre, *Critique*, p. 34.

26. Guérin, *La Lutte de classes* (1946), 1: 46.

27. *Ibid.*, 1: 46–62, especially p. 61.

28. Sartre, *Critique*, pp. 33–35.

29. *Ibid.*, pp. 36–40.

30. *Ibid.*, p. 37.

31. *Ibid.*, p. 33.

32. D. Guérin, 'Sartre, Lukács et la Gironde', *TM*, December 1957; reproduced in *La Lutte de classes* (1968) 2: 514–20.

33. *TM*, December 1957, p. 1137.

34. See D. Guérin, *Front populaire.– révolution manquée*, Paris, 1963.

35. ' "1984": Le mysticisme de la cruauté', *TM*, June–July 1955, pp. 2205–18; originally published as ' "1984" – The Mysticism of Cruelty' in I. Deutscher, *Heretics and Renegades*, London, 1955, pp. 35–50.

36. *TM*, July–August 1957, pp. 174–206; September 1957, pp. 478–99; October 1957, pp. 699–728.

37. I. Deutscher, *The Prophet Armed*, Oxford, 1970, pp. 249–324.

38. *Sit* VII, p. 132.

39. M. Scriven, *Sartre's Existential Biographies*, Basingstoke, 1984; D. Collins, *Sartre as Biographer*, Cambridge, Mass., 1980.

40. Ben Brewster told readers of *New Left Review* that the *Critique* 'has dispensed with the theoretical paraphernalia of the Stalin–Trotsky debate and is thus able to comprehend both positions'. 'Presentation of Gorz on Sartre', *New Left Review* 37 (May-June 1966), p. 31.

41. I first heard this analogy from the late Tony Cliff.

42. R. Aronson, 'Sartre and the Dialectic', in F. Jameson, ed., *Sartre after Sartre*, Yale French Studies 68: Yale, 1985, p. 96.

43. J-.P. Sartre, *Critique* tome II, p. 115.

44. 'N.S. Khrushchev's "Secret" Speech', in D. Jacobs, ed., *The New Communist Manifesto*, New York, 1962, p. 101.

45. Sartre, *Critique* tome II, p. 117.

46. H. Isaacs, *The Tragedy of the Chinese Revolution*, Stanford, 1961.

47. I. Deutscher, *The Prophet Unarmed*, Oxford, 1970, pp. 316–38; *The Prophet Outcast*, Oxford 1970, pp. 159–62.

48. Sartre, *Critique* tome II, pp. 111–12.

49. *Ibid.*, p. 177.

50. Sartre, *Critique*, p. 630.

51. Sartre, *Critique* tome II, p. 128.

52. *Ibid.*, p. 233.

Chapter 15

THE BATTLE OVER ALGERIA

The war for Algerian independence (1954–62) was bloody and protracted, fought ruthlessly on both sides, but with the defenders of French rule lapsing into the worst savageries of torture and mass repression. Like the Vietnam War for the United States a decade later, it tore through the very fabric of French society, and destroyed the fragile institutions of the Fourth Republic, bringing de Gaulle to power in 1958. Sartre again found himself in a triangular relation with the PCF and the anti-Stalinist left. Above all, the war led to a profound and lasting radicalisation of Sartre's position.

Between 1939 and 1962 France never enjoyed normal peacetime conditions for more than a few months. The Second World War and German Occupation were followed, first by eight years of war in Indo-China, then by the even more bitter Algerian War, which frequently between 1954 and 1962 threatened to spill over onto European territory. The bulk of Sartre's work was produced during this period and this state of permanent warfare is often reflected in his preoccupation with violence and conflict.

Before the outbreak of hostilities in 1954, a number of people in Sartre's circle had concerned themselves with the effects of French rule in North Africa. One was Francis Jeanson, a close associate of Sartre's and a regular contributor to *Les Temps modernes*, of which he was managing editor from 1951 to 1956. Jeanson had written a book about Sartre,[1] and had been the instigator of the celebrated quarrel with Camus. He and his wife Colette had spent several months in Algeria and in 1955 they published a book on the nature of French rule.[2] Another person concerned with North Africa was Claude Bourdet, who had a long and distinguished record of opposition to French imperialism.

There was also Daniel Guérin, who in 1953 contributed a powerful article to *Les Temps modernes* under the title 'Pitié pour le Maghreb', in which he anticipated the coming conflict.[3] He began with a variation on the theme of 'the main enemy is at home', which had exercised Sartre's mind during the debate about the Russian camps. Guérin told how, when extracts from his book on racism in the U.S.A. had appeared in the *Pittsburgh Courier*, he had received a letter from Atlanta, Georgia, advising him to keep his own French doorstep clean instead of concerning himself with the Southern U.S.A.[4] Guérin pointed out the arguments he could have used in reply, asserting the right of an internationalist to criticise abuses in any country. However, after a three-month journey through North Africa, he had decided his American critic had been right.

He gave a vivid account of the human suffering he had observed in Morocco, Algeria and Tunisia, stressing in the Algerian case both the wretchedness of urban overcrowding and unemployment and the way the authorities had 'tried to kill the soul of this country' by suppression of indigenous culture, especially the Arabic language and Islam. He concluded by noting that 'North Africa today is the last bastion of French capitalism' and predicting that the owners of the great plantations would be capable of letting the Maghreb be covered by fire and blood 'rather than give up any part of their power'. Yet he feared the French left, divided by Stalinism, would not rise to the challenge: 'The North African drama is, in the last analysis, in a way also the drama of the French left'.

It was a powerfully prophetic article and initiated a decade in which *Les Temps modernes* would play a very creditable role in its opposition to French imperialism. But the insurrection launched on 1 November 1954 was to put all sections of the French left to the test. Initially the PCF condemned 'the recourse to individual acts liable to play into the hands of the worst colonialists'.[5] In the early stages of the war the PCF kept a low profile; while condemning repression in Algeria and recognising the 'national demands' of the Algerians, it refused to advocate Algerian independence. There were two reasons for this. Firstly, Moscow had no particular desire to see an independent Algeria, fearing that if Algeria broke from France the United States would increase its influence in North Africa. A senior Russian official visiting Paris made clear to Sartre that an attempt to push the question of Algeria within the Communist-led Peace Movement would be inopportune.[6] And secondly, racist and imperialist attitudes were widespread in sections of the French working class, as well as among European settlers in Algeria; the PCF was apprehensive that if it stood out too firmly against such attitudes it might weaken its influence within the working class.

The initial opposition to the war, therefore, came from small groupings of the far left. Daniel Guérin was involved in attempting to organise the first public meeting against the war in Paris on 21 December 1954, a meeting sponsored by Trotskyists and anarchists. But the meeting never happened, since it was banned by the then Minister of the Interior, François Mitterrand.[7] The Trotskyist PCI, with a handful of members, was the only political organisation in 1954 to support Algerian independence.[8]

In the course of 1955 *Les Temps modernes* began to come out against the war. In May a concluding editorial note to the special issue on 'La Gauche' made reference to North Africa and colonialism, but said nothing specific on Algeria. But in October a much sharper editorial statement appeared under the title 'Refusal to Obey'. This described Algeria as a 'colony' (rejecting the official fiction that it was an integral part of France) subject to 'the most obvious exploitation'. It went on: 'A war is starting in North Africa; it is up to the government whether to stop it, or, on the contrary, to make it inevitable... To this war, we say no'.

The statement quoted *L'Express* as arguing that the presence in North Africa of conscripts and reservists was 'a duty which nobody could oppose without denying the very existence of the national collectivity', and commented: 'This pompous fraud indicates very precisely the difference between us and a "new left" whose prudent realism clearly tolerates quite happily what it claims to be fighting'.[9]

The following month's issue went even further. Under the title 'Algeria Is Not France' (a slogan which also appeared on the cover), it denounced the policy of 'integration' advocated by the government, and came very close to urging soldiers to fraternise with the enemy: 'Yesterday, Robert Barrat was arrested for having held a meeting with the "rebels". Tomorrow, on the trails of the Aurès mountains, perhaps the conscript soldiers will come to recognise them as brothers'.[10]

It is not likely that Sartre himself penned these editorial notes; they may well have been written by Francis Jeanson, still managing editor. But they committed the journal to a course of opposition to the war that would soon run up against the limits of legality, and it is hard to suppose that this was done without Sartre's conscious and willing acceptance.

Sartre, of course, was still at this point entangled in his *rapprochement* with the PCF, but this did not prevent him and *Les Temps modernes* from speaking out against the war. On 26 June 1955, at the World Peace Assembly at Helsinki, Sartre declared that the colonial era was at an end, and he demanded that the French government recognise the demands of the people of North Africa through peaceful negotiation.[11]

On 27 January 1956 a meeting was held at the *salle Wagram*, organised by the *Comité d'action des intellectuels contre la poursuite de la guerre en Afrique du Nord*. The speakers came from various sections of the independent left, and included a number who had crossed Sartre's path before: Guérin, Michel Leiris (a former surrealist and contributor to *Les Temps modernes*), Aimé Césaire (a contributor to Senghor's anthology of African and Caribbean poetry which Sartre had prefaced), Pierre Stibbe (former *pivertiste*), and Jean Rous (ex-Trotskyist and leading figure in the RDR).[12] Sartre was coming to recognise a group of allies from the independent left with whom he must associate on issues where he could not count on the PCF – as he clearly could not here. The PCF's daily paper reported the event in just three sentences, with no mention of the name of any speaker, even Sartre. Moreover, it was stated that the speakers had merely called for negotiations, when some of them had gone considerably further than this.[13]

Sartre's contribution[14] in particular went further, although his analysis of the war was still evolving. He seemed to have abandoned his earlier hopes for peaceful negotiations, and denounced those who suggested that the economic and social problems of Algeria could be solved within the existing framework: 'the leaders of the FLN have replied: "Even if we were happy under the French bayonets, we should fight." They are right'.

He declared that neither 'good' settlers nor metropolitan France could bring about the needed reforms: 'These reforms will be the job of the Algerian people itself, when it has won its freedom' – a clear statement of support for those fighting for national independence.

After an extensive account of the impact of colonialism on the history of Algeria, Sartre concluded by arguing that colonialism was the enemy of both the Algerians and the French: 'It makes our atmosphere stink: it is our shame, it mocks our laws and caricatures them; it infects us with its racism'. Hence the task of the French left was to struggle alongside the Algerian people 'in order to liberate *at the same time* Algerians and French from colonial tyranny'. Here Sartre showed real prescience; memories of the Algerian conflict continue to nourish the far right in France; a decade after the 'death of communism' Jean-Marie Le Pen was still very much alive.

In itself, this might seem like a vigorous encouragement to the building of an anti-war movement. Unfortunately, things were not so simple, and behind the scenes of the *salle Wagram* meeting there were deep political tensions. The struggle for Algerian independence was complicated by the fact that the independence movement itself was bitterly divided. On the one side stood the *Mouvement national algérien* (MNA), led by the veteran Messali Hadj, who had been the dominant figure in Algerian nationalism in the 1920s and 1930s. On the other was the *Front de libération nationale* (FLN), which had launched the insurrection of November 1954. Although there was no substantial difference in programme between the two organisations, there was a long and bitter struggle for hegemony over the independence movement, with many internecine killings in the streets of France.[15]

In a letter to the anarchist paper *Le Libertaire*,[16] Guérin, a friend and associate of Messali Hadj since the 1930s, described the manoeuvrings that had taken place prior to the *salle Wagram* meeting. On the previous Saturday a meeting had been held to allocate the topics for the meeting. Sartre was present and, according to Guérin, 'showed total objectivity'. Guérin was impressed by the apparent atmosphere of 'confidence, cordiality and cooperation', and agreed to speak on the continuity of the Algerian national struggle. But the same evening a further meeting took place, in the absence of Sartre and Guérin, and it was agreed that no mention should be made of the name of Messali Hadj.[17] This was obviously to avoid offence to the FLN – and to the PCF.[18] As a result Guérin received a *pneumatique* (express letter) from Jean Pouillon of the *Temps modernes* editorial board, asking him not to speak about the history of the Algerian independence movement.

Guérin, a man of high moral integrity and great personal courage, was not to be intimidated. Nearly a third of his contribution (which he later self-published as a small pamphlet)[19] was devoted to the role of Messali Hadj and the PPA (*Parti du peuple algérien*), as a conclusion to an account of Algeria before colonisation and the growth of national resistance. However, doubtless in an effort to be conciliatory, Guérin refrained from mentioning either the FLN or the MNA by name, and he was studiedly cautious (though subtly provocative) in his final summing up of the current situation:

> It's a duty *for us all* to recall the historic service which this movement and its founder have rendered to the cause of Algerian emancipation. Without them the various currents of the present resistance, engaged in the same struggle and victims of the same repression, would not be what they are. The means of struggle have changed, young people, inspired with a new spirit, have joined the ranks of the fighters in large numbers. We hail them as the glorious heirs of the great precursors.

When the meeting took place, nine-tenths of those attending were MNA sympathisers, Algerian workers in their work clothes (the MNA's main base was among Algerian workers in mainland France). Sartre, obviously not pleased by this, accused Guérin of having 'packed the meeting'.[20]

Sartre was only a bit player in this dispute, and Guérin does not seem to have held him personally to blame. But Sartre could not evade the continuing dispute. A number of those he had associated with in the RDR, especially those with a past in the anti-Stalinist left – Jean Rous, Yves Dechezelles – sympathised with the MNA. When Colette and Francis Jeanson's book *L'Algérie hors la loi* – sympathetic to the FLN – appeared in December 1955, it received a review from Daniel Guérin which, while commending the book as a valuable source of information, expressed sharp reservations about the authors' hostility to Messali Hadj.[21]

Sartre, doubtless under the influence of Jeanson, took the side of the FLN. In October 1955 he had warned Marcel Péju not to go too far in his support for the FLN in *Les Temps modernes*,[22] but he soon came to the position that support for Algerian independence must imply support for those bearing the brunt of the fighting. The logic seemed to be much the same as had led him to make his alliance with the PCF; the FLN were the force actually doing the fighting, and whatever criticisms one might have, they must be supported. As he told Jean Daniel in an unpublished interview in January 1958:

> Listen, whatever the FLN may be, it *is* the Algerian revolution. We have to take it as it is. If we can do anything, secretly, if we can have any sort of influence on it, I'm in favour of doing so. But it's impossible. The FLN repudiates France *en bloc*. You've seen the last two issues of *el Moudjahid* [the party organ of the FLN]. They're raving. But I don't think such stupidities should have been published. In their own interest, that sort of thing should not be put into circulation.[23]

At the same time the PCF was failing to give the necessary lead. In the first two years of the war there were various acts of open rebellion by soldiers, especially after reservists were sent to fight in Algeria by the decrees of August 1955. In September 1955 *France-Observateur* was seized for opposing sending conscripts to Algeria, and there were demonstrations of reservists at the *gare de Lyon*, and then in October at Rouen. If the PCF had encouraged these and tried to spread the action, it might have proved impossible for the French government to continue the war.

In fact things turned out very differently. At the beginning of 1956 a new government was formed under SFIO leader Guy Mollet, which decided to prosecute the war against the FLN with renewed vigour, and to this end brought in a set of 'special powers' designed to strengthen the hand of the French authorities in their repressive task. The PCF, whose current strategy was to form a new 'Popular Front' with other parties of the left, wanted to avoid confrontation with the SFIO and voted in favour of these powers.

An editorial, signed 'T.M.', in *Les Temps modernes* immediately condemned the special powers, which it saw as making a decisive turn away from the possibility of a peaceful settlement in Algeria. The author – presumably reflecting editor Sartre's own position – was ironic at the fact that the unity of the left parties (PCF and SFIO) which had been much demanded, notably by Sartre and *Les Temps modernes*, had now been achieved in the vote: 'The left, for once unanimous, has voted for the "special powers", powers which are totally useless for negotiation but indispensable for the pursuit and intensification of the war. This vote is scandalous and runs the risk of being irreparable'.

It was Mollet's SFIO which had initiated the powers and it, naturally enough, was the main target of the attack; there was no direct denunciation of the PCF, but a clear reference to the fact that the vote had been supported by 'M. Duclos, who argues that it is necessary to begin by recognising the fact of Algerian nationality'.[24]

In 'Le Fantôme de Staline', published early in 1957, Sartre made a much more vigorous attack on the PCF for its neglect of the Algerian question:

> They talk of Algeria, of course, but in moderate terms. So as not to lose face, the Party press complains a little. But it is understood that there will be no agitation. The 'Mouvement de la Paix', very active in the days of M. Bidault and the war in Vietnam, has dropped out of the picture: there is no national campaign, no meetings, no days of action; its activists are grumbling, some are resigning: no effort is made to hold on to them. As for the working class, the result, and perhaps the aim, of this policy is that it is entirely demobilised: nothing at all like the strikes by the Marseilles dockers or the demonstrations for the release of Henri Martin. The workers are sickened by the war in Algeria but they are left without instructions, without slogans. The PCF is reaping what it has sown: when it needs the masses, it will no longer find them.[25]

The bitter tone of Sartre's polemic was amply justified by the course of events. Eighteen months later, when the Algerian crisis led to the collapse of the Fourth Republic, the PCF's attempt to use its industrial strength quickly disintegrated, and in the ensuing parliamentary elections the Party lost over a million and a half votes. It had indeed reaped what it had sown.[26]

In a message to the court at the time of the trial of Francis Jeanson and his supporters in 1960, Sartre stated that intellectuals had no special role in the action against the war, that there were no 'noble tasks' and 'commonplace tasks'.[27] (This letter was composed on Sartre's behalf by Lanzmann and Péju while he was in Brazil, but there is no doubt that it reflected his views.) From 1956 through to the bitter end of the war in 1962 Sartre campaigned constantly on every level against French imperialism.

Sartre himself was rather too prominent a figure to 'carry suitcases' for the FLN (though Francis Jeanson did consider giving him some false documents and addresses to put the police on the wrong trail).[28] But many of those involved in Sartre's circle were directly involved – Lanzmann, Péju and Pingaud sheltered Algerian activists.[29] Serge Reggiani, the actor who played Frantz in *Les Séquestrés d'Altona*, was sheltering Francis Jeanson, on the run from the police, during the period the play was being performed.[30] In purely material terms the *Front d'Action et de Coordination* (FAC) (in which Sartre played a leading role) sent more than three tons of medical supplies to the Casbah between March and May 1962 (in comparison to just six tons from the USSR in the same period).[31]

Les Temps modernes consistently campaigned against the war; it was seized by the authorities in Algeria no less than four times in 1957. When Sartre's article 'Une Victoire' – dealing with the torture of Algerian Communist Henri Alleg – was published in *L'Express*, the weekly was promptly confiscated by the authorities. A reduced photograph of the offending article with large crosses through it was then published in *Le Canard enchaîné*; this could be read easily with the aid of a magnifying glass.[32]

Sartre also took up issues which were of some embarrassment to other sections of the left. In 1958 he wrote of the case of Fernand Iveton, an Algerian Communist who had planted a bomb in a power station (with no possible risk to life) and who was executed on the decision of the then Minister of the Interior, François Mitterrand. Iveton received only limited support from the PCF because he had gone beyond the limits of the party line in his desire to support Algerian independence.[33]

Looking back in 1965 Sartre was, as often, self-deprecating about his activity over the Algerian War:

> The affair was played out between three protagonists: de Gaulle, the army and the FLN, backed by the Algerian population in the towns. As for us, we frequently demonstrated in the streets. It was our job to do so because we were French. That served to show the Algerians that there did exist a minority of French people who considered the war to be iniquitous, but we recognise that we did not achieve any real results. Objectively, our opposition accomplished nothing.[34]

Sartre here clearly underestimated the extent to which the anti-war movement encouraged opposition among conscripts and the population in general, and thus made it more difficult for de Gaulle and the army to attempt to hold on to Algeria.

In general the PCF wished to keep Sartre's various initiatives at arm's length. While the PCF often argued, in accordance with the logic of the popular front, for a broad alliance against the OAS (an ultra-right terrorist organisation opposed to Algerian independence), Sartre considered it necessary also to oppose the Gaullist regime. A few individual members of the PCF worked with Sartre, notably Jean-Pierre Vigier, a distinguished physicist, who was critical of the PCF's passive line. Vigier and Laurent Schwartz (a Trotskyist from 1936 to the Liberation) worked with Sartre on the establishment of the *Ligue pour un rassemblement antifasciste*, which became the FAC.[35]

Other former comrades crossed Sartre's path. In November 1961 – just after the Paris police had murdered some hundreds of Algerians on the streets of Paris – Sartre participated in a demonstration in Paris. One of those present was Jean-René Chauvin (who had worked with Sartre at the time of the RDR): 'Chauvin, an obstreperous PSU member, shouted "Shoot then. Go on, shoot!" The cop (in plain clothes) shrugged, as if never, as long as any cop could remember, had a cop shot anyone'.[36]

In particular Sartre found himself cooperating with *La Voie communiste*, a rather loose grouping around the journal of the same name. A number of its leading figures were of Trotskyist formation – Denis Berger (expelled from the Fourth International and an expert in jail-breaks), Félix Guattari, J.-R. Chauvin and others. Sartre financed the first issue of *La Voie communiste* in 1958. Hamon and Rotman have claimed that in March 1958 Sartre was told by Claude Lanzmann of the Trotskyist connections of some members of *La Voie communiste* and withdrew his financial support.[37] Jean-René Chauvin did not recall any such dispute with Sartre.[38] And certainly Sartre did not break off relations with *La Voie communiste*; he gave two substantial interviews to the journal. In the first, an interview with Deville, Arrieux and Labre in February 1961, he argued that de Gaulle was reluctant to negotiate with the FLN because the Algerian revolution was 'not merely nationalist but also fundamentally social'. Referring to the recent Belgian general strike, he prophetically looked forward to something similar in France – but only after the end of the war. And he observed that a left which based itself on the principle of defending the USSR because this was in the French national interest found itself incapable of genuine internationalist solidarity.[39]

In the second interview – with Gérard Spitzer and Simon Blumenthal (both of whom had been expelled from the PCF) in June–July 1962 – Sartre focused on the difficulties of cooperating with the PCF, which had recently accused him of being soft on the OAS because of a difference about slogans. He pointed out that to work with dissidents in the PCF was difficult, because these were disavowed by the leadership and had to cover their own positions; on the other hand, to work with the leadership was equally unsatisfactory, because the PCF leadership demanded unanimity. He concluded that collaboration with the PCF was 'simultaneously necessary and impossible'.[40]

Sartre also spoke out in support of Michel Raptis (Pablo) and Sal Santen, leading figures in the Fourth International, who in 1960–61 were arrested, tried and imprisoned in the Netherlands, charged with forging papers and money and running guns to assist the FLN.[41]

But undoubtedly Sartre's most notorious act in support of Algerian independence was his involvement, in September 1960, with the celebrated Manifesto of the 121. The prime responsibility for this had to be concealed at the time, for obvious reasons, but in an interview with Bernard-Henri Lévy, Claude Simon stated that it was Maurice Blanchot and Maurice Nadeau who had drafted the original statement.[42] Novelist and critic Blanchot had been the subject of an essay by Sartre in 1943.[43] Nadeau, a Trotskyist in the 1930s and 1940s, had been centrally involved in the FIARI. From this experience, and his study of the history of surrealism, he had acquired a knowledge of the tradition of statements and petitions by intellectuals and artists. This one was to have more impact than most of its predecessors.

In an interview with Madeleine Chapsal, intended for *L'Express*, but not published, Nadeau explained what he hoped the Manifesto would achieve:

> Its first effect will be to bring encouragement to courageous young people who, obeying their conscience, have preferred prison or exile, the breaking of family links, to the peculiar task of 'pacification' that was required of them. They will feel less abandoned. They will know that they are not universally considered as 'swine' and 'traitors'.[44]

The statement was unequivocal in giving open encouragement to illegal activity:

> We respect and consider justified the refusal to take arms against the Algerian people.

> We respect and consider justified the actions of those French people who regard it as their duty to offer assistance and protection to Algerians oppressed in the name of the French people.

The signatories[45] brought together an unprecedented alliance of the various currents of the French left. Alfred Rosmer, a member of the tiny *Vie ouvrière* group who had opposed the First World War from day one, former member of the Executive of the Comintern and friend of Leon Trotsky, signed. So too did the widow and son of Marcel Martinet, another member of that group, and Robert Louzon, a veteran syndicalist from before 1914. From the *pivertistes* came Daniel Guérin, from the surrealists André Breton,

Michel Leiris and André Masson, veteran of the FIARI, who had designed the scenery for *Morts sans sépulture* and *La Putain respectueuse*, and on whom Sartre published an essay in 1960.[46] Some of Sartre's old adversaries were there too: Marguerite Duras, who had savaged *Les Mains sales*, and Henri Lefebvre, who had devoted a whole book to denouncing existentialism.[47] Very few of the signatories, however, came from the PCF, which took a dim view of the whole enterprise. Hélène Parmelin and Edouard Pignon were summoned before the Central Committee to explain why they had given their names.[48]

But there were also some notable absentees. In the case of some Trotskyist activists it may have been because they did not want to prejudice illegal solidarity work they were engaged in. Others who had been associated with opposition to the war had political reservations about the line of the Manifesto of the 121.

In October 1960 there appeared an appeal for 'a negotiated peace in Algeria'. As well as Roland Barthes , Edgar Morin, Jacques Prévert and others, this was signed by a number of people closely linked to the *Temps modernes* circle, notably Merleau-Ponty, Colette Audry and Claude Lefort. This was often seen as a 'soft' alternative to the Manifesto of the 121, for those who did not want to risk their freedom or their careers by signing an open appeal to illegal action. However, it did make clear its support for Algerian self-determination, and recognised that insubordination by young conscripts was 'inevitable'. It criticised the government for using the Manifesto of the 121 as an excuse for attacking civil liberties.[49] J.-F. Sirinelli considered it had a greater impact than the Manifesto of the 121.[50]

In her obituary of Merleau-Ponty the following year[51] Colette Audry related how she, Lefort and Merleau-Ponty had been instrumental in drafting the appeal because, although they had decided not to sign the Manifesto of the 121, they also did not intend to 'condemn or ignore it'. She described the choice not to sign as 'correct' but 'very disagreeable; and, unfortunately for us, it involved no immediate risk'. Audry added that her own position had been confirmed by the action of conscripts in Algiers in 1961, when a revolt by senior Army officers who wished to keep Algeria French had collapsed because conscript soldiers did not support it – 'when contempt for the law is blatant on the part of some officers, the place of conscripts is to confront those officers'. Her position could therefore reasonably be described as a 'left' criticism of the 121, adopting the Leninist position that soldiers should not desert but should organise inside the army.[52]

Audry told how, as she, Lefort and Merleau-Ponty were discussing this situation, they suddenly realised that all their efforts could be traced back to Sartre's action: 'We were chewing over all this before splitting up. Merleau-Ponty stopped in the middle of the road and said: "Bloody old Sartre!" (*Sacré Sartre!*) Suddenly we saw ourselves and the mess we had got into. We looked silly, even if we were right'.

By his consistent activity against the Algerian War Sartre had established a moral and political authority which even those who disagreed with him had to respect. Even more importantly, opposition to the war had led to the emergence of a clear political current to the left of the PCF; Sartre's role in the creation of this current and his continuing influence on it stand as the most important political achievement of his life.

Notes

1. F. Jeanson, *Le Problème moral et la pensée de Sartre*, Paris, 1947.
2. C. and F. Jeanson, *L'Algérie hors la loi*, Paris, 1955.
3. *TM*, January–February 1953, pp. 1190–1219.
4. The expression 'keeping one's own doorstep clean' (*balayer devant sa porte*) had been used by Bourdet when refusing to support Rousset's campaign on the Russian camps. See *Combat*, 14 November, 1949.
5. *L'Humanité*, 9 November 1954.
6. *Choses*, p. 361.
7. D. Guérin, *Quand l'Algérie s'insurgeait*, Claix, 1979, p. 62.
8. H. Hamon and P. Rotman, *Les Porteurs de valises*, Paris, 1981, p. 40.
9. 'Refus d'obéissance', *TM*, October 1955, pp. 385–88.
10. 'L'Algérie n'est pas la France', *TM*, November 1955, pp. 577–79.
11. M.-C. Granjon, 'Raymond Aron, Jean-Paul Sartre et le conflit algérien', in J.-P. Rioux and J.-F. Sirinelli, *La Guerre d'Algérie et les intellectuels français*, Paris, 1988, p. 80; *C&R*, p. 288.
12. *C&R*, p. 297; *Le Monde*, 29–30 January 1956; *Le Libertaire*, 2 February 1956.
13. *L'Humanité*, 28 January 1956.
14. J.-P. Sartre, 'Le colonialisme est un système', *Sit* V, pp. 25–48.
15. For a balanced account of the complex rivalry between MNA and FLN, see Guérin, *Quand l'Algérie*, in particular pp. 58–59, 116–23, 172–74.
16. *Le Libertaire*, 2 February 1956.
17. Edgar Morin, who was present, says that only he and the Trotskyist Chéramy opposed this, against the opposition of Stalinists and *sartriens* (E. Morin, *Autocritique*, Paris, 1959, pp. 188–89).
18. There had been bitter antagonism between Messali Hadj and the PCF in the 1930s, with Messali's organisation, the *Étoile nord-africaine*, even being described as 'fascist'. See Guérin, *Quand l'Algérie*, pp. 26–28.
19. D. Guérin, *L'Algérie n'a jamais été la France*, Paris, 1956.
20. Guérin, *Quand l'Algérie*, pp. 83–84.
21. *France Observateur*, 26 January 1956, p. 12.
22. R. Hayman, *Writing Against*, London, 1986, p. 295.
23. J. Daniel, *Le Temps qui reste*, Paris, 1973, p. 252.
24. 'Pouvoirs "spéciaux"', *TM*, March–April 1956, pp. 1345–53.
25. *Sit* VII, p. 299.
26. In a 1976 interview Roland Leroy, one of the Party's top leaders, rather grudgingly admitted that the PCF should have been more sympathetic to those involved in radical action against the war ('Le PCF, les intellectuels et la culture dans les vingt dernières années', *Cahiers d'histoire de l'institut Maurice Thorez* 15 (1976), pp. 126–48, especially pp. 139–40).
27. *Choses*, pp. 571, 573.
28. F. Jeanson, *Le Problème moral et la pensée de Sartre* (revised edition), Paris, 1965, p. 300.

29. Hamon and Rotman, *Les Porteurs*, p. 158.
30. *L'Humanité*, 14 April 1990.
31. M.-A. Burnier, *Les Existentialistes et la politique*, Paris, 1966, p. 151.
32. *L'Express*, 6 March 1958; *Le Canard enchaîné*, 12 March 1958. To the best of my knowledge this was Sartre's only 'collaboration' with *Le Canard enchaîné*, whose leftism represented a tradition of pacifist anarchism very different to Sartre's.
33. 'Nous sommes tous des assassins', *Sit* V, pp. 68–71; see J.-L. Einaudi, *Pour l'exemple*, Paris, 1986.
34. *Sit* VIII, pp. 14–15.
35. *Choses*, pp. 630–31, 637, 645.
36. *Choses*, p. 629.
37. Hamon and Rotman, *Les Porteurs*, p. 109. This claim is repeated, without source, in *L'Année sartrienne* No. 15, Paris, June 2001, pp. 129–30.
38. Interview with J.-R. Chauvin, 1997.
39. 'Entretien avec Jean-Paul Sartre', *La Voie communiste* nouvelle série No. 20, February 1961, pp. 3–4.
40. 'Entretien avec Jean-Paul Sartre', *La Voie communiste* nouvelle série No. 29, June–July 1962, p. 20.
41. K. Coates and J. Daniels, 'Free Raptis and Santen', *Socialist Review*, July–August 1961, pp. 6–7.
42. B.-H. Lévy, *Les Aventures de la liberté*, Paris, 1991, p. 15.
43. *Sit* I, pp. 113–32.
44. *Le Droit à l'insoumission*, Paris, 1961, p. 96.
45. Although the Manifesto had at least 172 signatories, it was always known as the Manifesto of the 121.
46. See *Sit* IV, pp. 387–407.
47. H. Lefebvre, *L'Existentialisme*, Paris, 1946.
48. J. Verdès-Leroux, 'La Guerre d'Algérie dans la trajectoire des intellectuels communistes', in Rioux and Sirinelli, *La Guerre d'Algérie*, p. 218; see also P. Daix, *J'ai cru au matin*, Paris, 1976, p. 380.
49. *Combat*, 6 October 1960.
50. J.-F. Sirinelli, 'Guerre d'Algérie, guerre de pétitions?', in Rioux and Sirinelli, *La Guerre d'Algérie*, p. 199.
51. *L'Express*, 11 May 1961, pp. 34–35.
52. This point was widely discussed during the Algerian War; many on the left argued that the particular conditions in the French Army in Algeria made political organisation impossible. The PCF invoked Leninist orthodoxy to justify its opposition to desertion, but its actual achievement in organising within the army was limited. While Audry was trying to explore the most effective way of opposing the war, the PCF was primarily concerned to stay within the framework of legality.

Chapter 16

REBUILDING THE LEFT

During the Algerian War, Sartre's conduct was that of an exemplary anti-imperialist. Even the PCF no longer dared to vilify him in the old way. But the broader task of rebuilding the French left proved more intractable. Here Sartre was still bound by the contradictions of his own past. In particular, he had not resolved the question of how to relate to the PCF.

And so, once the blood had dried on the pavements of Budapest, it was back to the hesitation waltz. Already by 1958 Sartre was making tentative moves towards renewed dialogue with the PCF, a process accelerated in 1962. Yet in an interview with an Italian newspaper in 1959, Sartre declared that 'joining a Communist Party today is joining a party which is effectively conservative'.[1]

When Sartre told *La Voie communiste* in 1962 that collaboration with the PCF was 'simultaneously necessary and impossible',[2] it seemed as though he had learned nothing and forgotten nothing since 1945. The formulation of this paradox revealed that Sartre had never understood the strategy of the united front. A united front approach to the PCF would have meant simultaneously cooperating on as many practical measures as possible and using that cooperation to expose the PCF's limitations.

Thus Sartre was violently opposed to de Gaulle's return to power in 1958, and wrote some powerful articles in *L'Express*. Yet he shrewdly noted the PCF's ambiguity; it had heard de Gaulle's slogan 'France alone' and was hoping for a possible withdrawal from NATO.[3] But in November 1965 *Les Temps modernes* published an editorial describing Mitterrand's presidential candidacy as 'a useless compromise'; Sartre was denounced in *L'Humanité* for complicity with Gaullism and made a last minute volte-face by calling for a vote for Mitterrand to prevent the SFIO's 'rush to the right'.[4]

Notes for this chapter begin on page 209.

Sartre's stance and analysis on these and many other issues can be considered on their merits; what is clear is that they did not constitute a strategy. The one thing Sartre excluded from 1956 onwards was the attempt to build a new organisation. In the 1956 *L'Express* interview he was dismissive of the various forces that constituted the so-called 'new left':

> The *nouvelle gauche* [new left] is full of highly intelligent people; alongside the intellectuals there are workers and petty bourgeois. But unless it grows enormously, at present it hardly represents more than perhaps two hundred thousand people throughout the country. It is very useful to achieve links. But the real problem lies elsewhere.[5]

That Sartre could be so disparaging of an estimated 200,000 people shows that he was still fixated on the 'big battalions' of the PCF, with its five million voters. This fixation may have had a rational core, since he was aware that the majority of the working class retained at least a passive loyalty to the PCF. Yet his past experience had apparently not taught him that only an independent organisational base would make it possible to approach those workers.

Sartre in fact showed little interest in the new publications and organisations that emerged in this period, despite the fact that many of his associates and contributors to *Les Temps modernes* were involved. The journal *Nouvelle Gauche* appeared twice monthly from April 1956 to November 1957, edited by Colette Audry, and with contributions from Daniel Guérin, Pierre Naville, Claude Bourdet and many others. Audry and Naville also contributed to *Arguments*, a review edited by a group including former Communists Edgar Morin and Henri Lefebvre, who tended to see *Les Temps modernes* as too sympathetic to the PCF. Even when the *nouvelle gauche* merged with a left split from the SFIO to form the Parti Socialiste Unifié (PSU) in 1960, an organisation in which Audry, Bourdet and Naville played a leading role, Sartre took little interest apart from some collaboration on Algeria, probably identifying the PSU as reformist because of its origins in the SFIO. Moreover the RDR experience had made him wary of such attempts at left regroupment.

Yet Sartre continued to influence and encourage a wide range of thinkers and activists on the left. Between 1956 and 1968 there was a whole layer of intellectuals uneasily hovering between reform and revolution. Among them may be mentioned André Gorz, who was heavily involved with *Les Temps modernes*. Gorz's politics – apart from occasional lurches into pro-student ultraleftism[6] – were to the right of Sartre's. In 1966 he gave the notorious lecture in which he prophesied that there would be no general strike by European workers in the foreseeable future.[7] Later he contributed regularly to the *Nouvel Observateur* under the name Michel Bosquet, and bade farewell to politics oriented to the working class in the influential *Adieux au prolétariat*.[8] Although he was an admirer and friend of Sartre, his reformist politics should not be identified too closely with

Sartre. Sartre also gave financial support to the ex-Communist Serge Mallet while he researched his important book *La Nouvelle classe ouvrière*.[9] *Les Temps modernes* published similar work by Pierre Belleville, another sociologist of the 'new working class'.[10]

But by the middle of the 1960s new paths were beginning to open up. Among PCF students new critical tendencies were beginning to emerge. There were some who looked to the Italian CP as an alternative model; many of these had been influenced by Sartre's critique of Stalinist dogmatism. Under the leadership of Togliatti, the Italian CP was destalinising much more rapidly than the PCF, adopting a position described as 'polycentrism' (relative independence of Moscow). But Togliatti was also guiding the Italian CP in a more openly reformist direction; he was very much a precursor of what subsequently came to be known as 'Eurocommunism'. In 1964 Sartre wrote an obituary of 'my friend Togliatti' in which, among other things, he praised Togliatti's positive attitude towards the Common Market. The warmth of his tribute contrasted visibly with the cursory and purely formal message sent on the death of PCF leader Maurice Thorez.[11] When, after the Sino-Soviet split of 1963, a section of the PCF students started to look to China, with its revolutionary rhetoric and its rejection of 'peaceful coexistence', Sartre attempted to encourage such dissidence as part of the process leading to effective destalinisation, while initially nurturing the unrealistic hope that the pro-Italian and pro-Chinese currents might converge.[12]

Sartre's lack of success in influencing the French left sometimes led him to take a highly pessimistic position. Thus he wrote in his 1960 essay on Nizan:

> The left, this great corpse, flat on its back, with worms in it? It stinks, this rotting carcass... We have nothing more to say to the young: fifty years of life in this backward province which France has become, it's humiliating. We have shouted, protested, signed and countersigned... And in the end here we are; we have accepted everything... From failure to failure, we have learnt only one thing: our total impotence'.[13]

It is in the context of this demoralisation that one of the least edifying episodes of his career should be located. Maria Craipeau, a Trotskyist militant in the 1930s and former wife of Yvan Craipeau, conducted an interview with Sartre in 1959 in which a cordial relationship seemed to have been established. She enquired whether Sartre felt vulnerable to criticisms; he responded that when such criticisms came from the left, he did.[14]

But the friendship was not to last. In 1963 Craipeau published a review of the third volume of de Beauvoir's autobiography, *La Force des choses*. She took a distinctly bleak view of the political evolution of Sartre and de Beauvoir: 'nothing but a long love affair with the Communist Party, which "objectively" represented the proletariat, and therefore history; a love that was endlessly spurned, deceived, taken and retaken'.

She argued that since they had never actually joined the Party they had a 'sense of guilt' which led to 'the most extraordinary masochism' with respect to the insults they received from the PCF. Craipeau went on to discuss de Beauvoir's thoughts on old age, and to compare her to revolutionaries of an earlier generation, like Vera Zasulich and Rosa Luxemburg, for whom old age meant simply that they had not much time left to do what had to be done – indeed, she noted, Luxemburg had not lived to enjoy old age.[15]

Sartre responded with one of the most intemperate letters of his career; clearly he was indeed 'vulnerable' to criticism from the left. *France-Observateur* (now edited by Gilles Martinet) found it necessary to preface his letter with a note saying that his conduct was more childish that that of the child described in his autobiography *Les Mots*. Sartre began by indignantly protesting that Craipeau had no right to compare an 'intellectual' like de Beauvoir to a 'politician' like Luxemburg (a peculiarly 'essentialist' distinction for an existentialist to make), and adding the cheap gibe that Craipeau was neither the one nor the other. Rather than defend his own record, Sartre went on to attack her personally, for being a member of the PSU ('that political nothingness') and for writing for *France-Observateur* ('an unreadable paper'). Craipeau was not in fact a member of the PSU; perhaps Sartre assumed she must automatically be a member of the same organisation as her ex-husband! Even more unwisely, he accused both the PSU and *France Observateur* of 'cowardice' during the Algerian War,[16] when in fact both had creditable records that would stand comparison with Sartre's own. Sartre had made a fool of himself; his 'vulnerability' was clearly based on the fact that he recognised the truth in Craipeau's criticisms.

Sartre's pessimism and sense of failure in this period led him to look to revolutionary developments outside France. His record on Algeria showed that he was certainly a consistent and principled opponent of imperialism, well to the left of the PCF. But was he, as he has often been described, a 'third worldist'? Had he merely switched the support he had previously given to the USSR to the emerging nationalist leaders and dictators of the third world? Annie Cohen-Solal has described his preface to Fanon's *Les Damnés de la terre* as being 'one of his most furiously third worldist texts'.[17]

It is true that in the period after 1958 Sartre was depressed at the seeming passivity of the mainstream French left. If a courageous but relatively small minority took action against the Algerian War, the mass parties of the left, the PCF and the SFIO, were at best sluggish in opposition and at worst complicit with imperialism. Sartre welcomed the struggles against imperialism developing in Africa, in Cuba and a little later in Vietnam, and hoped that these could help to revive and reinvigorate the international left. His visit to postrevolutionary Cuba in 1960, where he met Castro and Che Guevara, was of particular symbolic importance in this respect.

But there was a continuity in Sartre's thinking from the 1940s onwards. It was based on the principle summed up in Marx's statement that 'Any people that oppresses another people forges its own chains'.[18] For Marx a working class that supported the imperialism of its own nation necessarily subordinated itself to its own ruling class by seeing itself as sharing a common 'national interest' with it. It was the same logic as Liebknecht's principle, 'the main enemy is at home', which had oriented Sartre's strategy towards the USSR in the 1940s and 1950s. Sartre thus argued that the liberation of colonised or otherwise oppressed populations was inextricably linked to the emancipation of the proletariat in the imperialist nations, and that therefore working-class solidarity with liberation struggles was possible, although it was certainly not automatic and had to be fought for against tenacious opposition.

Thus in 1948, at the time of the RDR, Sartre had told a meeting of supporters of Moroccan independence:

> We shall not be worthy to demand our own freedom for as long as we have not been liberated from the shame and fear which belong to the oppressor, for as long as any man on earth is oppressed because of us.
>
> It is by struggling alongside you against our common oppressors that we shall liberate ourselves.[19]

In a 1959 interview with Francis Jeanson Sartre argued a similar position, claiming that as long as the colonial system was still functioning effectively it was inevitable that metropolitan workers would find themselves closer to their bosses than to the colonised populations. However, the colonial system contained the seeds of its own destruction within itself; as a result: '*Today*, French workers are in solidarity with the Algerian fighters because both of them have the most urgent interest in breaking the chains of colonisation'.[20]

Sartre therefore gave an important role in the struggle against imperialism to the working class. In this he remained much closer to classical Marxism than those 'third worldist' thinkers of the 1960s who, following Mao or Guevara, saw the peasantry as the main revolutionary class on a world scale. Indeed, Sartre was far less sympathetic to the peasantry than most French Marxists. In *Saint Genet* he contrasted the conservatism of the peasantry as compared with the working class – 'the peasant acquires the silent immobility of his field'.[21] That Sartre largely resisted the romanticisation of the peasantry widespread on the French left is another indication of how rooted his thought was in the classic traditions of the socialist left.

And while Sartre denounced the myth that there were 'good' settlers (*colons*) in Algeria or that any reform could be hoped for from such settlers, he made clear that this indictment did not include the 'poor whites', the working classes of Algeria (from which Camus had originated): 'I don't describe as settlers either the minor officials or the European workers who are simultaneously victims and innocent profiteers from the regime'.[22]

Hence Sartre's persistent and frequent willingness to stand up in solidarity with those of whatever political tendency who were fighting imperialism; thus in 1967 he appeared at a meeting in support of the imprisoned Trotskyist Hugo Blanco, threatened with the death sentence for having organised peasant trade unions in Peru.[23]

It may seem to many that the one major exception to this lies in Sartre's systematic sympathy for the state of Israel, which they would see as a loyal ally of U.S. imperialism and the oppressor of the Palestinian population. Sartre's tortuous position on the Middle East is a complex subject, and not really relevant to the subject of this book. Suffice it to say that Sartre's support for Israel was rooted in his recognition of the historic oppression of Jews, and while he always recognised the right of the Israeli state to exist, he also recognised Palestinian national rights.[24]

Sartre's preface to Fanon's *Les Damnés de la terre*[25] must be seen against this background. It was undoubtedly a passionate, angry and provocative text. But Sartre's anger was directed against the French left, and it was to this French left that Sartre addressed himself. True, he described the 'beautiful souls' of the French left as 'racist', but he clearly did not think they were incurably so, since his aim in the preface was to persuade them to read Fanon.[26]

Moreover, the fact that he chose Fanon to preface was significant, for Fanon was far from being an archetypal third worldist or black nationalist. The relation between Fanon and Sartre was a complex one; in formulating his thought Fanon had been deeply influenced by Sartre's work, especially *Réflexions sur la question juive*, which impressed him much more than 'Orphée noir', about which he had considerable reservations.[27] Moreover, Fanon was deeply rooted in the traditions of the European left, and in particular of the anti-Stalinist left. As a young man he had shown a great interest in Trotsky;[28] in *Peau noire masques blancs*, among many other sources including Sartre and Leiris, he drew on Pierre Naville's *Psychologie, marxisme, matérialisme* to argue that individual sexuality and dreams depend on the general conditions of civilisation, especially the class struggle.[29] He had little sympathy for Stalinism, especially as a result of the USSR's lack of enthusiasm for Algerian independence, and on occasion is said to have described Russia as being a form of 'state capitalism'.[30] In *L'An V de la révolution algérienne* he devoted an extended essay to the role of those Europeans in Algeria who had given material support to the struggle for national independence.[31] Indeed, if Fanon had not recognised an important role for the European left, he would not have spent so much time in his last year of life in intense discussion with Sartre; as he told Lanzmann: 'I'd pay twenty thousand francs a day to talk to Sartre from morning to night for a fortnight'.[32]

Sartre has been much criticised for the sympathy he showed to Castro's Cuba in the late 1950s and 1960s.[33] Again this must be set in the context of the period, when Sartre's pessimistic assessment of the French left meant that he was looking for new sources of inspiration. What is clear is that the flirtation with Castro was by no means a rerun of his *rapprochement* with the USSR. Sartre had learnt from that experience and had no desire to repeat it. The full story of his relation with Cuba was complex and contained a number of contradictions.[34] But if his support for the USSR between 1952 and 1956 was genuinely tragic, Cuba was to be no more than a one-act farce.

Sartre and de Beauvoir visited Cuba for a month in February and March 1960, a little over a year after Castro had taken power. They felt undoubted enthusiasm for the new regime; Sartre spoke of the 'honeymoon of the revolution', but at the same time he was aware of historical precedent – he doubtless shared de Beauvoir's sentiments when she commented: 'It wouldn't last for ever, but it was encouraging'.[35] What was encouraging was, primarily, the defeat of imperialism. Sartre was explicitly asked not to present the new Cuba as 'socialist'.[36] Castro had not yet discovered that he was a Marxist-Leninist; that was to come only after the U.S. economic boycott and the Bay of Pigs invasion forced him to seek trade and aid from Russia.

Sartre reported on his visit to Cuba in sixteen articles in *France-Soir*, under the general title 'Ouragan sur le sucre' (Storm over Sugar). These never appeared in book form in French, though they did in Spanish and English.[37] The articles were enthusiastic in celebrating the changes initiated by Castro's regime, although it was the democratic and welfare aspects that were stressed. However, at points Sartre's enthusiasm ran away with him. He described an occasion when Castro was served warm lemonade because of a defective refrigerator; the Cuban leader examined the fridge himself and warned the waitress to tell her managers that they would have problems with him. Sartre commented that 'It was the first time that I understood – still very vaguely – what the other day I referred to as "direct democracy" '.[38] The only response is that if this were in fact true, he ought to have got out more.

Yet in private Sartre remained deeply suspicious – he was not going to wait for another set of Khrushchev-style revelations. When Che Guevara was killed in Bolivia, Sartre insisted that the body photographed was not Che, and that Guevara had been killed by Castro in Havana for having criticised the Castroite bureaucracy.[39]

It was all to end in tears. In 1971, after Sartre had taken up the case of the imprisoned Cuban poet Heberto Padilla, he found himself being denounced by his erstwhile comrade Castro as being among the 'bourgeois liberal gentlemen... two-bit agents of colonialism... agents of the CIA and intelligence services of imperialism' who had dared to criticise Cuba.[40] Sartre responded with a plea to Castro to 'spare Cuba the dogmatic obscurantism, the cultural xenophobia and the repressive system which Stalinism imposed in the socialist countries'.[41]

Thus Sartre had not gone overboard for third worldism. Rather he was seeking some alternative to post-Stalinist Communism which might assist the reawakening of the left, in France and internationally.

This was shown by the fact that at the very same time as Sartre was enthusing about Cuba he was also continuing to praise the Italian Communist Party and Togliatti. While Togliatti was the hero of the open reformists, Castro was becoming the hero of the extreme left, including many Trotskyists who became his uncritical acolytes.

Yet Sartre was not being as inconsistent as it might seem, for Togliatti's reformism and Castro's guerrillaism were two faces of the same coin. Both professed an independence of Moscow which was verbal rather than a clean break with Stalinism; both represented a type of politics which involved acting for the working class rather than mobilising it to act for itself. Sartre was still on occasion failing to distinguish the working class from those who claimed to act in its name, and showed himself much more impressed by style than by substance.

So, in the decade following the Hungarian rising, Sartre's political achievements were at best ambiguous. In 1965 two former *pivertiste* colleagues from the 1930s, Colette Audry and Aimé Patri, debated publicly about Sartre. Patri was scornful about Sartre's 'exceptional political clumsiness', which he attributed to the facts that Sartre had come late to politics and that his philosophy prevented him from becoming a true Marxist. Audry, however, defended Sartre, arguing that if, in a hundred or 150 years' time, anyone wanted to understand the political thought of people of our time, 'it will be in Sartre that they will find the image of the difficulties and agonising conflicts that we have lived through'.[42]

In a sense both were right. Sartre's actual achievements were few, yet he undoubtedly did embody the contradictions of a whole historical period. That period, however, was coming to an end. By 1965 events were in progress which would open up a dramatic new phase, not just for Sartre, but for the whole international left.

Sartre had not been wrong in seeing, like Trotsky and many before him, a dialectical interaction between the struggles of the third world and those of the metropolitan working class. If the Algerian War had divided and demoralised the French left, the war in Vietnam would play a crucial role in its reawakening.

When the bombing of North Vietnam began in the spring of 1965, Sartre cancelled a proposed visit to an American university. He argued that while people in the third world would see such a visit as a betrayal of the Vietnamese cause, there was no valid anti-war movement in the U.S.A. which he could encourage; he saw the American opponents of the war as 'a tiny minority of intellectuals who, if they are not all politicised, are at least "moralised", and who understand the political absurdity and the shamefulness of what their country is doing in Vietnam. They are totally impotent'.[43]

Sartre was soon to be pleasantly surprised by the rapid growth of a mass anti-war movement, not only in the United States, but in France. And in France, as elsewhere, the movement soon divided along political lines. On the one hand, the PCF, ostensibly concerned with the broadest unity, put forward the anodyne slogan 'Peace in Vietnam'. On the other hand, the *Comité National Vietnam*, in which Sartre played a leading role alongside ex-Trotskyist Laurent Schwartz and one of the Trotskyist leaders of the upcoming student generation, Alain Krivine, adopted as its main slogan 'The NLF [National Liberation Front] will win'.[44] Once again Sartre was learning that when it came to the crunch, he was more likely to find his allies among the anti-Stalinist left.

In particular Sartre came to play an important role in the International War Crimes Tribunal, generally referred to as the Russell Tribunal because of the participation of the distinguished British philosopher Bertrand Russell, who had a record of anti-war activity stretching back to 1914. That two of the world's greatest philosophers, albeit from very different traditions, came together in opposition to the Vietnam War was undoubtedly a source of enormous encouragement to a new generation of politically active students.

The personnel of the Russell Tribunal came from different countries and a range of political positions, but many were in one way or another representatives of the independent non-Stalinist left. From the U.S.A. came Stokely Carmichael, a leading figure from the new wave of black militancy; from Italy, Lelio Basso of the PSIUP (roughly equivalent to the French PSU); from Yugoslavia Vladimir Dedijer, a former Communist leader who had been expelled from the Party Central Committee for defending the oppositionist Djilas; from France Sartre, de Beauvoir and Schwartz; from Britain Lawrence Daly, a miners' leader who broken with the Communist Party in 1956 and formed the Fife Socialist League, linked to *New Left Review*. Other participants included Isaac Deutscher, and Peter Weiss, a playwright who was later to write a drama on the life of Trotsky.[45] The central organiser was Ralph Schoenman, an American anti-war activist, who at the time had rather tense and ambiguous relations with the Fourth International in Britain. As de Beauvoir reported, he had 'the vices of his virtues, and a few more besides',[46] and was responsible for both the success of the Tribunal and many of its internal disputes.

The PCF was clearly not enthusiastic about such a venture which was out of its control and where Trotskyists clearly had a considerable foothold. Sartre, asked in a 1967 interview about the PCF's noncommittal attitude, attempted, obviously in the interests of unity, to play this down, pointing to support from the Italian and Swedish CPs, and to the involvement of Jean-Pierre Vigier of the PCF.[47] (By 1968 Vigier was to leave the Party in favour of the revolutionary left.)

In 1968, at the time of the Russian invasion of Czechoslovakia, Sartre was told by Vietnamese representatives in Paris that West Germany was preparing a capitalist takeover of Czechoslovakia. Sartre told them that if they used such standards of evidence in documenting U.S. war crimes they would be undermining their own case, and had a representative of the Tribunal sent to Hanoi to explain the point to Ho Chi Minh.[48]

Vietnam was to have a major impact in reawakening the international left. Meanwhile, at home in France a new social force was emerging. The vast expansion of higher education under de Gaulle was leading to radicalisation among students, who faced overcrowding, poor conditions, archaic syllabuses and regulations and the fact that a university education was no longer a passport to a prosperous middle-class career. The Algerian War had politicised many students, but the fundamental cause of student radicalisation was the same in France as everywhere else, the changing social role of students from being a small elite minority destined for privileged status in society to something involving a much broader layer of society.

This radicalisation posed problems for the PCF. Many of its intellectual members held university teaching posts and did not welcome a challenge to their authority by discontented students. The PCF 's adaptation to bourgeois academic life can be seen from an article called 'Concerning "Student Power" ', published in June 1968:

> Without paternalism vis-à-vis the students, and without demagogy, we are acting in a responsible way in strongly criticising the very principle of 'student power' no matter what its form.

> A student in the first or second cycle (secondary school and first years of university) cannot judge the scientific value of a professor. He can and ought, naturally, possibly to criticise his technique in transmitting knowledge but his criticism must stop there.

> By the third cycle things are no doubt different but even there the idea of challenging basics cannot be accepted without extreme caution.[49]

Louis Althusser's famous defence of the 'autonomy of theory' (the principle that theoretical and scientific questions cannot be reduced to political ones) was an important component in the PCF's reaction to student demands.[50]

In 1964 *Les Temps modernes* carried a major article by Marc Kravetz on the development of student trade-unionism. He argued that what students learnt at the university was primarily 'passivity and submission', that neocapitalism needed 'human robots' and that a long struggle was required to build student unions that could fight for 'fundamental reform' of the university system.[51] Kravetz, a young man in his early twenties, was a member of the generation who had been radicalised by the Algerian War. Through contacts with *La Voie communiste* and *Socialisme ou barbarie* he had inherited some of the traditions of the anti-Stalinist left.[52]

It was not only the PCF intellectuals who felt threatened by this new wave of revolt. Kravetz's article in *Les Temps modernes* was immediately followed by a note signed J.-B.P. (J.-B. Pontalis – a lecturer at the *Centre national de la recherche scientifique* and later at the *Ecole pratique des hautes études*). Ostensibly this was a call for further debate with contributions from both students and lecturers. But in fact Pontalis was making clear his own reservations, noting that readers will find 'something to take exception to on almost every page'.[53] Sartre himself, who had a gift for aligning himself with the oppressed even though the theoretical justification might be contorted or contradictory, sided with Kravetz and against Pontalis and Bernard Pingaud.[54] Just as that gift had led him to side with the workers of Budapest against the bureaucrats of the PCF, so it was to lead him into another confrontation with French Stalinism. The next battle was to be on Sartre's own doorstep.

Notes

1. *Il Messagero di Roma*, 25 August 1959; *C&R*, p. 335.
2. 'Entretien avec Jean-Paul Sartre', *La Voie communiste* No. 29, p. 20.
3. *L'Express*, 22 May 1958; *Sit* V, p. 93.
4. M.-A. Burnier, 'On ne peut pas être sartrien...'. *TM* October–December 1990, pp. 927–28; *TM*, November 1965, pp. 769–75; *Le Monde*, 4 December 1965.
5. Sartre, 'Après Budapest', *L'Express*, 9 November 1956, p.16.
6. For example his 1970 piece 'Détruire l'université', in which he argued: 'The University cannot function; it must therefore be prevented from functioning so that this impossibility becomes obvious. No reform of any kind can make this institution viable; we must therefore oppose reforms... because they are illusory' (*TM*, April 1970, pp. 1553–58, especially p. 1553).
7. A. Gorz, 'Reform and Revolution', in R. Miliband and J. Saville, eds., *The Socialist Register 1968*, London, 1968, p. 111. Gorz's article was based on a lecture series originally delivered in Sweden in April 1966.
8. A. Gorz, *Adieux au prolétariat*, Paris, 1980.
9. S. Mallet, *La Nouvelle classe ouvrière*, Paris, 1963.
10. A. Hirsh, *The French Left*, Montreal, 1982, p. 155.
11. *Sit* IX, pp. 137–51; *C&R*, p. 400.
12. *Raison*, pp. 61–62.
13. *Sit* IV, p. 138.
14. 'Jean-Paul Sartre: "Le Silence de ceux qui reviennent..." ', *France-Observateur* 10 September 1959, pp. 12–13; cf. J.-P. Boulé, *Sartre médiatique*, Fleury sur Orne, 1992, pp. 58–60.
15. M. Craipeau, 'La Vie en marge', *France-Observateur*, 5 December 1963, pp. 13–14.
16. *France Observateur*, 12 December 1963, p. 2.
17. A. Cohen-Solal, *Sartre*, Paris, 1985, p. 720.
18. K. Marx and F. Engels, *Collected Works*, London and Moscow, 1975–2001, 21:120.
19. *Combat*, 19 November 1948.
20. *C&R*, p. 727.
21. J.-P. Sartre, *Saint Genet*, Paris, 1952, pp. 18–19.
22. *Sit* V, p. 27.
23. *Solidarité Pérou* No. 6, May 1967, pp. 1–2, 8.
24. See N. Lamouchi, *Jean-Paul Sartre et le tiers monde*, Paris, 1996, 151–65; E. Ben-Gal, *Mardi, chez Sartre*, Paris, 1992, pp. 281–308, 315–27.
25. *Sit* V, pp. 167–93; originally appeared as preface to F. Fanon, *Les Damnés de la terre*, Paris, 1961.
26. *Sit* V, p. 182.

27. I.L. Gendzier, *Frantz Fanon*, London, 1973, pp. 30–35, 56–57.
28. Gendzier, *Frantz Fanon*, p. 20.
29. F. Fanon, *Peau noire, masques blancs*, Paris, 1952, pp. 109–10.
30. See T. Bergmann and M. Kessler, eds., *Ketzer im Kommunismus*, Mainz, 1993, p. 273.
31. 'La Minorité européenne d'Algérie', in F. Fanon, *L'An V de la révolution algérienne*, Paris, 1960, pp. 141–60. First appeared in *TM*, June 1959, pp. 1841–67.
32. *Choses*, p. 619.
33. E.g., J. Verdès-Leroux, *La Lune et le caudillo*, Paris, 1989.
34. See Jay Murphy, 'Sartre on Cuba Revisited', *Sartre Studies International* Vol. 2, No. 2 (1996), pp. 27–48.
35. *Choses*, p. 515.
36. A. Astruc and M. Contat, *Sartre*, Paris, 1977, p. 119.
37. *France-Soir*, 28 June to 15 July 1960; *Sartre visita a Cuba*, Havana, 1960; *Sartre on Cuba*, New York, 1961.
38. *France-Soir*, 13 July 1960.
39. E. Ben-Gal, *Mardi chez Sartre*, Paris, 1992, p. 138.
40. F. Castro, speech to the First National Congress on Education and Culture, April 1971.
41. *Le Monde*, 22 May 1971. See *L'Année sartrienne* No. 15, Paris, June 2001, pp. 211–13.
42. *Figaro*, 25 February 1965.
43. *Sit* VIII, p. 16.
44. R. Hayman, *Writing Against*, London, 1986, p. 385; H. Hamon and P. Rotman, *Génération*, 2 vols, Paris, 1990,1: 309, 426.
45. *Trotski im Exil*, Frankfurt am Main, 1970; *Trotsky in Exile*, London, 1971.
46. *Compte*, p. 382.
47. *Sit* VIII, p. 67.
48. V. Dedijer and R. Rizman, *The Universal Validity of Human Rights*, Kamnik (Yugoslavia), 1982, pp. 14–15.
49. *L'Humanité*, 15 June 1968.
50. J. Rancière, *La Leçon d'Althusser*, Paris, 1974, pp. 84–88.
51. M. Kravetz, 'Naissance d'un syndicalisme étudiant', *TM*, February 1964, pp. 1447–75.
52. Hamon and Rotman, *Génération*, 1: 191–92.
53. J.-B. P., 'Un Couple menacé', *TM*, February 1964, pp. 1476–78.
54. *Compte*, p. 154.

Chapter 17

MAY TO DECEMBER

The events of 1968, often ignorantly dismissed as no more than a year of 'student revolt', undermined the political certainties that had endured since 1945. In Vietnam, the world's strongest power was proved vulnerable in face of a national liberation struggle. The Russian invasion of Czechoslovakia marked a definitive end to Moscow's hegemony over the world's Communist Parties. In France a general strike of over nine million workers, the biggest general strike in human history, showed that the power of the working class could not be ignored; an anti-Stalinist left that had been confined to the margins of political life found itself in the full glare of public attention.

These events redrew the map of the French left. For Sartre this was to be the last major turning point of his career. In the early days of May he made the final break with the PCF, and aligned himself unambiguously with the revolutionary left.

On 8 May *Le Monde* published a brief press statement urging 'all workers and intellectuals to give moral and material support to the struggle launched by students and teachers'.[1] The small group of Sartre's fellow-signatories read almost like a cast-list for *This is Your Life*: Simone de Beauvoir; Colette Audry, the *pivertiste* comrade from the 1930s; Daniel Guérin, regular writer for *Les Temps modernes* and pioneer campaigner for Algerian independence; Michel Leiris, former surrealist and long-time contributor to *Les Temps modernes*.[2] And on 10 May a further statement appeared, signed not only by Sartre, but by Maurice Nadeau and Maurice Blanchot, organisers of the Manifesto of the 121, and by André Gorz and Henri Lefebvre.[3]

Meanwhile Georges Marchais of the PCF was taking a very different stance. On 3 May he had published a long tirade against the 'false revolutionaries' and 'leftist *groupuscules*' led by the 'German anarchist' Cohn-

Bendit, whose activities 'fitted into the pattern of the anti-Communist campaign of the Gaullist authorities'. Whereas the PCF in the 1940s had feared that Sartre was challenging its hegemony among students, the Party now saw the student movement in the hands of dissidents, and was outraged that some of these were daring to appear 'more and more frequently... at the factory gates'.[4] Ironically, Marchais chose this article to cite Anatole France's remark about 'no enemies on the left'. Like Sartre, the PCF had chosen their side.

Sartre continued to identify himself with the revolutionary students, and by many of them he was perceived as one of the few representatives of the older generation they could trust.[5] A number of the student leaders had first come into politics in opposition to the Algerian War, and had respected Sartre's role in that struggle.

The events of 1968 drew the lines between Sartre and Stalinism very clearly. Although the PCF suffered a serious electoral setback in 1968 as a result of the strategy it had opted for, it quickly recovered this ground, and indeed, during the 1970s had its most substantial period of growth since the 1940s, rising from 425,000 in 1966 to 700,000 in the mid-1970s. But although the PCF recruited – including many former 1968 activists – it now did so as an openly reformist party, which for a considerable part of the 1970s boasted of its alliance with Mitterrand's newly reconstituted Socialist Party. Those who decided to join the PCF after 1968 were making a conscious decision to reject the revolutionary left. For intellectuals the PCF was a safe choice which would not interfere with their careers. Jacques Rancière quoted a PCF academic as telling his pupils that he was in the PCF 'because it is the only organisation that does not require me to be an activist'.[6]

Sartre's loss of faith in the PCF was now rapid. In 1969 he pointed to the 'complete inadequacy of the "historic" institutions of the Communist Party to the tasks which we have a right to assign to it'. Sartre now rejected the popular front strategy once and for all, and applied the critique retrospectively by recognising that in 1945 the Western CPs had been required by Moscow to abandon any attempt to take power[7] (thus admitting that Germain-Mandel had been right in their 1952 exchange).

Sartre's view of Russia also showed radical development, as he moved closer to the positions advanced by Rousset and Lefort in the 1940s and 1950s. In a 1964 interview Sartre had still insisted that: 'If there were to be conflicts in the USSR, they would take the form of a *reformism* and not of a revolution. There would be no class to be overthrown, but new arrangements (*aménagements*) might be demanded, which is a very different matter'.[8]

But after the Russian invasion of Czechoslovakia he spoke of 'Soviet imperialism', while saying that it followed different laws from U.S. imperialism.[9] Recalling that friends in the USSR had told him that progress was slow but irreversible, he commented: 'I sometimes feel that nothing was irreversible except the continuous and implacable degradation of Soviet socialism'.[10] At a meeting in January 1971 he said that for a correct policy on Jews in the USSR to be applied, 'it would be necessary for the Soviet working classes to take the power which has been stolen from them'.[11]

Such statements were unambiguous; but there was no trace of the theoretical analysis which Lefort and his comrades of *Socialisme ou barbarie* had put into their analysis of Russian society (though such questions lay behind the uncompleted second volume of the *Critique*). Yet neither was there any evidence that Sartre was adopting the rather grotesque theory current in some Maoist circles that Russia became a new class society after the death of Stalin. Stalinism for Sartre still lay at the heart of the problem. Coming back to his 1940s thoughts on the dialectic of ends and means, he affirmed: 'It is impossible to reach socialism by starting from Stalinism, for one will never reach anything except something whose instrument has been Stalinism'.[12]

In an interview with the German magazine *Der Spiegel* in 1973, Sartre developed the argument further by claiming that there was nothing specifically socialist about nationalisation. If an enterprise was nationalised while the capitalist structure was preserved (*bewahrt*), then what resulted was 'state capitalism'. And he pointed out that the Renault factory, whose security staff had killed a sacked worker in 1972, was a nationalised enterprise.[13] Although Sartre's thought remained fluid, it was clear that the debates that he had been engaged in since the 1940s had not left him untouched, and that he was coming to recognise that there was nothing socialist, in however degenerated a form, about the USSR, and that state ownership could in no way be equated with socialism.

The PCF was equally well aware that the old relationship was gone for good. On 21 October 1970 Maoists announced to workers at Renault Billancourt by leaflet that Sartre would speak in the Bir-Hakeim square at 2.10 p.m. as the shift was leaving. The PCF, anxious to preserve its proletarian base from contamination, was quite happy to exploit Sartre's pro-Israel sympathies in order to discourage the large number of North African workers. A report in a Trotskyist paper described events:

The same morning a PCF leaflet headed 'Warning' set the tone…

'WHO IS SARTRE?

'He is the man who took the initiative for a statement by intellectuals, greeting the Israeli–American aggression against the Arab peoples. That is why he has been declared unwelcome in all the Arab countries'.

So that this warning should have full effect, by 2.00 p.m. there was an array of CGT militants, PCF members, posted at the Zola gate to inform the workers: 'Beware. It's a provocation. The Bir-Hakeim square is crawling with cops. Don't go there, take the Yves-Kermen road, etc'. And the cordon of PCF members gently guided the workers to the Yves-Kermen road. The detour was obviously intended to avoid the Bir-Hakeim square, where there was no sign of any cops, but where Sartre was explaining to between one and two hundred people the meaning of the Geismar trial and Maoists from the factory – sacked or about to be so – were calling for 'popular resistance'.[14]

In 1974 *L'Humanité* published a biting attack on Sartre by none other than Jean Genet – Zhdanov's former whipping boy – who accused Sartre of 'bankruptcy' in his failure to support the struggle of immigrant workers. *L'Humanité*'s comments on Genet's attack made clear what was really at stake – Sartre's refusal to call for a vote for François Mitterrand, described as 'the only candidate of the left, who defends them'.[15]

After 1968 the revolutionary left had come out of the shadows. The claim that socialism could be identified exclusively with the twin bureaucracies of Stalinism and social democracy was no longer plausible. Those individuals and groups of the anti-Stalinist left with whom Sartre had sometimes cooperated, sometimes polemicised fiercely, had seen their long and often wearisome task fulfilled, and a new left created. That new left was real, real enough to cause considerable anxiety to the existing regime and to provoke quite serious repression. But it was also a left that was deeply divided by factionalism, often wildly overoptimistic and hence ultraleft in its perspectives.

Initially Sartre found himself politically closest to such militant students as Daniel Cohn-Bendit, who had been influenced by the traditions of the anti-Stalinist left and in particular by the ideas of *Socialisme ou barbarie*. (Unfortunately *Socialisme ou barbarie*'s politics had led it ever further from the task of building a revolutionary organisation; it had dissolved itself in 1967 and was not able to take advantage of its success.)

Sartre had played his part in the birth of a new left. But the warring currents of the far left offered him no obvious home. It is often claimed that he became a 'Maoist'. In fact things were not quite so simple. In his preface to Michèle Manceaux's 1972 book *Les Maos en France*, Sartre began by asserting: 'I am not a Maoist'.[16]

In fact defining what constituted being a Maoist was a rather difficult operation. The post-1968 pro-Chinese left was fragmented, and its policies, to say the least, fluid. Sartre never showed any detailed interest in the economic and social structure of Communist China, and had little contact with the pro-Chinese 'Marxist-Leninists' who stressed their attachment to Beijing orthodoxy.[17] As a result he seems to have been little affected by the disillusion with China that affected many Maoists after the death of Mao.

For Sartre 'Maoism' above all meant the activism of the post-1968 French Maoists, their enthusiasm for spontaneity, their willingness to use violence, their rejection of bourgeois legality, and what he saw as their stress on morality: 'They prove that in fact, when one engages in politics, it is wrong to consider morality as a mere superstructure, but it must be considered that it exists on the same level as what are called infrastructures, which has always been my opinion'.[18]

Certainly the Maoists enabled Sartre to develop a militant practice which he never previously had (except perhaps very briefly in the RDR period). He sold papers on the streets, just as his friend Colette Audry had sold *Le Populaire* nearly forty years earlier. Like Gorky's *Mother*, Sartre was learning his activism from the younger generation. He gave his name as responsible for a number of revolutionary newspapers at the time of state repression against leftism in the early 1970s, on the basis that the authorities would think twice about imprisoning anyone so distinguished. But he did so primarily as a defence of civil liberties, and the fact that these papers were mainly Maoist (including the ex-Trotskyist and semi-Maoist *Révolution!*) did not necessarily indicate political alignment. Doubtless, if asked, Sartre would have extended his protection to the Trotskyist press, but in fact journals such as *Rouge* and *Lutte ouvrière* were sufficiently well organised not to need his services.[19]

But the very spontaneity and activism which attracted Sartre to the Maoists was inseparable from their political volatility. In 1970 Sartre and Alain Geismar of the *Gauche prolétarienne* were interviewed together in the *Nouvel Observateur*. Geismar insisted that the Maoists 'are not seeking – like the Trotskyists, like the PSU – to create the conditions for taking power in a month'. He argued that political revolutions must be preceded by 'ideological revolution', which in France would take the form of 'popular guerrilla warfare', and that their struggle might take 'ten years, twenty years, perhaps more'. Sartre spoke much less than Geismar and expressed only the mildest reservations.[20] But ten years later neither Geismar nor Maoism was much in evidence.

Yet Sartre remained extremely distrustful of the Trotskyist tradition despite – perhaps because of – its greater stability. In part this may be seen as a hangover from an earlier period, a recollection of polemics with Rousset and Naville, Mandel and Lefort, and a sense that in the post-1968 era something new was needed.

When de Gaulle resigned in 1969, Alain Krivine, leading figure in the *Ligue communiste*, announced his intention to run for the presidency as a revolutionary alternative to the PCF and the SFIO. Sartre signed a statement in his support, along with such longstanding associates as de Beauvoir, Nadeau, Leiris and Audry (as well as erstwhile adversaries like Marguerite Duras and Dionys Mascolo).[21] Yet Sartre retained his deep distrust of electoral politics; he explained later: 'I expected Krivine to say, when he first appeared on TV: thanks for having listened to me, I wanted nothing else. Do what you like with your votes, but don't vote for me, because I'm no longer a candidate'.[22]

This showed a very limited understanding of what could be achieved through an election campaign. In fact Sartre gave no further support to Krivine after the initial statement.[23] Sartre's basic political criticism of the Trotskyists was that they wished to use legal means where possible:

> The weakness of the PSU and the LCR is that they try to use sometimes illegality – for example, by going ahead with a banned demonstration – and sometimes legality – by, for example, putting up candidates in elections. In fact, if you respect legality, you can't act against the system: you're inside it. Voting, for example, as Kravetz says, is voting for the vote, that is for the delegation of powers. This way you will never destroy the system.[24]

Here Sartre, who had claimed *Les Mains sales* was inspired by Lenin's *Left-Wing Communism*, revealed that he had never understood that text. On one occasion Sartre told Krivine that the Trotskyists had a programme but that their action was legalistic, whereas the Maoists had no programme but useful activity; therefore, he urged, the two tendencies should fuse.[25] It was a charming testimony to Sartre's political naivety.

In the course of the 1970s the entire European far left went through a massive crisis. As it became clear that the expectations raised by 1968 were not being delivered as quickly as had been hoped, many turned in disillusion to reformism or even to the political right. Others sought to substitute their own impatience for the dilatoriness of the masses by engaging in terrorism. And in general it was the Trotskyists who weathered the storm far better than the Maoists. In those countries like Germany and Italy, where the anti-Stalinist left had been weak before 1968, the left grew rapidly in the 1970s and then collapsed into chaos and terrorism.

Contrary to frequent allegations, Sartre did not have any sympathy for terrorism. His notorious visit to Andreas Baader in jail in December 1974 was a protest against governmental repression rather than an act of solidarity with Baader. In fact nobody was pleased; the right denounced Sartre for supporting terrorism, while Baader complained: 'I expected a friend and I see a judge instead'. Sartre summed up the episode as a 'failure', but added: 'If I had to do it again, I'd do it'.[26]

In France the situation was more complex. By the end of the 1970s the Maoist left had largely disappeared; some of its leading figures had joined the ranks of the *nouveaux philosophes* (a grouping of anti-socialist writers launched by the Grasset publishing house). *Libération*, the daily paper Sartre had put such efforts into launching, became by the 1980s a loyal supporter of Mitterrand's Socialist Party, differing from *Le Monde* only in having a more up-to-date style. The Trotskyists of *Lutte ouvrière* and the LCR survived, though battered.

More significantly, reformism had recovered much more than had seemed possible in 1968. During the 1970s François Mitterrand rebuilt his Socialist Party and reduced the PCF to a minority position. Sartre never really came to terms with this revival of reformism. In an interview published in July 1968 he had rather rashly prophesied: 'I am convinced that the present leaders of the left will no longer represent anything in ten years time and I don't see what danger there would be in a revolutionary movement being formed outside the PCF and to its left'.[27] The strategic judgement that the time was ripe for a new revolutionary organisation marked a significant break with the past; but the suggestion that Mitterrand would simply evaporate was, to say the least, rash.

Yet, while stretching the time-scale a little, Sartre stood by this position; in a discussion with Benny Lévy shortly before his death, he asserted: 'I say quite simply that at present the parties are screwed (*foutus*). It's quite clear that in twenty or thirty years from now the great parties of the left will no longer be what they are now'.[28] In a sense Sartre was correct here. Two decades after his death the PCF was a tiny rump, which maintained its parliamentary representation only by courtesy of the Socialist Party, while the Socialist Party itself had moved ever closer to the political centre, abandoning most of its distinctive identity as a party of the left. Yet Sartre gave only the vaguest idea of what new sort of organisation would replace traditional parties. His distrust of party organisation, dating back to his earliest years, though brutally negated during his *rapprochement* with Stalinism in the 1950s, was one of the great weaknesses in his political strategy.

Many of Sartre's most successful interventions came as a result of what he himself called his 'star role'.[29] (Sartre's self-critical view of his own 'star role' can perhaps be seen as a continuity of the critique of 'spectacular demonstrations' which was made in the Sartre–Chauvin resolution for the 1949 RDR Conference.) But precisely the deployment of this 'star role' could not be adopted as a strategy by others. Sartre could defy the police because the government was embarrassed to imprison him (at the time of the Manifesto of 121 de Gaulle was reputed to have said, 'One does not put Voltaire in jail';[30] if the actual words were apocryphal,[31] the logic was certainly present); but the selfsame police would be only too happy to beat up the ordinary militants accompanying him.

Sartre's last years have been the subject of much controversy. Some have seized on his handshake with his old enemy Raymond Aron at a demonstration in support of Vietnamese 'boat people' in 1979, or his alleged expressions of interest in Judaism, as an indication that he had renounced his old ideas. But although a number of ambiguities and confusions undoubtedly persisted, Sartre clearly remained a revolutionary socialist. If he abandoned the term 'Marxist' in the 1970s, it was not any indication of a move to the right. On the contrary, as he told Michel Rybalka in 1975, he now used the term 'libertarian socialism'.[32] It was an echo, conscious or unconscious, of the title of a book by his old comrade Daniel Guérin, *Jeunesse du socialisme libertaire*.[33]

In 1977 he gave an interview to the Italian revolutionary paper *Lotta Continua*, on the occasion of a far left rally in Bologna. The Bologna municipality had been controlled by the Italian Communist Party since the Second World War; in March 1977 the authorities had cracked down on a demonstration by students and unemployed, and a student was shot dead by police. Sartre stated: 'I cannot accept that a young militant should be killed in the streets of a city run by the Communist Party. Every time the state police shoots at a young militant, I am alongside him'.[34]

Sartre gave his very last interview to a gay newspaper, *Le Gai Pied*.[35] Here he spoke at length about homosexuality and literature, especially in relation to Genet, and observed that both fascism and Stalinism had committed terrible crimes against homosexuals. Given the vigorous condemnation of homosexuality – as grave a sin as eating an owl – in Leviticus,[36] his conversion to Judaism had obviously not gone as far as all that. The interview revealed a remarkable continuity with Sartre's work of earlier decades, as he recalled *Saint Genet* and even 'L'Enfance d'un chef'. His willingness to stand on the side of the oppressed, his hatred of hierarchy and authoritarianism, were as powerful as ever. Sartre died as he had lived for many years, as a revolutionary socialist.

Notes

1. *Le Monde*, 8 May 1968.
2. This was not the first such declaration. On 7 May 1968 *Le Monde* had carried a rather more cautious statement, supporting the higher education teachers' union and stressing that the students were not proposing an examination boycott. This was signed by, among others, Audry, Guérin, Leiris, David Rousset (still a Gaullist!) and Jean-Pierre Vigier.
3. *Le Monde*, 10 May 1968.
4. G. Marchais, 'De Faux Révolutionnaires à démasquer', *L'Humanité*, 3 May 1968.
5. For a detailed account see D. Drake, 'Sartre and May 1968', *Sartre Studies International* Vol. 3, No. 1 (1997), pp. 43–65.
6. J. Rancière, *La Leçon d'Althusser*, Paris, 1974, p. 137.
7. *Sit* VIII, p. 212.
8. *Sit* VIII, p. 139.
9. *TDS*, p. 368.
10. *Sit* IX, p. 227.
11. Speech at Mutualité, 7 January 1971, in E. Ben-Gal, *Mardi*, Paris, 1992, p. 308.
12. *Sit* VIII, p. 354.
13. J.-P. Sartre, 'Volksfront nicht besser als Gaullisten', *Der Spiegel*, 12 February 1973, p. 88.
14. *Lutte ouvrière*, 27 October 1970.
15. *L'Humanité*, 3 May 1974.
16. *Sit* X, p. 38.
17. Sartre had spent two months in China with Simone de Beauvoir in 1955, following which she had written a book – *La Longue Marche*, Paris, 1957 – which was largely sympathetic to the regime, though not wholly uncritical. This was, of course, well before the Sino-Soviet split and the period of the 'Cultural Revolution' which produced such enthusiasm among certain elements in the West.
18. A. Astruc and M. Contat, *Sartre*, Paris, 1977, p. 100. The Chinese Maoists did indeed deploy the concept of morality, notably in the matter of 'non-material incentives', which were presented as an alternative to higher wages (material incentives), and hence were a means of increasing the exploitation of Chinese workers. Sartre never confronted any Maoist thinker on morals with the seriousness which he had devoted to Trotsky's *Their Morals and Ours*.
19. Sartre's Maoist connections led him into some strange territory on occasion. The special issue of *Les Temps modernes* in 1972 on the Irish Question contained an article by Bernard Kouchner (later head of the UN occupation forces in Kosovo), which hailed the 'Irish Maoists' of the ICO (Irish Communist Organisation), a bizarre Stalinist sect which supported the national rights of Ulster Protestants, and a piece by Jean-Yves Bériou which dismissed the IRA as a 'fascist racket' (*TM*, June 1972, pp. 1947, 2118).
20. 'Jean-Paul Sartre fait parler les "casseurs" ', *Le Nouvel Observateur*, 18–24 May 1970, pp. 47–50, 53–56.

21. *Le Monde,* 10 May 1969.
22. *Raison,* pp. 84–85.
23. R. Hayman, *Writing Against,* London, 1986, p. 402.
24. *Raison,* p. 76.
25. *Le Monde,* 21 November 1973.
26. *Sit X,* p. 158.
27. *Sit VIII,* p. 223.
28. J.-P. Sartre and B. Lévy, *L'Espoir maintenant,* Lagrasse, 1991, pp. 31–32.
29. See Sartre, 'Volksfront', *Der Spiegel,* 12 February 1973, p. 95.
30. A. Cohen-Solal, *Sartre,* Paris, 1985, p. 694.
31. See *L'Année sartrienne,* No. 15, Paris, June 2001, p. 122.
32. In P.A. Schilpp, ed., *The Philosophy of Jean-Paul Sartre,* La Salle, Ill., 1981, p. 21.
33. D. Guérin, *Jeunesse du socialisme libertaire,* Paris, 1959.
34. Cited *Le Monde,* 24 September 1977.
35. 'Jean-Paul Sartre et les homosexuels', *Le Gai Pied,* April 1980, pp. 1, 11–14.
36. Leviticus, XI 17, XVIII 22.

Chapter 18

CONCLUSION: SARTRE'S CENTURY?

'Revolutionaries of the J.-P. Sartre style have never disturbed the sleep of any banker in the world'.[1] So asserted Raymond Aron in 1952, and in the absence of any more extensive research on insomnia in the financial services industry we shall have to take his word for it. Yet bankers, by the nature of their trade, are immersed in the short term, the day-to-day fluctuations of the market. They are not the most sensitive judges of the long-term permeation of ideas and values which can eventually have a major impact on social change.

An honest assessment of Sartre's achievements and of their limits requires that he be rescued from his friends as well as his enemies. As Lenin pointed out in *The State and Revolution*, the bourgeoisie converts dead revolutionaries into 'harmless icons'.[2] The tributes paid to Sartre on his death would fill a volume on their own. But one, from Maurice Nadeau, cut through the nonsense and the hypocrisy. Nadeau, Trotskyist in the 1930s, organiser of the Manifesto of the 121, had known Sartre since 1941; he mocked the pious tributes which seemed to suggest that President Giscard d'Estaing read *L'Être et le néant* when he had difficulty sleeping:

> Amid this funereal din, we shall not play our part. From respect for the writer, from the time when he was seen as 'wallowing in the sordid'; for the philosopher, still considered by some as a 'demoraliser of youth'; for the militant, described over there as a 'monkey with a typewriter', and over here as a 'traitor to the West'; and finally for the man called Jean-Paul Sartre, whose life and work refused in advance that death should make him into a great man.[3]

A balance sheet of Sartre's political contribution – leaving aside the aesthetic value of his plays and novels, and the validity of his strictly philosophical work – would have to list the following positive points:

Notes for this chapter begin on page 224.

- the creation of *Les Temps modernes*, which provided a forum for confrontation of views from different sections of the left and a platform for dissident thinkers otherwise condemned to obscure marginal publications;
- his steadfast opposition to racism from 'L'enfance d'un chef' through *Réflexions sur la question juive* to *La Putain respectueuse*;
- his strenuous efforts, at the time of the RDR, to establish a left current independent of both Stalinism and social democracy;
- his consistent anti-imperialism, and especially his courage and outspokenness in the service of Algerian independence;
- his contribution, with *Question de méthode*, to the rebirth after 1956 of Marxism as a critical and radical method of thought rather than a sterile dogmatism;
- his widespread influence on the generation of students and young people who contributed to the political breakthrough of 1968;
- his uncompromising defence of the student movement in 1968;
- his defence of the revolutionary left against repression after 1968, and his lifelong adherence to the principles of revolutionary socialism.

On the negative side can be listed:

- first and foremost, his defence during the period 1952 to 1956, and occasionally thereafter, of reactionary and authoritarian regimes in the Eastern bloc, which by his own criteria did not deserve the name of socialism;
- his failure to complete the *Critique de la raison dialectique* and to fulfil the programme he set for himself therein;
- his failure to provide adequate strategic guidance for the revolutionary left in the 1960s and 1970s.

That Sartre had a real influence on a generation of young people, largely but far from exclusively students, who grew up in the 1950s and 1960s, not only in France but throughout the world, seems impossible to deny. M.-A. Burnier, who was deeply influenced by Sartre before repudiating him, recalled the end of Sartre's story 'L'Enfance d'un chef', where Lucien, having found that anti-Semitism had given him a meaning in life, decided to grow a moustache. He asked: 'Is it an exaggeration to claim that Sartre has prevented a good many Lucien Fleuriers from letting their moustaches grow?'[4] If even that were true, it would be no mean achievement.

The unity of theory and practice was at the heart of all Sartre wrote. This set him firmly in opposition to postmodernism, which is based on a quite willing disjunction of theory and practice, leading to a fatalistic attitude towards both knowledge and action. Postmodernist thought insists that there is no unitary self, that the human individual is fractured and divided. Such a claim immediately allows a disintegration of the unity of theory and practice; if my self is not unitary, then I can hardly be expected to act in a consistent way, or to relate my theoretical positions to my day-to-day conduct. For Sartre the centring of human activity on freedom and choice meant that there could be no excuses; at any given time there was a single, undivided agent; there could be no compromise or evasion, but only choice.

By raising the links between individual morality and Marxism, Sartre asked important questions for political practice which had been neglected in the classic Marxist tradition. Marx argued that class struggle was the motor of history; Lenin contended that a revolutionary party was necessary for the conquest of state power. But neither of them posed the existential question: 'Why should *I* join, why should *I* get involved?'

There is no Sartrean line in political action, there are no Sartreans to rival Leninists or Trotskyists. Sartre's main attempt at a theoretical synthesis, the *Critique de la raison dialectique*, was incomplete and must be accounted a failure. But as de Beauvoir wrote of a very different figure, the marquis de Sade, 'he never produced a proof; but at least he challenged all the excessively easy answers'.[5] Sartre too will continue to be more valuable for the questions he asked than for the answers he gave.

In his study *Le Siècle de Sartre*, Bernard-Henri Lévy has attempted to recuperate Sartre by stressing the pessimistic themes in his work as the healthy ones. Lévy saw the root of all totalitarianism in the desire to create a 'better world'.[6] But Levy's compassionate conservatism proved not very convincing in the face of Sartre's life work; for the central theme that ran throughout all Sartre's writings was that we are free to change the world for the better and that we have a responsibility to do so.

In fact Sartre's philosophy has long been caricatured, by both Stalinists and conservatives, as a philosophy of gloom and squalor; yet, as Sartre responded in 1945: 'I wonder if their resentment is not at its pessimism, but rather at its optimism'.[7] The insistence that we are free to act, and that the world can be changed, is the most radical theme in Sartre's thought.

For Lévy 'Sartre's century' was the bleak twentieth, the age of Stalin and Hitler, when the best hopes of revolutionary change were betrayed and the worst nightmares of racism were put into practice. But now a new generation is emerging, who were scarcely out of nappies when the Berlin Wall fell. The problems of the world they face – extremes of poverty and wealth, famine, war, rapacious multinationals and ecological disaster – can scarcely be blamed on 'totalitarian communism', of which they know only from the history books; their problems clearly have their roots in the unbridled free market.

It is scarcely likely that a new generation of 'anti-capitalists' will see much to attract them in Stalinism, and they may safely disregard Sartre's defence of the indefensible. But other Sartrean themes may prove more lasting. Sartre's continuing stress on human freedom, the insistence that no human institutions should be taken as given and unchangeable, finds a powerful echo in the anti-capitalist slogan: 'Another world is possible'. In the age of globalisation, Sartre's persistent claim that 'man is responsible for all men'[8] acquires a new relevance.

And if a new generation discover the true Sartre, they will find a man of dialogue, one constantly willing to learn through debate and cooperation with the anti-Stalinist left. Through him they may encounter other representatives of the authentic left, largely hidden from history during the long night of Stalinist domination – Colette Audry, Daniel Guérin, Victor Serge, Pierre Naville, the pioneers of *Socialisme ou barbarie*. It may yet be that 'Sartre's century' will be the twenty-first.

Notes

1.   R. Aron, *Polémiques*, Paris, 1955, p. 38.
2.   V.I. Lenin, *Collected Works*, Moscow and London, 1960, 24: 385.
3.   M. Nadeau, 'La Mort de Sartre', *La Quinzaine littéraire*, 1/15 May 1980, p. 5.
4.   M.-A. Burnier, *Les Existentialistes et la politique*, Paris, 1966, p. 186.
5.   S. de Beauvoir, *Faut-il brûler Sade?* Paris, 1972, p. 82.
6.   B.-H. Lévy, *Le Siècle de Sartre*, Paris, 2000, pp. 216, 318.
7.   J.-P. Sartre, *L'Existentialisme*, Paris, 1966, p. 15.
8.   J.-P. Sartre, *L'Existentialisme*, p. 24.

BIBLIOGRAPHY

Abbreviations in brackets are those used in references.

Works by Sartre

Sartre J.-P., *Cahiers pour une morale*. Paris, 1983.
———. *Critique de la raison dialectique*. Paris, 1960.
———. *Critique de la raison dialectique* tome II. Paris, 1985.
———. *L'Être et le néant*. Paris, 1943.
———. *L'Existentialisme est un humanisme*. Paris, 1966 (first edition 1946).
———. *L'Imaginaire*. Paris, 1966 (first edition 1940).
———. *Le Diable et le Bon Dieu*. Paris, 1951.
———. *Les Carnets de la drôle de guerre*. Paris, 1983. English: *War Diaries: Notebooks from a Phoney War*. trans. Quintin Hoare. London, 1984.
———. *Les Mains sales*. Paris, 1948; republished in Methuen's Twentieth Century Texts, ed. G. Brereton, London, 1963.
———. *Les Mots*. Paris, 1964.
———. *Lettres au Castor*. 2 vols. Paris, 1983.
———. *Nekrassov*. Paris, 1956.
———. *Oeuvres romanesques*. Paris, 1981.
———. *Réflexions sur la question juive*. Paris, 1954 (first edition 1946).
———. *Saint Genet*. Paris, 1952.
———. *Situations*, volumes I–X, Paris, 1947–76. (*Sit*)
———. *Un Théâtre de situations*. Paris, 1973. (*TDS*)
———. (English) *The Communists and Peace*, trans. Irene Clephane. London, 1969.
———. (English) *Sartre on Cuba*. New York, 1961.
———. (Spanish) *Sartre visita a Cuba*. Havana, 1960.
Sartre, J.-P., Ph Gavi and P. Victor. *On a raison de se révolter*. Paris, 1974. (*Raison*).
Sartre, J.-P. and B. Lévy. *L'Espoir maintenant*. Lagrasse, 1991.
Sartre, J.-P., B. Pingaud and D. Mascolo, *Du Rôle de l'intellectuel dans le mouvement révolutionnaire*. Paris, 1971.
Sartre J.-P., D. Rousset and G. Rosenthal, *Entretiens sur la politique*. Paris, 1949.
Sartre J.-P. and M. Merleau-Ponty, 'Les Lettres d'une rupture', *Magazine littéraire*, No. 320, April 1994, pp. 67–86.

Other Books Cited

Anderson, P. *Considerations on Western Marxism*. London, 1976.
Aragon, L. *Persécuté persécuteur*. Paris [1931]; trans. E.E. Cummings, *The Red Front*, Chapel Hill, NC, 1933.
Aron, R. *Polémiques*. Paris, 1955.
Aronson, R. *Jean-Paul Sartre: Philosophy in the World*. London, 1980.
Aronson, R. and A. van den Hoven, eds. *Sartre Alive*. Detroit, 1991.
Astruc, A. and M. Contat. *Sartre*. Paris, 1977.
Audry, C. *Connaissance de Sartre*. Paris, 1955.
Audry, C. *Sartre et la réalité humaine*. Paris, 1966.
Audry, C. *La Statue*, Paris. 1983.
Bair, D. *Simone de Beauvoir*. London, 1990.
Beauvoir, S. de, *Faut-il brûler Sade?* Paris, 1972.
———. *L'Amérique au jour le jour*. Paris, 1948.
———. *La Cérémonie des adieux*. Paris, 1981. (*Adieux*)
———. *Le Deuxième Sexe*. 2 vols. Paris, 1949.
———. *La Force de l'âge*. Paris, 1960. (*Force*). English: *The Prime of Life*, trans. Peter Green, Harmondsworth, 1965.
———. *La Force des choses*. Paris, 1963. (*Choses*)
———. *Lettres à Sartre*. 2 vols. Paris, 1990.
———. *La Longue Marche*. Paris, 1957.
———. *Les Mandarins*. Paris, 1954.
———. *Pour une morale de l'ambiguïté*. Paris, 1947.
———. *Tout compte fait*. Paris, 1972. (*Compte*)
Bellanger, C. et al. *Histoire générale de la presse française*, Vol. IV. Paris, 1975.
Ben-Gal, E. *Mardi, chez Sartre*. Paris, 1992.
Bergmann, T. and M. Kessler, eds. *Ketzer im Kommunismus*. Mainz, 1993.
Bouchardeau, H. *Simone Weil*. Paris, 1995.
Boulé, J.-P., *Sartre médiatique*. Fleury sur Orne, 1992.
Breton, A. *Manifestes du surréalisme*. Paris, 1963.
Broué, P. and R. Vacheron. *Meurtres au maquis*. Paris, 1997.
Broyelle C and J, *Les Illusions retrouvées*, Paris, 1982.
Bruhat, J. *Il n'est jamais trop tard*. Paris, 1983.
Burnier, M.-A. *L'Adieu à Sartre*. Paris, 2000.
———. *Les Existentialistes et la politique*. Paris, 1966.
———. *Le Testament de Sartre*. Paris, 1982.
Camus, A. *Actuelles*. Paris, 1950.
———. *Actuelles* II. Paris, 1953.
———. *Carnets*. Paris, 1964.
Cau, J. *Croquis de mémoire*. Paris, 1985.
Charpier, F. *Histoire de l'extrême-gauche trotskiste*. Paris, 2002.
Chebel d'Appollonia, A. *Histoire politique des intellectuels en France*, 2 vols. Brussels, 1991.
Chiodi, P. *Sartre and Marxism*. Hassocks, 1976.
Cliff, T. *The Darker the Night the Brighter the Star*. London, 1993.
———. *The Employers' Offensive*. London, 1970.

Cohen-Solal, A. *Sartre*. Paris. 1985.

Cohen, M. *The Wager of Lucien Goldmann*. Princeton NJ, 1994.

Collins D., *Sartre as Biographer*. Cambridge, Mass., 1980.

Colombel, J. *La Nostalgie de l'espérance*. Paris, 1997.

Contat, M. and M. Rybalka. *Les Écrits de Sartre*. Paris, 1970. (*C&R*).

Craipeau, Y. *Contre vents et marées*. Paris, 1977.

———. *La Libération confisquée*. Paris, 1978.

Crossman, R. ed. *The God that Failed*. London, 1950.

Daix, P. *J'ai cru au matin*. Paris, 1976.

Daniel, J. *Le Temps qui reste*. Paris, 1973.

Danos, J. and M. Gibelin. *Juin 36*. Paris, 1952.

Davies, H. *Sartre and 'Les Temps modernes'*. Cambridge, 1987.

Dedijer, V. and R. Rizman. *The Universal Validity of Human Rights*. Kamnik (Yugoslavia), 1982.

Desanti, D. *Les Staliniens (1944–1956)*. Paris, 1975.

Deutscher, I. *Heretics and Renegades*. London, 1955.

———. *The Prophet Armed*. Oxford, 1970.

———. *The Prophet Outcast*. Oxford 1970.

———. *The Prophet Unarmed*. Oxford, 1970.

Dommanget, M. *Le Drapeau rouge*. Paris, 1966.

Drake, D. *Intellectuals and Politics in Post-War France*. Basingstoke, 2002.

Le Droit à l'insoumission. Paris, 1961.

Dujardin, P. *Simone Weil – idéologie et politique*. Grenoble, 1975.

Einaudi, J.-L. *Pour l'exemple*. Paris, 1986.

Fanon, F. *L'An V de la révolution algérienne*. Paris, 1960.

———. *Les Damnés de la terre*. Paris, 1961.

———. *Peau noire, masques blancs*. Paris, 1952.

Ferniot, J. *Je recommencerais bien*. Paris, 1991.

Galster, I. ed. *La Naissance du phénomène Sartre*. Paris, 2001.

Galster, I. *Sartre, Vichy et les intellectuels*. Paris, 2001.

Garaudy, R. *Les Fossoyeurs de la littérature*. Paris, 1947.

Garaudy, R. et al. *Mésaventures de la dialectique*. Paris, 1956.

Gendzier, I.L. *Frantz Fanon*. London, 1973.

Gerassi, J. *Jean-Paul Sartre – Hated Conscience of His Century*, Vol. I. Chicago, 1989.

Ginsbourg, A. *Paul Nizan*. Paris, 1966.

Goldmann, L. *Le Dieu caché*. Paris, 1955.

Gorz, A. *Adieux au prolétariat*. Paris, 1980.

Gottraux, P. *"Socialisme ou Barbarie"*. Lausanne, 1997.

Grimshaw, A. ed. *The CLR James Reader*. Oxford, 1992.

Guérin, D. *L'Algérie n'a jamais été la France*. Paris, 1956.

———. *Fascisme et grand capital*. Paris, 1969 (first edition 1936).

———. *Front populaire – révolution manquée*. Paris, 1963.

———. *Jeunesse du socialisme libertaire*. Paris, 1959.

———. *La Lutte de classes sous la première république*. 2 vols. Paris, 1946; revised edition Paris, 1968.

———. *La Peste brune*. Paris, 1969.

———. *Quand l'Algérie s'insurgeait*. Claix, 1979.

Halimi, S. *Sisyphe est fatigué*. Paris, 1993.

Hamon, H. and P. Rotman. *Génération*. 2 Vols. Paris, 1990.

———. *Les Porteurs de valises*. Paris, 1981.

Hayman, R. *Writing Against*. London, 1986.

Hervé, P. *La Révolution et les fétiches*. Paris, 1956.

Hirsh, A. *The French Left*. Montreal, 1982.

Hook, S. *Out of Step*. New York, 1987.

Howe, I. ed. *The Basic Writings of Trotsky*. London, 1964.

Isaacs, H. *The Tragedy of the Chinese Revolution*. Stanford, 1961.

Jacobs, D. ed. *The New Communist Manifesto*. New York, 1962.

Jameson, F. ed. *Sartre after Sartre*. Yale French Studies 68: Yale, 1985.

Jeanson, C. and F. *L'Algérie hors la loi*. Paris, 1955.

Jeanson, F. *Le Problème moral et la pensée de Sartre*. Paris, 1947; (revised edition) Paris, 1965.

———. *Sartre dans sa vie*. Paris, 1974.

Joseph, G. *Une si douce occupation*. Paris, 1991.

Judt, T. *Past Imperfect*. Berkeley and Los Angeles, 1992.

Kanapa, J. *Comme si la lutte entière*. Paris, 1946.

———. *L'Existentialisme n'est pas un humanisme*. Paris, 1947.

Kergoat, J. *Le Parti socialiste*. Paris. 1983.

Kravchenko, V.-A. *J'ai choisi la liberté*. Paris, 1947.

Kriegel, A. *Les Communistes*. Paris, 1968.

Lamouchi, N. *Jean-Paul Sartre et le tiers monde*. Paris, 1996.

Landau, K. *Le Stalinisme en Espagne*. Paris, 1938, preface by Alfred Rosmer; English translation as 'Stalinism in Spain', in *Revolutionary History* Vol. 1, No. 2 (1988), pp. 40–55.

Lefebvre, H. *L'Existentialisme*. Paris, 1946.

Lefort, C. *Eléments d'une critique de la bureaucratie*. Paris, 1979.

———. *Un Homme en trop*. Paris, 1986.

Lefranc, G. *Juin 36*. Paris, 1966.

Lenin, V.I. *Collected Works*. 45 vols., Moscow & London, 1960.

Levine, I.D. *The Mind of an Assassin*. New York, 1959.

Lévy, B.-H. *Le Siècle de Sartre*. Paris, 2000.

———, *Les Aventures de la liberté*. Paris, 1991, p 15.

Linet, R. *Renault. 1947–58*, Paris, 1997.

Lottman, H. *Camus*. London, 1981.

Lukács G., *Existentialisme ou marxisme?* Paris, 1948.

Maitron, J. and C. Pennetier, *Dictionnaire biographique du mouvement ouvrier français*. Paris, 1964ff.

Malgorn, A. *Jean Genet: Qui êtes-vous?* Lyon, 1988.

Mallet, S. *La Nouvelle classe ouvrière*. Paris, 1963.

Mandel, E. *La Longue marche de la révolution*. Paris, 1976.

Marie, J.-J. *Trotsky, le trotskysme et la IVe internationale*. Paris, 1980.

Martinet, M. *La Maison à l'abri*. Paris, 1919.

Marx, K. and F. Engels. *Collected Works*, 49 vols. (to date). London and Moscow, 1975–2001.

———. *Selected Correspondence*. Moscow, 1956.

Mascolo, D. *Le Communisme*. Paris, 1953.

McCall, D. *The Theatre of Jean-Paul Sartre*. New York, 1969.

McLellan, D. *Simone Weil*. Basingstoke, 1989.

Merleau-Ponty, M. *Les Aventures de la dialectique*. Paris, 1955.

————. *Humanisme et terreur*. Paris, 1947.

————. *Sens et non-sens*. Paris, 1966.

————. *Signes*. Paris, 1960.

Mészáros, I. *The Work of Sartre*. Brighton, 1979.

Moraly, J.-B. *Jean Genet – la vie écrite*. Paris, 1988.

Morin, E. *Autocritique*. Paris, 1959.

Mothé, D. *Journal d'un ouvrier*. Paris, 1959.

Nadeau, M. *Grâces leur soient rendues*. Paris, 1990.

————. *Histoire du surréalisme*. Paris, 1964.

Naville, P. *Les Conditions de la liberté*. Paris, 1947.

————. *D'Holbach et la philosophie scientifique au XVIIIe siècle*. Paris, 1967 (first edition 1942).

————. *Mémoires imparfaites*. Paris, 1987.

————. *Le Nouveau Léviathan*. Paris, 1967.

————. *La Psychologie du comportement*. Paris, 1963 (first edition 1942).

————. *Psychologie, marxisme, matérialisme*. Paris, 1948.

————. *La Révolution et les intellectuels*. Paris, 1975.

Newsinger, J. *Orwell's Politics*. Basingstoke, 1999.

Orwell, G. *Coming Up For Air*. Harmondsworth, 1962.

Le Parti communiste dans la résistance. Paris, 1967.

Paul Nizan: intellectuel communiste. 2 vols. Paris, 1970.

Perrin, M. *Avec Sartre au stalag 12D*. Paris, 1980.

Plisnier, C. *Faux Passeports*. 1937.

Pluet-Despatin, J. *Les Trotskystes et la guerre*. Paris, 1980.

Podhoretz, N. *The Bloody Crossroads*. New York, 1986.

Politzer, G. *Ecrits I: La Philosophie et les mythes*. Paris, 1969.

Polizzotti, M. *Revolution of the Mind: The Life of André Breton*. London, 1995.

Popper, K. *Conjectures and Refutations*. London, 1972.

Rancière, J. *La Leçon d'Althusser*. Paris, 1974.

Read, B. ed. *Flowers and Revolution*. London, 1997.

Rioux, J.-P. and J.-F. Sirinelli, *La Guerre d'Algérie et les intellectuels français*. Paris, 1988.

Robrieux, P. *Histoire intérieure du parti communiste*. 4 vols. Paris, 1980–84.

Romano, P. and R. Stone. *The American Worker*. Detroit, 1972.

Ronsac, C. *Trois noms pour une vie*. Paris, 1988, p. 234.

Rosmer, A. and M. and L.D. Trotsky, *Correspondance 1929–1939*. Paris, 1982.

Rous, J. and D. Gauthiez. *Un Homme de l'ombre*. Paris, 1983.

Rousset, D. *Une Vie dans le siècle*. Paris, 1991.

Rykner, A. *Nathalie Sarraute*. Paris, 1991.

Schilpp, P.A. ed. *The Philosophy of Jean-Paul Sartre*. La Salle, Illinois, 1981.

Scriven, M. *Paul Nizan: Communist Novelist*. Basingstoke, 1988.

————. *Sartre's Existential Biographies*. Basingstoke, 1984.

Serge, V. *Carnets*. Paris, 1952.

———. *16 Fusillés à Moscou*. Paris, 1984.

Streiff, G. *Jean Kanapa*. Paris, 1998.

Thody, P. *Jean-Paul Sartre*. Basingstoke, 1992.

Todd, O. *Albert Camus*. Paris, 1996.

———. *Fils rebelle*. Paris, 1981.

Trotsky, L. *Against Individual Terrorism*. New York, 1974.

———. *Fascism, Stalinism and the United Front*. London, 1989.

———. *My Life*. New York, 1960.

———. *Writings 1939–40*. New York, 1973.

Verdès-Leroux, J. *La Lune et le caudillo*. Paris, 1989.

Wald, A. *The New York Intellectuals*. Chapel Hill, 1987.

Weiss, P. *Trotski im Exil*. Frankfurt am Main, 1970. English translation: Weiss, P. *Trotsky in Exile*. London, 1971.

White, E. *Genet*. London, 1993.

Williams, P.M. *Crisis and Compromise*. London, 1964.

Winock, M. *Histoire politique de la revue "Esprit" 1930–1950*. Paris, 1975.

———. *La République se meurt. 1956–1958*. Paris, 1985.

Wolfe, B. *Memoirs of a Not Altogether Shy Pornographer*. New York, 1972.

———. *The Great Prince Died*. London, 1959.

Wurmser, A. *Fidèlement vôtre*. Paris, 1979.

Zhdanov, A.A. *On Literature, Music and Philosophy*. London, 1950.

Articles in Journals

Adereth, M. 'Sartre and Communism', *Journal of European Studies* XVII (1987), pp. 1–48.

Aronson, R. 'Sartre and Marxism: A Double Retrospective', in *Sartre Studies International* Vol. I, Nos 1–2 (1995), pp. 21–36.

Audry, C. 'Une philosophie du fascisme allemand: l'oeuvre de Martin Heidegger', *L'Ecole émancipée* 14 October, 1934, pp. 34–35; 21 October, p. 53.

Bell, L.A. 'Different Oppressions', *Sartre Studies International* Vol. 3, No. 2 (1997), pp. 1–20.

———. 'Identity Politics?', *Sartre Studies International* Vol. 4, No. 2 (1998), pp. 79–84.

Birchall, I.H. 'Neither Washington nor Moscow?' *Journal of European Studies*, XXIX (1999), pp. 365–404.

———. 'Prequel to the Heidegger Debate', *Radical Philosophy* 88 (March–April 1998), pp. 19–27.

———. 'Sartre's Encounter with Daniel Guérin', *Sartre Studies International* Vol. 2, No. 1 (1996), pp. 41–56.

———. 'Socialism or Identity Politics', *Sartre Studies International* Vol. 4, No. 2 (1998), pp. 69–78 .

———. 'With the Masses, Against the Stream', *Revolutionary History* Vol. 1, No. 4 (1988), pp. 34–38.

———. 'Camus contre Sartre: quarante ans plus tard', in D. Walker ed., *Albert Camus, les extrêmes et l'équilibre*, Amsterdam, 1994, pp. 129–50.

———. 'The labourism of Sisyphus: Albert Camus and revolutionary syndicalism', *Journal of European Studies* xx (1990), pp. 135–65.

———, 'Voltaire and Collective Action', *British Journal for Eighteenth-Century Studies*, Vol. xiii, No. 1 (Spring 1990), pp. 19–29.

Carlin, N. 'Daniel Guérin and the Working Class in the French Revolution', *International Socialism* 47 (1990), pp. 197–223.

Drake, D. '*Les Temps modernes* and the French War in Indochina', *Journal of European Studies* xxviii (1998), pp. 25–41.

———. 'Sartre and May 1968', *Sartre Studies International* Vol. 3, No. 1 (1997), pp. 43–65.

Gorz, A. 'Reform and Revolution', in R. Miliband and J. Saville, eds, *The Socialist Register 1968*, London, 1968.

Greeman, R. 'The Victor Serge Affair and the French Literary Left', *Revolutionary History* Vol. 5, No. 3 (Autumn 1994), pp. 142–74.

Kelly, M. 'Towards a Heuristic Method: Sartre and Lefebvre', *Sartre Studies International* Vol. 5, No. 1 (1999), pp. 1–15.

Leroy, R. 'Le PCF, les intellectuels et la culture dans les vingt dernières années', *Cahiers d'histoire de l'institut Maurice Thorez* 15 (1976), pp. 126–48.

Murphy, J. 'Sartre on Cuba Revisited', *Sartre Studies International* Vol. 2/No. 2 (1996), pp. 27–48.

Pronteau, J. and M. Kriegel-Valrimont (interview), 'The Khrushchev Speech, the PCF and the PCI', in R. Miliband and J. Saville, eds, *The Socialist Register 1976*, London, (1976), pp. 58–60.

Walsh, J.L. 'Sartre and the Marxist Ethics of Revolution', *Sartre Studies International* Vol. 6, No. 1 (2000), pp. 116–24.

Newspapers and Reviews Cited

Action
Adam
L'Année sartrienne
La Bataille socialiste
Le Cahier du propagandiste
Le Canard enchaîné
Carrefour
Clé
Combat
La Correspondance internationale
L'Ecole émancipée
Etudes sartriennes
Europe
L'Express
Figaro
Franc-Tireur
France-Observateur
France-Soir
France–URSS
Le Gai Pied
La Gauche RDR
Gavroche
Heures claires des femmes françaises
L'Humanité
Jeune Afrique
Les Lettres françaises
Les Lettres nouvelles
Libération (1944–64)
Le Libertaire
Lutte ouvrière
Masques
Il Messagero di Roma
Le Monde
New Left Review
New York Herald Tribune (Paris edition)
Le Nouvel Observateur
La Nouvelle critique
Les Nouvelles littéraires
L'Observateur
Paris-Presse l'intransigeant
Partisan Review
La Pensée socialiste

Le Populaire
Preuves
La Quinzaine littéraire
RDR Bulletin intérieur
La Révolution prolétarienne
Revolutionary History
La Revue des revues
La Revue internationale
Revue socialiste
Samedi Soir
Socialisme ou barbarie
Socialist Review
Solidarité Pérou
Der Spiegel
Sunday Times
Telos
Les Temps modernes (TM)
La Vérité
La Vérité des travailleurs
La Voie communiste

INDEX